Most people do not wish to be associated with animal suffering but just don't realize how ingrained the use of animals has become in today's society.

This book challenges the barriers that we have used to separate ourselves from the rest of the earth's inhabitants.

This is a book that can change your life.

The more people who read it, the fewer animals will pay for human ignorance with their lives.

Please, pass "Animal Liberation" on to a friend or to your local library when you've finished reading it. It could make a difference in someone else's life.

From: *To:*   *Date*

_____

_____

_____

_____

PETER SINGER was born in Melbourne, Australia, in 1946. He was educated at both the University of Melbourne and Oxford, where he was Radcliffe lecturer in philosophy at University College between 1971 and 1973. "I first became aware," he writes, "of the prejudice that I, in common with most others, had against taking seriously the interests of animals when I was a student at Oxford. It was at this time that I met others who were vegetarians because of their concern for animals, and after making myself acquainted with the facts of our treatment of animals, I decided that there was no way in which the present situation could be justified ethically. I therefore became a vegetarian and began the research that has culminated in ANIMAL LIBERATION."

Mr. Singer is the author of *Democracy and Disobedience* and has contributed articles to the philosophical journals as well as *The New York Times Magazine* and *The New York Review of Books*. His article on "Animal Liberation" in *The New York Review* attracted national attention and is the basis for this present volume.

ANIMAL LIBERATION

PETER SINGER

A DISCUS BOOK/PUBLISHED BY AVON BOOKS

AVON BOOKS
A division of
The Hearst Corporation
1790 Broadway
New York, New York 10019

First Discus Printing, September, 1977

DISCUS TRADEMARK REG. U.S. PAT. OFF. AND IN
OTHER COUNTRIES, MARCA REGISTRADA,
HECHO EN U.S.A.

Printed in Canada

UNV 15

*To Richard and Mary, and Ros and Stan,
and—especially—to Renata*

CONTENTS

viii CONTENTS

PREFACE

This book is about the tyranny of human over nonhuman animals. This tyranny has caused and today is still causing an amount of pain and suffering that can only be compared with that which resulted from the centuries of tyranny by white humans over black humans. The struggle against this tyranny is a struggle as important as any of the moral and social issues that have been fought over in recent years.

Most readers will take what they have just read to be a wild exaggeration. Five years ago I myself would have laughed at the statements I have now written in complete seriousness. Five years ago I did not know what I know today. If you read this book carefully, paying special attention to the second and third chapters, you will then know as much of what I know about the oppression of animals as it is possible to get into a book of reasonable length. Then you will be able to judge if my opening paragraph is a wild exaggeration or a sober estimate of a situation largely unknown to the general public. So I do not ask you to believe my opening paragraph now. All I ask is that you reserve your judgment until you have read the book.

Soon after I began work on this book my wife and I were invited to tea—we were living in England at the time —by a lady who had heard that I was planning to write about animals. She herself was very interested in animals, she said, and she had a friend who had already written a book about animals and would be *so* keen to meet us.

When we arrived our hostess's friend was already there, and she certainly was keen to talk about animals. "I do love animals," she began, "I have a dog and two cats, and do you know they get on together wonderfully well. Do you know Mrs. Scott? She runs a little hospital for sick pets . . ." and she was off. She paused while refreshments were served, took a ham sandwich, and then asked us what pets we had.

We told her we didn't own any pets. She looked a little surprised, and took a bite of her sandwich. Our hostess, who had now finished serving the sandwiches, joined us and took up the conversation: "But you *are* interested in animals, aren't you, Mr. Singer?"

We tried to explain that we were interested in the prevention of suffering and misery; that we were opposed to arbitrary discrimination; that we thought it wrong to inflict needless suffering on another being, even if that being were not a member of our own species; and that we believed animals were ruthlessly and cruelly exploited by humans, and we wanted this changed. Otherwise, we said, we were not especially "interested in" animals. Neither of us had ever been inordinately fond of dogs, cats, or horses in the way that many people are. We didn't "love" animals. We simply wanted them treated as the independent sentient beings that they are, and not as a means to human ends—as the pig whose flesh was now in our hostess's sandwiches had been treated.

This book is not about pets. It is not likely to be comfortable reading for those who think that love for animals involves no more than stroking a cat or feeding the birds in the garden. It is intended rather for people who are concerned about ending oppression and exploitation wherever they occur, and in seeing that the basic moral principle of equal consideration of interests is not arbitrarily restricted to members of our own species. The assumption that in order to be interested in such matters one must be an "animal-lover" is itself an indication of the absence of the slightest inkling that the moral standards that we apply among human beings might extend to other animals. No one, except a racist concerned to smear his opponents as "nigger-lovers," would suggest that in order to be concerned about equality for mistreated racial minorities you have to love those minorities, or regard them as cute and cuddly. So why make this assumption about people who work for improvements in the conditions of animals?

The portrayal of those who protest against cruelty to animals as sentimental, emotional "animal-lovers" has had the effect of excluding the entire issue of our treatment of nonhumans from serious political and moral discussion. It is easy to see why we do this. If we did give the issue serious consideration, if, for instance, we looked closely at the conditions in which animals live in the modern "factory farms" that produce our meat, we might be made uncomfortable about ham sandwiches, roast beef, fried chicken, and all those other items in our diet that we prefer not to think of as dead animals.

This book makes no sentimental appeals for sympathy toward "cute" animals. I am no more outraged by the slaughter of horses or dogs for meat than I am by the slaughter of pigs for this purpose. When the United States Defense Department finds that its use of beagles to test lethal gases has evoked a howl of protest and offers to use rats instead, I am not appeased.

This book is an attempt to think through, carefully and consistently, the question of how we ought to treat nonhuman animals. In the process it exposes the prejudices that lie behind our present attitudes and behavior. In the chapters that describe what these attitudes mean in practical terms—how animals suffer from the tyranny of human beings—there are passages that will arouse some emotions. These will, I hope, be emotions of anger and outrage, coupled with a determination to do something about the practices described. Nowhere in this book, however, do I appeal to the reader's emotions where they cannot be supported by reason. When there are unpleasant things to be described it would be dishonest to try to describe them in some neutral way that hid their real unpleasantness. You cannot write objectively about the experiments of the Nazi concentration camp "doctors" on those they considered "subhuman" without stirring emotions; and the same is true of a description of some of the experiments performed today on nonhumans in laboratories in America, Britain, and elsewhere. The ultimate justification for opposition to both these kinds of experiments, though, is not emotional.

It is an appeal to basic moral principles which we all accept, and the application of these principles to the victims of both kinds of experiment is demanded by reason, not emotion.

The title of this book has a serious point behind it. A liberation movement is a demand for an end to prejudice and discrimination based on an arbitrary characteristic like race or sex. The classic instance is the Black Liberation movement. The immediate appeal of this movement, and its initial, if limited, success, made it a model for other oppressed groups. We soon became familiar with Gay Liberation and movements on behalf of American Indians and Spanish-speaking Americans. When a majority group —women—began their campaign some thought we had come to the end of the road. Discrimination on the basis of sex, it was said, was the last form of discrimination to be universally accepted and practiced without secrecy or pretense, even in those liberal circles that have long prided themselves on their freedom from prejudice against racial minorities.

We should always be wary of talking of "the last remaining form of discrimination." If we have learned anything from the liberation movements we should have learned how difficult it is to be aware of latent prejudices in our attitudes to particular groups until these prejudices are forcefully pointed out to us.

A liberation movement demands an expansion of our moral horizons. Practices that were previously regarded as natural and inevitable come to be seen as the result of an unjustifiable prejudice. Who can say with any confidence that none of his or her attitudes and practices can legitimately be questioned? If we wish to avoid being numbered among the oppressors, we must be prepared to rethink all our attitudes to other groups, including the most fundamental of them. We need to consider our attitudes from the point of view of those who suffer by them, and by the practices that follow from them. If we can make this unaccustomed mental switch we may discover a pattern in our attitudes and practices that operates so as consistently to benefit the same group—usually the group to which we ourselves belong—at the expense of another group. So we come to see that there is a case for a new liberation movement.

The aim of this book is to lead you to make this mental switch in your attitudes and practices toward a very large group of beings: members of species other than our own. I believe that our present attitudes to these beings are based on a long history of prejudice and arbitrary discrimination. I argue that there can be no reason—except the selfish desire to preserve the privileges of the exploiting group—for refusing to extend the basic principle of equality of consideration to members of other species. I ask you to recognize that your attitudes to members of other species are a form of prejudice no less objectionable than prejudice about a person's race or sex.

In comparison with other liberation movements, Animal Liberation has a lot of handicaps. First and most obvious is the fact that the exploited group cannot themselves make an organized protest against the treatment they receive (though they can and do protest to the best of their abilities individually). We have to speak up on behalf of those who cannot speak for themselves. You can appreciate how serious this handicap is by asking yourself how long blacks would have had to wait for equal rights if they had not been able to stand up for themselves and demand it. The less able a group is to stand up and organize against oppression, the more easily it is oppressed.

More significant still for the prospects of the Animal Liberation movement is the fact that almost all of the oppressing group are directly involved in, and see themselves as benefiting from, the oppression. There are few humans indeed who can view the oppression of animals with the detachment possessed, say, by Northern whites debating the institution of slavery in the Southern states of the Union. People who eat pieces of slaughtered nonhumans every day find it hard to believe that they are doing wrong; and they also find it hard to imagine what else they could eat. On this issue, anyone who eats meat is an interested party. They benefit—or at least they think they benefit— from the present disregard of the interests of nonhuman animals. This makes persuasion more difficult. How many Southern slaveholders were persuaded by the arguments used by the Northern abolitionists, and accepted by nearly all of us today? Some, but not many. I can and do ask you to put aside your interest in eating meat when considering the arguments of this book; but I know from my own experience that with the best will in the world this is not an easy thing to do. For behind the mere momentary desire to eat meat on a particular occasion lie many years of habitual meat-eating which have conditioned our attitudes to animals.

Habit. That is the final barrier that the Animal Liberation movement faces. Habits not only of diet but also of thought and language must be challenged and altered. Habits of thought lead us to brush aside descriptions of cruelty to animals as emotional, for "animal-lovers only"; or if not that, then anyway the problem is so trivial in comparison to the problems of human beings that no sensible person could give it his time and attention. This too is a prejudice—for how can one know that a problem is trivial until one has taken the time to examine its extent? Although in order to allow a more thorough treatment this book deals with only two of the many areas in which humans cause other animals to suffer, I do not think anyone who reads it to the end will ever again think that the only problems that merit time and energy are problems concerning humans.

The habits of thought that lead us to disregard the interests of animals can be challenged, as they are challenged in the following pages. This challenge has to be expressed in a language, which in this case happens to be English. The English language, like other languages, reflects the prejudices of its users. So an author who wishes to challenge these prejudices is in a well-known type of bind: either he uses language which reinforces the very prejudices he wishes to challenge, or else he fails to communicate with his audience. This book has already been forced along the former of these paths. We commonly use the word "animal" to mean "animals other than human beings." This usage sets humans apart from other animals, implying that we are not ourselves animals—an implication that everyone who has had elementary lessons in biology knows to be false.

In the popular mind the term "animal" lumps together beings as different as oysters and chimpanzees, while placing a gulf between chimpanzees and humans, although our relationship to those apes is much closer than the oyster's. Since there exists no other short term for the nonhuman animals, I have, in the title of this book and elsewhere in these pages, had to use "animal" as if it did not include the human animal. This is a regrettable lapse from the standards of revolutionary purity but it seems necessary for effective communication. Occasionally, however, to remind you that this is a matter of convenience only, I shall use longer, more accurate modes of referring to what was once called "the brute creation." In other cases, too, I have tried to avoid language which tends to degrade animals or disguise the nature of the food we eat.

The basic principles of Animal Liberation are very simple. I have tried to write a book that is clear and easy to understand, requiring no expertise of any kind. It is necessary, however, to begin with a discussion of the principles that underlie what I have to say. While there should be nothing here that is difficult, readers unused to this kind of discussion might find the first chapter rather abstract. Don't be put off. In the next chapters we get down to the little-known details of how our species oppresses others under our control. There is nothing abstract about this oppression, or about the chapters that describe it.

If the recommendations made in the following chapters are accepted, millions of animals will be spared considerable pain. Moreover, millions of humans will benefit too. As I write, people are starving to death in many parts of the world; and many more are in imminent danger of starvation. The United States government has said that because of poor harvests and diminished stocks of grain it can provide only limited—and inadequate—assistance; but as Chapter 4 of this book makes clear, the heavy emphasis in affluent nations on rearing animals for food wastes several times as much food as it produces. By ceasing to rear and kill animals for food, we can make so much extra food available for humans that, properly distributed, it would eliminate starvation and malnutrition from this planet. Animal Liberation is Human Liberation too.

ACKNOWLEDGMENTS

It is normal practice to thank those who have assisted in the writing of a book; but in the present instance my debts are of a special kind, which can only be indicated by a brief narrative.

In the fall of 1970 I was a graduate student at the University of Oxford. Although I had specialized in moral and social philosophy, it had not occurred to me—any more than it occurs to most people—that our relations with animals raised a serious moral issue. I knew, of course, that some animals were cruelly treated, but I assumed that these were incidental abuses, and not an indication of anything fundamentally wrong.

My complacency was disturbed when I met Richard Keshen, a fellow student at Oxford and a vegetarian. Over lunch I asked him why he did not eat meat, and he began to tell me about the conditions in which the animal whose body I was eating had lived. Through Richard and his wife Mary, my wife and I became friendly with Roslind and Stanley Godlovitch, also vegetarians studying philosophy at Oxford. In long conversations with these four—and particularly with Roslind Godlovitch, who had worked out her ethical position in considerable detail—I became convinced that by eating animals I was participating in a systematic form of oppression of other species by my own species. The central ideas of this book derive from these conversations.

Reaching a theoretical conclusion is one thing; putting it into practice is another. Without the support and encouragement of Renata, my wife, who had become equally convinced that our friends were right, I might still be eating meat, though with a guilty conscience.

The idea of writing a book arose from the enthusiastic response to my review of *Animals, Men and Morals*, edited by Stanley and Roslind Godlovitch and John Harris, which appeared in *The New York Review of Books* (April 5, 1973). I am grateful to the editors of *The New York Review* for publishing this unsolicited discussion of a book on an unfashionable topic. The review would, however, never have turned into a book without the encouragement and assistance of the following:

Eleanor Seiling of United Action for Animals, New York, made her organization's unique collection of documents on experimental uses of animals available to me; and Alois Acowitz's summaries of the experimenters' reports enabled me to find what I wanted in a fraction of the time that would otherwise have been needed.

Richard Ryder generously lent me material he had gathered for his own book, *Victims of Science*.

Joanne Bower, of the Farm and Food Society, London, provided me with information on the conditions of farm animals in Britain.

Kathleen Jannaway, of the Vegan Society of the United Kingdom, helped me to locate reports on the nutritional adequacy of plant foods.

John Norton, of the Animal Rescue League of Boston, and Martha Coe, of Argus Archives, New York, provided materials on the transport and slaughter of animals in the United States.

The Scottish Society for the Prevention of Vivisection was of assistance in obtaining photographs of experiments on animals.

Dudley Giehl, of Animal Liberation, Inc., New York, allowed me to use material he had collected on intensive farming and vegetarianism.

Alice Herrington and Joyce Lambert, of Friends of Animals, New York, assisted in many ways, and Jim Mason, of the same organization, arranged visits to intensive farms.

An invitation to take up a visiting position in the Department of Philosophy at New York University for the academic year 1973/4 provided me with a congenial atmosphere and an ideal location for research and writing, and my colleagues and students gave me valuable comments and criticism. I also had the opportunity to subject my views on animals to the critical scrutiny of students and faculty of the philosophy departments at the following universities: Brown University, Fordham University, Long Island University, North Carolina State University at Raleigh, Rutgers University, State University of New York at Brockport, State University of New York at Stony Brook, Tufts University, University of California at Berkeley, University of Miami and Williams College; and at the Yale Law School and a meeting of the Society for Philosophy and Public Affairs, New York. Chapters 1 and 6 of this book benefited considerably from the discussions following my talks.

Finally I must thank the editors and publisher of *The New York Review of Books* for their support for the book; especially Robert Silvers, whose thoughtful editorial advice has considerably improved the original manuscript. It remains only to add that responsibility for any remaining imperfections is mine alone.

P.S.
February, 1975

1

All Animals Are Equal . . .

or why supporters of liberation
for Blacks and Women should
support Animal Liberation too.

"Animal Liberation" may sound more like a parody of
other liberation movements than a serious objective. The
idea of "The Rights of Animals" actually was once used to
parody the case for women's rights. When Mary Wollstonecraft, a forerunner of today's feminists, published her *Vindication of the Rights of Women* in 1792, her views were
widely regarded as absurd, and before long an anonymous
publication appeared entitled *A Vindication of the Rights
of Brutes*. The author of this satirical work (now known
to have been Thomas Taylor, a distinguished Cambridge
philosopher) tried to refute Mary Wollstonecraft's arguments by showing that they could be carried one stage
further. If the argument for equality was sound when applied to women, why should it not be applied to dogs,
cats, and horses? The reasoning seemed to hold for these
"brutes" too; yet to hold that brutes had rights was mani-
festly absurd; therefore the reasoning by which this conclusion had been reached must be unsound, and if unsound
when applied to brutes, it must also be unsound when applied to women, since the very same arguments had been
used in each case.

1

In order to explain the basis of the case for the equality of animals, it will be helpful to start with an examination of the case for the equality of women. Let us assume that we wish to defend the case for women's rights against the attack by Thomas Taylor. How should we reply?

One way in which we might reply is by saying that the case for equality between men and women cannot validly be extended to nonhuman animals. Women have a right to vote, for instance, because they are just as capable of making rational decisions about the future as men are; dogs, on the other hand, are incapable of understanding the significance of voting, so they cannot have the right to vote. There are many other obvious ways in which men and women resemble each other closely, while humans and animals differ greatly. So, it might be said, men and women are similar beings and should have similar rights, while humans and nonhumans are different and should not have equal rights.

The reasoning behind this reply to Taylor's analogy is correct up to a point, but it does not go far enough. There *are* important differences between humans and other animals, and these differences must give rise to *some* differences in the rights that each have. Recognizing this obvious fact, however, is no barrier to the case for extending the basic principle of equality to nonhuman animals. The differences that exist between men and women are equally undeniable, and the supporters of Women's Liberation are aware that these differences may give rise to different rights. Many feminists hold that women have the right to an abortion on request. It does not follow that since these same feminists are campaigning for equality between men and women they must support the right of men to have abortions too. Since a man cannot have an abortion, it is meaningless to talk of his right to have one. Since a dog can't vote, it is meaningless to talk of its right to vote. There is no reason why either Women's Liberation or Animal Liberation should get involved in such nonsense. The extension of the basic principle of equality from one group to another does not imply that we must treat both groups in exactly the same way, or grant exactly the same rights to both groups. Whether we should do so will depend on the nature of the members of the two groups. The basic principle of equality does not require equal or identical *treatment;* it requires equal *consideration.* Equal consideration for different beings may lead to different treatment and different rights.

So there is a different way of replying to Taylor's attempt to parody the case for women's rights, a way that does not deny the obvious differences between humans and nonhumans but goes more deeply into the question of equality and concludes by finding nothing absurd in the idea that the basic principle of equality applies to so-called "brutes." At this point such a conclusion may appear odd; but if we examine more deeply the basis on which our opposition to discrimination on grounds of race or sex ultimately rests, we will see that we would be on shaky ground if we were to demand equality for blacks, women, and other groups of oppressed humans while denying equal consideration to nonhumans. To make this clear we need to see, first, exactly why racism and sexism are wrong.

When we say that all human beings, whatever their race, creed, or sex, are equal, what is it that we are asserting? Those who wish to defend hierarchical, inegalitarian societies have often pointed out that by whatever test we choose it simply is not true that all humans are equal. Like it or not we must face the fact that humans come in different shapes and sizes; they come with different moral capacities, different intellectual abilities, different amounts of benevolent feeling and sensitivity to the needs of others, different abilities to communicate effectively, and different capacities to experience pleasure and pain. In short, if the demand for equality were based on the actual equality of all human beings, we would have to stop demanding equality.

Still, one might cling to the view that the demand for equality among human beings is based on the actual equality of the different races and sexes. Although, it may be said, humans differ as individuals there are no differences between the races and sexes *as such.* From the mere fact that a person is black or a woman we cannot infer anything about that person's intellectual or moral capacities. This, it may be said, is why racism and sexism are wrong. The white racist claims that whites are superior to blacks, but this is false—although there are differences among individuals, some blacks are superior to some whites in all of the capacities and abilities that could conceivably be relevant. The opponent of sexism would say the same: a person's sex is no guide to his or her abilities, and this is why it is unjustifiable to discriminate on the basis of sex.

The existence of individual variations that cut across the lines of race or sex, however, provides us with no defense at all against a more sophisticated opponent of equality, one who proposes that, say, the interests of all those with IQ scores below 100 be given less consideration than the interests of those with ratings over 100. Perhaps those scoring below the mark would, in this society, be made the slaves of those scoring higher. Would a hierarchical society of this sort really be so much better than one based on race or sex? I think not. But if we tie the moral principle of equality to the factual equality of the different races or sexes, taken as a whole, our opposition to racism and sexism does not provide us with any basis for objecting to this kind of inegalitarianism.

There is a second important reason why we ought not to base our opposition to racism and sexism on any kind of actual equality, even the limited kind that asserts that variations in capacities and abilities are spread evenly between the different races and sexes: we can have no absolute guarantee that these capacities and abilities really are distributed evenly, without regard to race or sex, among human beings. So far as actual abilities are concerned there do seem to be certain measurable differences between both races and sexes. These differences do not, of course, appear in each case, but only when averages are taken. More important still, we do not yet know how much of these differences is really due to the different genetic endowments of the different races and sexes, and how much is due to poor schools, poor housing, and other factors that are the result of past and continuing discrimination. Perhaps all of the important differences will eventually prove to be environmental rather than genetic. Anyone opposed to racism and sexism will certainly hope that this will be so, for it will make the task of ending discrimination a lot easier; nevertheless it would be dangerous to rest the case against racism and sexism on the belief that all significant differences are environmental in origin. The opponent of, say, racism who takes this line will be unable to avoid conceding that *if* differences in ability do after all prove to have some genetic connection with race, racism would in some way be defensible.

Fortunately there is no need to pin the case for equality to one particular outcome of a scientific investigation. The appropriate response to those who claim to have found evidence of genetically based differences in ability between the races or sexes is not to stick to the belief that the genetic explanation must be wrong, whatever evidence to the contrary may turn up: instead we should make it quite clear that the claim to equality does not depend on intelligence, moral capacity, physical strength, or similar matters of fact. Equality is a moral idea, not an assertion of fact. There is no logically compelling reason for assuming that a factual difference in ability between two people justifies any difference in the amount of consideration we give to their needs and interests. *The principle of the equality of human beings is not a description of an alleged actual equality among humans: it is a prescription of how we should treat humans.*

Jeremy Bentham, the founder of the reforming utilitarian school of moral philosophy, incorporated the essential basis of moral equality into his system of ethics by means of the formula: "Each to count for one and none for more than one." In other words, the interests of every being affected by an action are to be taken into account and given the same weight as the like interests of any other being. A later utilitarian, Henry Sidgwick, put the point in this way: "The good of any one individual is of no more importance, from the point of view (if I may say so) of the Universe, than the good of any other." More recently the leading figures in contemporary moral philosophy have shown a great deal of agreement in specifying as a fundamental presupposition of their moral theories some similar requirement which operates so as to give everyone's interests equal consideration—although these writers generally cannot agree on how this requirement is best formulated.[1]

It is an implication of this principle of equality that our concern for others and our readiness to consider their interests ought not to depend on what they are like or on what abilities they may possess. Precisely what this concern or consideration requires us to do may vary according to the characteristics of those affected by what we do: concern for the well-being of a child growing up in America would require that we teach him to read; concern for the well-being of a pig may require no more than that we leave him alone with other pigs in a place where there is adequate food and room to run freely. But the basic element—the taking into account of the interests of the being, whatever those interests may be—must, according to the principle of equality, be extended to all beings, black or white, masculine or feminine, human or nonhuman.

Thomas Jefferson, who was responsible for writing the principle of the equality of men into the American Declaration of Independence, saw this point. It led him to oppose slavery even though he was unable to free himself fully from his slaveholding background. He wrote in a letter to the author of a book that emphasized the notable intellectual achievements of Negroes in order to refute the then common view that they had limited intellectual capacities:

> Be assured that no person living wishes more sincerely than I do, to see a complete refutation of the doubts I have myself entertained and expressed on the grade of understanding allotted to them by nature, and to find that they are on a par with ourselves . . . but whatever be their degree of talent it is no measure of their rights. Because Sir Isaac Newton was superior to others in understanding, he was not therefore lord of the property or person of others.[2]

Similarly when in the 1850s the call for women's rights was raised in the United States a remarkable black feminist named Sojourner Truth made the same point in more robust terms at a feminist convention:

. . . they talk about this thing in the head; what do they call it? ["Intellect," whispered someone near by.] That's it. What's that got to do with women's rights or Negroes' rights? If my cup won't hold but a pint and yours holds a quart, wouldn't you be mean not to let me have my little half-measure full?[3]

It is on this basis that the case against racism and the case against sexism must both ultimately rest; and it is in accordance with this principle that the attitude that we may call "speciesism," by analogy with racism, must also be condemned. Speciesism—the word is not an attractive one, but I can think of no better term—is a prejudice or attitude of bias toward the interests of members of one's own species and against those of members of other species. It should be obvious that the fundamental objections to racism and sexism made by Thomas Jefferson and Sojourner Truth apply equally to speciesism. If possessing a higher degree of intelligence does not entitle one human to use another for his own ends, how can it entitle humans to exploit nonhumans for the same purpose?[4]

Many philosophers and other writers have proposed the principle of equal consideration of interests, in some form or other, as a basic moral principle; but not many of them have recognized that this principle applies to members of other species as well as to our own. Jeremy Bentham was one of the few who did realize this. In a forward-looking passage written at a time when black slaves had been freed by the French but in the British dominions were still being treated in the way we now treat animals, Bentham wrote:

The day *may* come when the rest of the animal creation may acquire those rights which never could have been withholden from them but by the hand of tyranny. The French have already discovered that the blackness of the skin is no reason why a human being should be abandoned without redress to the caprice of a tormentor. It may one day come to be recognized that the number of the legs, the villosity of the skin, or the termination of the *os sacrum* are reasons equally insufficient for abandoning a sensitive being to the

same fate. What else is it that should trace the insuperable line? Is it the faculty of reason, or perhaps the
faculty of discourse? But a full-grown horse or dog is
beyond comparison a more rational, as well as a more
conversable animal, than an infant of a day or a week
or even a month, old. But suppose they were otherwise, what would it avail? The question is not, Can
they *reason?* nor Can they *talk?* but, *Can they suffer?*[5]

In this passage Bentham points to the capacity for suffering as the vital characteristic that gives a being the right
to equal consideration. The capacity for suffering—or more
strictly, for suffering and/or enjoyment or happiness—is
not just another characteristic like the capacity for language
or higher mathematics. Bentham is not saying that those
who try to mark "the insuperable line" that determines
whether the interests of a being should be considered happen to have chosen the wrong characteristic. By saying
that we must consider the interests of all beings with the
capacity for suffering or enjoyment Bentham does not arbitrarily exclude from consideration any interests at all—as
those who draw the line with reference to the possession
of reason or language do. The capacity for suffering and
enjoyment is *a prerequisite for having interests at all,* a
condition that must be satisfied before we can speak of interests in a meaningful way. It would be nonsense to say
that it was not in the interests of a stone to be kicked
along the road by a schoolboy. A stone does not have interests because it cannot suffer. Nothing that we can do to
it could possibly make any difference to its welfare. A
mouse, on the other hand, does have an interest in not
being kicked along the road, because it will suffer if it is.

If a being suffers there can be no moral justification for
refusing to take that suffering into consideration. No matter
what the nature of the being, the principle of equality
requires that its suffering be counted equally with the like
suffering—in so far as rough comparisons can be made—
of any other being. If a being is not capable of suffering,
or of experiencing enjoyment or happiness, there is nothing
to be taken into account. So the limit of sentience (using
the term as a convenient if not strictly accurate shorthand

for the capacity to suffer and/or experience enjoyment) is the only defensible boundary of concern for the interests of others. To mark this boundary by some other characteristic like intelligence or rationality would be to mark it in an arbitrary manner. Why not choose some other characteristic, like skin color?

The racist violates the principle of equality by giving greater weight to the interests of members of his own race when there is a clash between their interests and the interests of those of another race. The sexist violates the principle of equality by favoring the interests of his own sex. Similarly the speciesist allows the interests of his own species to override the greater interests of members of other species. The pattern is identical in each case.

Most human beings are speciesists. The following chapters show that ordinary human beings—not a few exceptionally cruel or heartless humans, but the overwhelming majority of humans—take an active part in, acquiesce in, and allow their taxes to pay for practices that require the sacrifice of the most important interests of members of other species in order to promote the most trivial interests of our own species.

There is, however, one general defense of the practices to be described in the next two chapters that needs to be disposed of before we discuss the practices themselves. It is a defense which, if true, would allow us to do anything at all to nonhumans for the slightest reason, or for no reason at all, without incurring any justifiable reproach. This defense claims that we are never guilty of neglecting the interests of other animals for one breathtakingly simple reason: they have no interests. Nonhuman animals have no interests, according to this view, because they are not capable of suffering. By this is not meant merely that they are not capable of suffering in all the ways that humans are—for instance, that a calf is not capable of suffering from the knowledge that it will be killed in six months time. That modest claim is, no doubt, true; but it does not clear humans of the charge of speciesism, since it allows that animals may suffer in other ways—for instance, by being given electric shocks, or being kept in small, cramped cages. The defense I am about to discuss is the much more sweeping, although correspondingly less plausible, claim that animals are incapable of suffering in any way at all; that they are, in fact, unconscious automata, possessing neither thoughts nor feelings nor a mental life of any kind.

Although, as we shall see in a later chapter, the view that animals are automata was proposed by the seventeenth-century French philosopher René Descartes, to most people, then and now, it is obvious that if, for example, we stick a sharp knife into the stomach of an unanesthetized dog, the dog will feel pain. That this is so is assumed by the laws in most civilized countries which prohibit wanton cruelty to animals. Readers whose common sense tells them that animals do suffer may prefer to skip the remainder of this section, moving straight on to page 16, since the pages in between do nothing but refute a position which they do not hold. Implausible as it is, though, for the sake of completeness this skeptical position must be discussed.

Do animals other than humans feel pain? How do we know? Well, how do we know if anyone, human or non-human, feels pain? We know that we ourselves can feel pain. We know this from the direct experiences of pain that we have when, for instance, somebody presses a lighted cigarette against the back of our hand. But how do we know that anyone else feels pain? We cannot directly experience anyone else's pain, whether that "anyone" is our best friend or a stray dog. Pain is a state of consciousness, a "mental event," and as such it can never be observed. Behavior like writhing, screaming, or drawing one's hand away from the lighted cigarette is not pain itself; nor are the recordings a neurologist might make of activity within the brain observations of pain itself. Pain is something that we feel, and we can only infer that others are feeling it from various external indications.

In theory, we *could* always be mistaken when we assume that other human beings feel pain. It is conceivable that our best friend is really a very cleverly constructed robot, controlled by a brilliant scientist so as to give all the signs of feeling pain, but really no more sensitive than any other machine. We can never know, with absolute certainty, that this is not the case. But while this might present a puzzle for philosophers, none of us has the slightest real doubt that our best friends feel pain just as we do. This is an inference, but a perfectly reasonable one, based on observations of their behavior in situations in which we would feel pain, and on the fact that we have every reason to assume that our friends are beings like us, with nervous systems like ours that can be assumed to function as ours do, and to produce similar feelings in similar circumstances.

If it is justifiable to assume that other humans feel pain as we do, is there any reason why a similar inference should be unjustifiable in the case of other animals?

Nearly all the external signs which lead us to infer pain in other humans can be seen in other species, especially the species most closely related to us—other species of mammals, and birds. Behavioral signs—writhing, facial contortions, moaning, yelping or other forms of calling, attempts to avoid the source of pain, appearance of fear at the prospect of its repetition, and so on—are present. In addition, we know that these animals have nervous systems very like ours, which respond physiologically as ours do when the animal is in circumstances in which we would feel pain: an initial rise of blood pressure, dilated pupils, perspiration, an increased pulse rate, and, if the stimulus continues, a fall in blood pressure. Although humans have a more developed cerebral cortex than other animals, this part of the brain is concerned with thinking functions rather than with basic impulses, emotions, and feelings. These impulses, emotions, and feelings are located in the diencephalon, which is well developed in many other species of animals, especially mammals and birds.[6]

We also know that the nervous systems of other animals were not artificially constructed to mimic the pain behavior of humans, as a robot might be artificially constructed. The nervous systems of animals evolved as our own did, and in fact the evolutionary history of humans and other animals, especially mammals, did not diverge until the central features of our nervous systems were already in existence. A capacity to feel pain obviously enhances a species' prospects of survival, since it causes members of the species to avoid sources of injury. It is surely unreasonable to suppose that nervous systems which are virtually identical physiologically, have a common origin and a common evolutionary function, and result in similar forms of behavior in similar circumstances should actually operate in an entirely different manner on the level of subjective feelings.

It has long been accepted as sound policy in science to search for the simplest possible explanation of whatever it is we are trying to explain. Occasionally it has been claimed that it is for this reason "unscientific" to explain the behavior of animals by theories that refer to the animal's conscious feelings, desires, and so on—the idea being that if the behavior in question can be explained without invoking consciousness or feelings, that will be the simpler theory. Yet we can now see that such explanations, when placed in the over-all context of the behavior of both human and nonhuman animals, are actually far more complex than their rivals. For we know from our own experience that explanations of our own behavior that did not refer to consciousness and the feeling of pain would be incomplete; and it is simpler to assume that the similar behavior of animals with similar nervous systems is to be explained in the same way than to try to invent some other explanation for the behavior of nonhuman animals as well as an explanation for the divergence between humans and nonhumans in this respect.

The overwhelming majority of scientists who have addressed themselves to this question agree. Lord Brain, one of the most eminent neurologists of our time, has said:

> I personally can see no reason for conceding mind to my fellow men and denying it to animals. . . . I at least cannot doubt that the interests and activities of animals are correlated with awareness and feeling in the same way as my own, and which may be, for aught I know, just as vivid.[7]

While the author of a recent book on pain writes:

> Every particle of factual evidence supports the contention that the higher mammalian vertebrates experience

pain sensations at least as acute as our own. To say that they feel less because they are lower animals is an absurdity; it can easily be shown that many of their senses are far more acute than ours—visual acuity in certain birds, hearing in most wild animals, and touch in others; these animals depend more than we do today on the sharpest possible awareness of a hostile environment. Apart from the complexity of the cerebral cortex (which does not directly perceive pain) their nervous systems are almost identical to ours and their reactions to pain remarkably similar, though lacking (so far as we know) the philosophical and moral overtones. The emotional element is all too evident, mainly in the form of fear and anger.[8]

In Britain, three separate expert government committees on matters relating to animals have accepted the conclusion that animals feel pain. After noting the obvious behavioral evidence for this view, the Committee on Cruelty to Wild Animals said:

> . . . we believe that the physiological, and more particularly the anatomical, evidence fully justifies and reinforces the commonsense belief that animals feel pain.

And after discussing the evolutionary value of pain they concluded that pain is "of clear-cut biological usefulness" and this is "a third type of evidence that animals feel pain." They then went on to consider forms of suffering other than mere physical pain, and added that they were "satisfied that animals do suffer from acute fear and terror." In 1965, reports by British government committees on experiments on animals, and on the welfare of animals under intensive farming methods, agreed with this view, concluding that animals are capable of suffering both from straightforward physical injuries and from fear, anxiety, stress, and so on.[9]

That might well be thought enough to settle the matter; but there is one more objection that needs to be considered. There is, after all, one behavioral sign that humans have when in pain which nonhumans do not have. This is a developed language. Other animals may communicate with each other, but not, it seems, in the complicated way we do. Some philosophers, including Descartes, have thought it important that while humans can tell each other about their experience of pain in great detail, other animals cannot. (Interestingly, this once neat dividing line between humans and other species has now been threatened by the discovery that chimpanzees can be taught a language.)[10] But as Bentham pointed out long ago, the ability to use language is not relevant to the question of how a being ought to be treated—unless that ability can be linked to the capacity to suffer, so that the absence of a language casts doubt on the existence of this capacity.

This link may be attempted in two ways. First, there is a hazy line of philosophical thought, stemming perhaps from some doctrines associated with the influential philosopher Ludwig Wittgenstein, which maintains that we cannot meaningfully attribute states of consciousness to beings without language. This position seems to me very implausible. Language may be necessary for abstract thought, at some level anyway; but states like pain are more primitive, and have nothing to do with language.

The second and more easily understood way of linking language and the existence of pain is to say that the best evidence that we can have that another creature is in pain is when he tells us that he is. This is a distinct line of argument, for it is not being denied that a non-language-user conceivably *could* suffer, but only that we could ever have sufficient reason to *believe* that he is suffering. Still, this line of argument fails too. As Jane Goodall has pointed out in her study of chimpanzees, *In the Shadow of Man*, when it comes to the expressions of feelings and emotions language is less important than in other areas. We tend to fall back on nonlinguistic modes of communication such as a cheering pat on the back, an exuberant embrace, a clasp of the hands, and so on. The basic signals we use to convey pain, fear, anger, love, joy, surprise, sexual arousal, and many other emotional states are not specific to our own species.[11]

Charles Darwin made an extensive study of this subject,

and the book he wrote about it, *The Expression of the Emotions in Man and Animals,* notes countless nonlinguistic modes of expression. The statement "I am in pain" may be one piece of evidence for the conclusion that the speaker is in pain, but it is not the only possible evidence, and since people sometimes tell lies, not even the best possible evidence.

Even if there were stronger grounds for refusing to attribute pain to those who do not have a language, the consequences of this refusal might lead us to reject the conclusion. Human infants and young children are unable to use language. Are we to deny that a year-old child can suffer? If not, language cannot be crucial. Of course, most parents understand the responses of their children better than they understand the responses of other animals; but this is just a fact about the relatively greater knowledge that we have of our own species, and the greater contact we have with infants, as compared to animals. Those who have studied the behavior of other animals, and those who have pet animals, soon learn to understand their responses as well as we understand those of an infant, and sometimes better. Jane Goodall's account of the chimpanzees she watched is one instance of this, but the same can be said of those who have observed species less closely related to our own. Two among many possible examples are Konrad Lorenz's observations of geese and jackdaws, and N. Tinbergen's extensive studies of herring gulls.[12] Just as we can understand infant human behavior in the light of adult human behavior, so we can understand the behavior of other species in the light of our own behavior—and sometimes we can understand our own behavior better in the light of the behavior of other species.

So to conclude: there are no good reasons, scientific or philosophical, for denying that animals feel pain. If we do not doubt that other humans feel pain we should not doubt that other animals do so too.

Animals can feel pain. As we saw earlier, there can be no moral justification for regarding the pain (or pleasure) that animals feel as less important than the same amount of pain (or pleasure) felt by humans. But what exactly does this mean, in practical terms? To prevent misunderstanding I shall spell out what I mean a little more fully.

If I give a horse a hard slap across its rump with my open hand, the horse may start, but it presumably feels little pain. Its skin is thick enough to protect it against a mere slap. If I slap a baby in the same way, however, the baby will cry and presumably does feel pain, for its skin is more sensitive. So it is worse to slap a baby than a horse, if both slaps are administered with equal force. But there must be some kind of blow—I don't know exactly what it would be, but perhaps a blow with a heavy stick—that would cause the horse as much pain as we cause a baby by slapping it with our hand. That is what I mean by "the same amount of pain" and if we consider it wrong to inflict that much pain on a baby for no good reason then we must, unless we are speciesists, consider it equally wrong to inflict the same amount of pain on a horse for no good reason.

There are other differences between humans and animals that cause other complications. Normal adult human beings have mental capacities which will, in certain circumstances, lead them to suffer more than animals would in the same circumstances. If, for instance, we decided to perform extremely painful or lethal scientific experiments on normal adult humans, kidnaped at random from public parks for this purpose, every adult who entered a park would become fearful that he would be kidnaped. The resultant terror would be a form of suffering additional to the pain of the experiment. The same experiments performed on non-human animals would cause less suffering since the animals would not have the anticipatory dread of being kidnaped and experimented upon. This does not mean, of course, that it would be right to perform the experiment on animals, but only that there is a reason, which is *not* speciesist, for preferring to use animals rather than normal adult humans, if the experiment is to be done at all. It should be noted, however, that this same argument gives us a reason for preferring to use human infants—orphans perhaps—or retarded humans for experiments, rather than adults, since infants and retarded humans would also have no idea of what was going to happen to them. So far as this argument is concerned nonhuman animals and infants and retarded humans are in the same category; and if we use this argument to justify experiments on nonhuman animals we have to ask ourselves whether we are also prepared to allow experiments on human infants and retarded adults; and if we make a distinction between animals and these humans, on what basis can we do it, other than a barefaced—and morally indefensible—preference for members of our own species?

There are many areas in which the superior mental powers of normal adult humans make a difference: anticipation, more detailed memory, greater knowledge of what is happening, and so on. Yet these differences do not all point to greater suffering on the part of the normal human being. Sometimes an animal may suffer more because of his more limited understanding. If, for instance, we are taking prisoners in wartime we can explain to them that while they must submit to capture, search, and confinement they will not otherwise be harmed and will be set free at the conclusion of hostilities. If we capture a wild animal, however, we cannot explain that we are not threatening its life. A wild animal cannot distinguish an attempt to overpower and confine from an attempt to kill; the one causes as much terror as the other.

It may be objected that comparisons of the sufferings of different species are impossible to make, and that for this reason when the interests of animals and humans clash the principle of equality gives no guidance. It is probably true that comparisons of suffering between members of different species cannot be made precisely, but precision is not essential. Even if we were to prevent the infliction of suffering on animals only when it is quite certain that the interests of humans will not be affected to anything like the extent that animals are affected, we would be forced to make radical changes in our treatment of animals that would involve our diet, the farming methods we use, experimental procedures in many fields of science, our approach to wildlife and to hunting, trapping and the wearing of furs, and areas of entertainment like circuses, rodeos, and zoos. As a result, a vast amount of suffering would be avoided.

So far I have said a lot about the infliction of suffering on animals, but nothing about killing them. This omission has been deliberate. The application of the principle of equality to the infliction of suffering is, in theory at least, fairly straightforward. Pain and suffering are bad and should be prevented or minimized, irrespective of the race, sex, or species of the being that suffers. How bad a pain is depends on how intense it is and how long it lasts, but pains of the same intensity and duration are equally bad, whether felt by humans or animals.

The wrongness of killing a being is more complicated. I have kept, and shall continue to keep, the question of killing in the background because in the present state of human tyranny over other species the more simple, straightforward principle of equal consideration of pain or pleasure is a sufficient basis for identifying and protesting against all the major abuses of animals that humans practice. Nevertheless, it is necessary to say something about killing.

Just as most humans are speciesists in their readiness to cause pain to animals when they would not cause a similar pain to humans for the same reason, so most humans are speciesists in their readiness to kill other animals when they would not kill humans. We need to proceed more cautiously here, however, because people hold widely differing views about when it is legitimate to kill humans, as the continuing debates over abortion and euthanasia attest. Nor have moral philosophers been able to agree on exactly what it is that makes it wrong to kill humans, and under what circumstances killing a human being may be justifiable.

Let us consider first the view that it is always wrong to take an innocent human life. We may call this the "sanctity of life" view. People who take this view oppose abortion and euthanasia. They do not usually, however, oppose the killing of nonhumans—so perhaps it would be more accurate to describe this view as the "sanctity of *human* life" view.

The belief that human life, and only human life, is sacrosanct is a form of speciesism. To see this, consider the following example.

Assume that, as sometimes happens, an infant has been

born with massive and irreparable brain damage. The damage is so severe that the infant can never be any more than a "human vegetable," unable to talk, recognize other people, act independently of others, or develop a sense of self-awareness. The parents of the infant, realizing that they cannot hope for any improvement in their child's condition and being in any case unwilling to spend, or ask the state to spend, the thousands of dollars that would be needed annually for proper care of the infant, ask the doctor to kill the infant painlessly.

Should the doctor do what the parents ask? Legally, he should not, and in this respect the law reflects the sanctity of life view. The life of every human being is sacred. Yet people who would say this about the infant do not object to the killing of nonhuman animals. How can they justify their different judgments? Adult chimpanzees, dogs, pigs, and many other species far surpass the brain-damaged infant in their ability to relate to others, act independently, be self-aware, and any other capacity that could reasonably be said to give value to life. With the most intensive care possible, there are retarded infants who can never achieve the intelligence level of a dog. Nor can we appeal to the concern of the infant's parents, since they themselves, in this imaginary example (and in some actual cases), do not want the infant kept alive.

The only thing that distinguishes the infant from the animal, in the eyes of those who claim it has a "right to life," is that it is, biologically, a member of the species Homo sapiens, whereas chimpanzees, dogs, and pigs are not. But to use *this* difference as the basis for granting a right to life to the infant and not to the other animals is, of course, pure speciesism.* It is exactly the kind of arbitrary difference that the most crude and overt kind of racist uses in attempting to justify racial discrimination.

* I am here putting aside religious views, for example the doctrine that all and only humans have immortal souls, or are made in the image of God. Historically these views have been very important, and no doubt are partly responsible for the idea that human life has a special sanctity. (For further historical discussion see Chapter 5.) Logically, however, these religious views are unsatisfactory, since a reasoned explanation of why it should be that all humans and no nonhumans have immortal souls is not

This does not mean that to avoid speciesism we must hold that it is as wrong to kill a dog as it is to kill a normal human being. The only position that is irredeemably speciesist is the one that tries to make the boundary of the right to life run exactly parallel to the boundary of our own species. Those who hold the sanctity of life view do this because while distinguishing sharply between humans and other animals they allow no distinctions to be made within our own species, objecting to the killing of the severely retarded and the hopelessly senile as strongly as they object to the killing of normal adults.

To avoid speciesism we must allow that beings which are similar in all relevant respects have a similar right to life—and mere membership in our own biological species cannot be a morally relevant criterion for this right. Within these limits we could still hold that, for instance, it is worse to kill a normal adult human, with a capacity for self-awareness, and the ability to plan for the future and have meaningful relations with others, than it is to kill a mouse, which presumably does not share all of these characteristics; or we might appeal to the close family and other personal ties which humans have but mice do not have to the same degree; or we might think that it is the consequences for other humans, who will be put in fear of their own lives, that makes the crucial difference; or we might think it is some combination of these factors, or other factors altogether.

Whatever criteria we choose, however, we will have to admit that they do not follow precisely the boundary of our own species. We may legitimately hold that there are some features of certain beings which make their lives more valuable than those of other beings; but there will surely be some nonhuman animals whose lives, by any standards, are more valuable than the lives of some humans. A chimpanzee, dog, or pig, for instance, will have a higher degree of self-awareness and a greater capacity for

offered. This belief too, therefore, comes under suspicion as a form of speciesism. In any case, defenders of the "sanctity of life" view are generally reluctant to base their position on purely religious doctrines, since these doctrines are no longer as widely accepted as they once were.

meaningful relations with others than a severely retarded infant or someone in a state of advanced senility. So if we base the right to life on these characteristics we must grant these animals a right to life as good as, or better than, such retarded or senile humans.

Now this argument cuts both ways. It could be taken as showing that chimpanzees, dogs, and pigs, along with some other species, have a right to life and we commit a grave moral offense whenever we kill them, even when they are old and suffering and our intention is to put them out of their misery. Alternatively one could take the argument as showing that the severely retarded and hopelessly senile have no right to life and may be killed for quite trivial reasons, as we now kill animals.

Since the focus of this book is on ethical questions concerning animals and not on the morality of euthanasia I shall not attempt to settle this issue finally. I think it is reasonably clear, though, that while both of the positions just described avoid speciesism, neither is entirely satisfactory. What we need is some middle position which would avoid speciesism but would not make the lives of the retarded and senile as cheap as the lives of pigs and dogs now are, nor make the lives of pigs and dogs so sacrosanct that we think it wrong to put them out of hopeless misery. What we must do is bring nonhuman animals within our sphere of moral concern and cease to treat their lives as expendable for whatever trivial purposes we may have. At the same time, once we realize that the fact that a being is a member of our own species is not in itself enough to make it always wrong to kill that being, we may come to reconsider our policy of preserving human lives at all costs, even when there is no prospect of a meaningful life or of existence without terrible pain.

I conclude, then, that a rejection of speciesism does not imply that all lives are of equal worth. While self-awareness, intelligence, the capacity for meaningful relations with others, and so on are not relevant to the question of inflicting pain—since pain is pain, whatever other capacities, beyond the capacity to feel pain, the being may have —these capacities may be relevant to the question of taking life. It is not arbitrary to hold that the life of a self-aware being, capable of abstract thought, of planning for the future, of complex acts of communication, and so on, is more valuable than the life of a being without these capacities. To see the difference between the issues of inflicting pain and taking life, consider how we would choose within our own species. If we had to choose to save the life of a normal human or a mentally defective human, we would probably choose to save the life of the normal human; but if we had to choose between preventing pain in the normal human or the mental defective—imagine that both have received painful but superficial injuries, and we only have enough painkiller for one of them—it is not nearly so clear how we ought to choose. The same is true when we consider other species. The evil of pain is, in itself, unaffected by the other characteristics of the being that feels the pain; the value of life is affected by these other characteristics.

Normally this will mean that if we have to choose between the life of a human being and the life of another animal we should choose to save the life of the human; but there may be special cases in which the reverse holds true, because the human being in question does not have the capacities of a normal human being. So this view is not speciesist, although it may appear to be at first glance. The preference, in normal cases, for saving a human life over the life of an animal when a choice *has* to be made is a preference based on the characteristics that normal humans have, and not on the mere fact that they are members of our own species. This is why when we consider members of our own species who lack the characteristics of normal humans we can no longer say that their lives are always to be preferred to those of other animals. This issue comes up in a practical way in the following chapter. In general, though, the question of when it is wrong to kill (painlessly) an animal is one to which we need give no precise answer. As long as we remember that we should give the same respect to the lives of animals as we give to the lives of those humans at a similar mental level, we shall not go far wrong.

In any case, the conclusions that are argued for in this book flow from the principle of minimizing suffering alone.

The idea that it is also wrong to kill animals painlessly gives some of these conclusions additional support which is welcome, but strictly unnecessary. Interestingly enough, this is true even of the conclusion that we ought to become vegetarians, a conclusion which in the popular mind is generally based on some kind of absolute prohibition on killing.

The reader may already have thought of some objections to the position I have taken in this chapter. What, for instance, do I propose to do about animals that may cause harm to humans? Should we try to stop animals from killing each other? How do we know that plants cannot feel pain, and if they can, must we starve? To avoid interrupting the flow of the main argument I have chosen to discuss these and other objections in a separate chapter, and the reader who is impatient to have his objections answered may look ahead to Chapter 6.

The next two chapters explore two examples of speciesism in practice. I have limited myself to two examples so that I would have space for a reasonably thorough discussion, although this limit means that the book contains no discussion at all of other practices that exist only because we do not take seriously the interests of other animals—practices like hunting, whether for sport or for furs; farming minks, foxes, and other animals for their fur; capturing wild animals (often after shooting their mothers) and imprisoning them in small cages for humans to stare at; tormenting animals to make them learn tricks for circuses, and tormenting them to make them entertain the folks at rodeos; slaughtering whales with explosive harpoons; and generally ignoring the interests of wild animals as we extend our empire of concrete and pollution over the surface of the globe.

While I shall say nothing about any of these things, the examples that I have chosen are very central and important forms of speciesism. I have not selected isolated examples of cruelty, like the revelations of the existence of organized dog-fighting contests that *The New York Times* featured so prominently in the summer of 1974. Most people have nothing to do with, and no sympathy for, these isolated occurrences. Readers of *The New York Times* no doubt said to themselves what a shocking thing it was, and how it should be suppressed, and then went on living their lives as before.

The practices discussed in the next two chapters are different. First, they involve not merely the few hundred animals that may have suffered in dog fights, but in one case tens of millions of animals, and in the other case, literally billions of animals every year. Second, we cannot pretend that we have nothing to do with these practices. One of them—experimentation on animals—is promoted by the government we elect, and largely paid for out of the taxes we pay. The other—rearing animals for food—is possible only because most people buy and eat the products of this practice. That is why I have chosen to discuss these particular forms of speciesism. They are the central ones. They cause more suffering to a greater number of animals than anything else that humans do. To stop them we must change the policies of our government, and we must change our own lives, to the extent of changing our diet. If these officially promoted and almost universally accepted forms of speciesism can be abolished, abolition of the other speciesist practices cannot be far behind.

NOTES

1. For Bentham's moral philosophy, see his *Introduction to the Principles of Morals and Legislation*, and for Sidgwick's see *The Methods of Ethics* (the passage quoted is from the seventh edition, p. 382). As examples of leading contemporary moral philosophers who incorporate a requirement of equal consideration of interests, see R. M. Hare, *Freedom and Reason* (New York: Oxford University Press, 1963) and John Rawls, *A Theory of Justice* (Cambridge: Harvard University Press, Belknap Press, 1972). For a brief account of the essential agreement on this issue between these and other positions, see R. M. Hare, "Rules of War and Moral Reasoning," *Philosophy and Public Affairs*, vol. 1, no. 2 (1972).

2. Letter to Henri Gregoire, February 25, 1809.

3. Reminiscences by Francis D. Gage, from Susan B. Anthony, *The History of Woman Suffrage*, vol. 1; the passage is to be found in the extract in Leslie Tanner, ed., *Voices from Women's Liberation* (New York: Signet, 1970).

4. I owe the term "speciesism" to Richard Ryder.

5. *Introduction to the Principles of Morals and Legislation*, chapter 17.

6. Lord Brain, "Presidential Address" in C. A. Keele and R. Smith, eds., *The Assessment of Pain in Men and Animals* (London: Universities Federation for Animal Welfare, 1962).

7. Ibid., p. 11.

8. Richard Serjeant, *The Spectrum of Pain* (London: Hart-Davis, 1969), p. 72.

9. See the reports of the Committee on Cruelty to Wild Animals (Command Paper 8266, 1951), paragraphs 36-42; the Departmental Committee on Experiments on Animals (Command Paper 2641, 1965), paragraphs 179-182; and the Technical Committee to Enquire into the Welfare of Animals Kept under Intensive Livestock Husbandry Systems (Command Paper 2836, 1965), paragraphs 26-28 (London: Her Majesty's Stationery Office).

10. One chimpanzee, Washoe, has been taught the sign language used by deaf people, and acquired a vocabulary of 350 signs. Another, Lana, communicates in structured sentences by pushing buttons on a special machine. For a brief account of Washoe's abilities, see Jane van Lawick-Goodall, *In the Shadow of Man* (Boston: Houghton Mifflin, 1971), pp. 252-254; and for Lana, see *Newsweek*, 7 January 1974, and *New York Times*, 4 December 1974.

11. *In the Shadow of Man*, p. 225; Michael Peters makes a similar

point in "Nature and Culture," in Stanley and Roslind Godlovitch
and John Harris, eds., *Animals, Men and Morals* (New York: Taplinger Publishing Co., 1972).

   12. Konrad Lorenz, *King Solomon's Ring* (New York: T. Y. Crowell,
1952); N. Tinbergen, *The Herring Gull's World*, rev. ed. (New
York: Basic Books, 1974).

2

Tools for Research . . .

or what the public doesn't know
it is paying for.

In July 1973 Congressman Les Aspin of Wisconsin learned
through an advertisement in an obscure newspaper that the
United States Air Force was planning to purchase 200
beagle puppies, with vocal cords tied to prevent normal
barking, for tests of poisonous gases. Shortly afterward it
became known that the army was also proposing to use
beagles—400 this time—in similar tests.

Aspin began a vigorous protest, supported by antivivi-
section societies. Advertisements were placed in major newspapers across the country. Letters from an outraged public
began pouring in. An aide from the House of Representatives Armed Services Committee said that the committee
received more mail on the beagles than it had received on
any other subject since Truman sacked General Mac-
Arthur, while an internal Department of Defense memo
released by Aspin said that the volume of mail the department had received was the greatest ever for any single
event, surpassing even the mail on the bombings of North
Vietnam and Cambodia.[1] After defending the experiments
intially, the Defense Department then announced that it
was postponing them, and looking into the possibility of
replacing the beagles with other experimental animals.

All this amounted to a rather curious incident; curious because the public furor over this particular experiment implied a remarkable ignorance of the nature of quite standard experiments performed by the armed services, research establishments, universities, and commercial firms of many different kinds. True, the proposed air force and army experiments were designed so that many animals would suffer and die without any certainty that this suffering and death would save a single human life, or benefit humans in any way at all; but the same can be said for tens of thousands of other experiments performed in the United States alone each year. For instance, limiting ourselves for the moment just to experiments done on beagles, the following should, one might think, have provoked as much protest as those planned by the air force and the army:

At the Lovelace Foundation, Albuquerque, New Mexico, experimenters forced sixty-four beagles to inhale radioactive strontium 90 as part of a larger "Fission Product Inhalation Program" which began in 1961 and has been paid for by the US Atomic Energy Commission. In this particular experiment twenty-five of the dogs eventually died. One of the deaths occurred during an epileptic seizure; another from a brain hemorrhage. Other dogs, before death, became feverish and anemic, lost their appetites, had hemorrhages and bloody diarrhea.

The experimenters, in their published report, compared their results with the results of other experiments at the University of Utah and at Argonne National Laboratory, in Illinois, in which beagles were injected with strontium 90. They concluded that the various experiments had led to similar results on the dose of strontium 90 needed to produce "early deaths" in 50 percent of a sample group of beagles, but that there was a difference in the number of deaths occurring later, because dogs injected with strontium 90 retain more of the radioactive substance than dogs forced to inhale it.[2]

At the University of Rochester School of Medicine a team of experimenters placed fifty beagles in wooden boxes and irradiated them with different levels of radiation by X-rays. Twenty-one of the dogs died between the ninth and thirty-ninth day after irradiation. The experimenters determined the dose at which 50 percent of the animals will die with "95 percent confidence." The irradiated dogs vomited, had diarrhea, and lost their appetites. Later they hemorrhaged from the mouth and the anus. In their report these experimenters summarized nine other experiments in which more than 700 beagles and other dogs were irradiated with X-rays, and they said that the injuries produced in their own experiments were "typical of those described for the dog."[3]

Experimenters working for the US Food and Drug Administration gave thirty beagles and thirty pigs large amounts of methoxychlor (a pesticide) in their food, seven days a week for six months, "in order to ensure tissue damage." Within eight weeks, eleven dogs showed signs of "abnormal behavior" including nervousness, salivation, muscle tremors, spasms, and convulsions. Dogs in convulsions breathed as rapidly as 200 times a minute before lack of oxygen caused them to collapse. Upon recovery from an episode of convulsion and collapse, the dogs were uncoordinated, apparently blind, and "any stimulus such as dropping a feed pan, squirting water, or touching the animals initiated another convulsion." After further experiments on an additional twenty beagles, the experimenters concluded that massive daily doses of methoxychlor produce different effects in dogs from those produced in pigs.[4]

These three examples should be enough to show that the air force beagle experiments were in no way exceptional. Note that all of these experiments, according to the experimenters' own reports, obviously caused the animals to suffer considerably before dying. No steps were taken to prevent this suffering, even when it was clear that the radiation or poison had made the animals extremely sick. Note, too, that these experiments are parts of series of similar experiments, repeated with only minor variations, that are being carried out all over the country. Note, finally, that these experiments do not save human lives. We already knew that strontium 90 was unhealthy before the beagles died; and the experimenters who poisoned dogs and pigs with methoxychlor knew beforehand that the large amounts they were feeding the animals (amounts no human would ever consume) would cause damage. In any case, as the differing results they obtained on dogs and pigs make clear, it is not possible to reach any firm conclusions about the effects of a substance on humans from tests on other species. The same is true of radioactive substances, and so the precision with which experimenters determine the dose necessary to make 50 percent of a sample group of beagles die has no application to humans.

Nor should we limit ourselves to dogs. People tend to care about dogs because they have dogs as pets; but other animals are as capable of suffering as dogs are. Dogs are only one species of many that are used in experiments. In Britain sentimental attachment to dogs and cats has gone so far that the law regulating experiments on animals requires an experimenter to obtain a special certificate for performing an experiment on unanesthetized dogs and cats; apes and monkeys, however, receive no such protection; nor, of course, does the common laboratory rat. Few people feel sympathy for rats. Yet the laboratory rat is an intelligent, gentle animal, the result of many generations of special breeding, and there can be no doubt that the rats are capable of suffering, and do suffer from the countless painful experiments performed on them.

The practice of experimenting on nonhuman animals as it exists today throughout the world reveals the brutal consequences of speciesism. Experiments are performed on animals that inflict severe pain without the remotest prospect of significant benefits for humans or any other animals. These are not isolated instances, but part of a major industry. In Britain, where experimenters are required to report the number of experiments performed, official government figures show that around 5 million experiments on animals are now performed each year. In the United States there are no figures of comparable accuracy. Under the Animal Welfare Act of 1970 the US Department of Agriculture publishes a report listing the number of animals used by facilities registered with it, but this list is incomplete in many ways. It does not include rats, mice, birds, reptiles, frogs, or domestic farm animals used for experimental purposes; it does not include animals used in secondary schools, or by government agencies; and it does not include experiments performed by facilities that do not transport animals interstate or receive grants or contracts from the federal government. According to this very incomplete report, the following animals were used in experimentation in 1973: dogs, 195,157; cats, 66,195; primates, 42,298; rabbits, 447,570; hamsters, 454,986; guinea pigs, 408,970; "wild animals" (species not given), 38,169; a total of 1,653,385.[5]

No one really knows how many animals of all kinds are used in the United States. An official of the US Department of Agriculture has stated that the number of rats and mice used annually for research purposes is estimated at 40 million.[6] In testimony before congressional committees in 1966, the Laboratory Animal Breeders Association estimated that the number of mice, rats, guinea pigs, hamsters, and rabbits used for experimental purposes in 1965 had totaled around 60 million; and they projected a figure of 97 million for these species by 1970. They estimated the number of dogs and cats used in 1965 as between 500,000 and 1 million.[7] A 1971 survey carried out by Rutgers University College of Agriculture and Environmental Sciences produced the following estimates of the number of animals used each year in U.S. laboratories: 85,000 primates, 500,000 dogs, 200,000 cats, 700,000 rabbits, 46,000 pigs, 23,000 sheep, 1.7 million birds, 45 million rodents, 15–20 million frogs, and 200,000 turtles, snakes, and lizards; a total of more than 63 million animals.[8]

These estimates are somewhat lower than the Laboratory Animal Breeders Association estimates for the species included in their survey for 1965; and much lower than their projections for 1970. These projections may, of course, have been overoptimistic expectations about the continued growth of the animal breeding industry, which had grown phenomenally in preceding years. Assuming then that the Rutgers University figures are a reasonable, and certainly not exaggerated, estimate, it is still clear that the official Animal Welfare Act report covers only a very small fraction of the animals experimented upon in the United States.

Of this vast number of experiments, only a few contribute to important medical research. Huge numbers of animals are used in university departments from Forestry to Psychology, and many more are used for commercial purposes, to test new cosmetics, shampoos, food coloring agents and other inessential items. All this can go on only because of our prejudice against taking seriously the suffering of a being that is not a member of our own species. The typical defender of experiments on animals does not deny that animals suffer. He cannot use this argument because he needs to stress the similarities between humans and other animals in order to claim that his experiment may have some relevance for human purposes. The researcher who forces rats to choose between starvation and electric shock to see if they develop ulcers (they do) does so because he knows that the rat has a nervous system very similar to man's, and presumably feels an electric shock in a similar way.

There has been opposition to experimenting on animals for a long time. This opposition has made little headway because experimenters, backed by commercial firms who profit by supplying laboratory animals and equipment, have been able to convince legislators and the public that opposition comes from sentimental cranks who consider the interests of animals more important than the interests of human beings. But to be opposed to what is going on now it is not necessary to insist that all experiments stop immediately. All that we need to say is that experiments serving no direct and urgent purpose should stop immediately, and in the remaining areas of research, methods involving animals should be replaced as soon as possible by alternative methods not involving animals.

To understand why this seemingly modest change would be so important we need to know something about the type of experiments that are now being performed, and have been performed for the past sixty or seventy years. Then we will be able to assess the claim by defenders of the present situation that experiments on animals are done only for important objectives. The following pages, there-

fore, describe some experiments on animals. Reading the
reports of these experiments is not a pleasant experience;
but we have an obligation to inform ourselves about what
is done in our own community, especially since we are
paying, through our taxes, for most of this research. If the
animals have to go through these experiments, the least
we can do is read the reports and inform ourselves about
them. That is why I have not attempted to tone down or
gloss over some of the things that are done to animals. At
the same time I have not tried to make these things worse
than they really are. The reports that follow are all drawn
from the accounts written by the experimenters themselves,
and published by them in the scientific journals in which
experimenters communicate with each other.

This source is, inevitably, more favorable to the experimenters than a report by an outside observer would
be. There are two reasons for this. One is that the experimenters will not emphasize suffering that they have
inflicted unless it is necessary to do so in order to communicate the results of the experiment. Thus a good deal
of suffering goes unreported in the journals. For instance,
when the inevitable accidents occur and electric shock devices are left on when they should have been turned off, or
animals recover consciousness in the midst of an operation
because of an improperly administered anesthetic, the experimenter will not include these "irrelevant" items in his
report. The second reason why scientific journals are a
source favorable to experimenters is that they include only
those experiments that the experimenters and editors of
the journals consider significant. The British government
committee that investigated experiments on animals found
that only about one quarter of the experiments performed
ever found their way into print.[9] There is no reason to believe that a higher proportion of experiments are published
in the United States; indeed since the proportion of minor
colleges with researchers of lesser talents is much higher
here than in Britain, it seems probable that an even smaller
proportion of experiments yield results of any significance
at all.

So in reading the following pages bear in mind that they
are drawn from sources favorable to the experimenters;

and if the results of the experiments do not appear to be of sufficient importance to justify the suffering that they caused, remember that these examples are all taken from the small fraction of experiments performed that researchers and editors considered significant enough to publish.

One last warning. The reports published in the journals always appear under the names of the experimenters. I have not deleted these names, since I see no reason to protect experimenters behind a cloak of anonymity. Nevertheless it should not be assumed that the people named are especially evil or cruel people. They are doing what they were trained to do, and what thousands of their colleagues do. The experiments are intended to illustrate not sadism on the part of individual experimenters, but the more widespread mentality of speciesism that makes it possible for these experimenters to do these things without serious consideration of the interests of the animals they are using.

Many of the most painful experiments are performed in the field of psychology. To give some idea of the numbers of animals experimented on in psychology laboratories, take as an example one small area of the subject—that involving experiments on the brain of living animals, including cutting, coagulating, and removing brain tissue, and stimulating the brain by electrical and chemical means. The international journal *Psychological Abstracts* reports about 700 papers dealing with this particular subject each year. Nearly all the experiments use more than ten animals, and sometimes many more, and as we have seen, for every experiment published there are probably three that are never published. This suggests, at a conservative estimate, around 50,000 animals experimented on every year in this one area of psychological research.[10]

Still more common are experiments designed to find out how animals react to various forms of punishment. The punishment, which is usually an electric shock, can be quite severe. The following is a straightforward case:

Erling Boe of the University of Pennsylvania trained eighty rats to press a lever to obtain food pellets. When the training was completed the apparatus was changed so that pressing the levers caused an electric current to flow through the metal grid floor of the cages in which the rats lived. Different levels of current were tried, and also a variable current. Boe found that the variable current was almost as effective in suppressing the trained behavior as the highest level of punishment, 110 volts.[11]

In another instance P. Baddia, S. Culbertson, and J. Harsh of Bowling Green State University, Ohio, tested whether a signal warning the rats when they were going to receive an electric shock made a difference to the severity of the punishment. They used ten rats. Electric current was again delivered to the rats' feet through a grid floor. The test sessions were six hours long and frequent shock was "at all times unavoidable and inescapable." The rats could press either of two levers within the test chamber in order to receive warning of a coming shock. The experimenters concluded that the rats preferred to be warned of a shock even when the warning signal led to a longer and stronger shock.[12]

Not surprisingly, animals are more sensitive to shocks administered on some parts of their bodies than on others; and this being so, researchers have thought it necessary to test the effects of varying the place of administration. For this purpose O. S. Ray and R. J. Barrett, working in the psychology research unit of the Veterans Administration Hospital, Pittsburgh, gave electric shocks to the feet of 1,042 mice. They then caused convulsions by giving more intense shocks through cup-shaped electrodes applied to the animals' eyes or through clips attached to their ears. They reported that unfortunately some of the mice who "successfully completed Day One training were found sick or dead prior to testing on Day Two."[13]

As an additional refinement, the animals can be provided with a means of turning off the electric current, but made to endure a prescribed length of shock before doing so. Perrin Cohen of the University of Pennsylvania hung six dogs in hammocks with legs protruding and electrodes taped to their hind feet. Their heads were placed between two panels. If a dog learned to press its head against the left panel the shock was turned off: otherwise it remained on indefinitely. Three of the dogs were required to wait periods of two to seven seconds while being shocked before making the response that turned off the current. If they did not wait they received further shocks. Each dog was given from twenty-six to forty-six sessions in the hammock, each session consisting of eighty "trials" or shocks, administered at intervals of one minute. Cohen reported that the dogs, who were unable to move in their hammocks, barked or bobbed their heads when the current was applied. He found a delay in the dogs' responses that increased proportionately to the time the dogs were required to endure the shock; but a gradual increase in the intensity of the shock had no systematic effect on the timing of the response.[14]

At Harvard University R. Solomon, L. Kamin, and L. Wynne tested the effects of electric shock on the behavior of dogs. They placed forty dogs in a device called a "shuttlebox" which consists of a box divided into two compartments separated by a barrier. Initially the barrier was set at the height of the dog's back. Hundreds of intense electric shocks were delivered to the dogs' feet through a grid floor. At first the dogs could escape the shock if they learned to jump the barrier into the other compartment. In an attempt to "discourage" one dog from jumping, the experimenters forced the dog to jump *into* shock 100 times. They said that as the dog jumped he gave a "sharp anticipatory yip which turned into a yelp when he landed on the electrified grid." They then blocked the passage between the compartments with a piece of plate glass and tested the same dog again. The dog "jumped forward and smashed his head against the glass." Initially dogs showed symptoms such as "defecation, urination, yelping and shrieking, trembling, attacking the apparatus" and so on, but after ten or twelve days of trials dogs that were prevented from escaping shock ceased to resist. The experimenters reported themselves "impressed" by this, and concluded that a combination of the plate glass barrier and foot shock was "very effective" in eliminating jumping by dogs.[15]

Although the experiment just described took place more than twenty years ago, dogs are still being shocked in shuttleboxes. At Cornell University and the University of Pennsylvania, Martin Seligman has carried out a series of experiments of this type. In a report written with two colleagues, Steven Maier and James Geer, Seligman has described his work as follows:

> When a normal, naive [untrained] dog receives escape/avoidance training in a shuttlebox, the following behavior typically occurs: at the onset of electric shock the dog runs frantically about, defecating, urinating and howling until it scrambles over the barrier and so escapes from shock. On the next trial the dog, running and howling, crosses the barrier more quickly, and so on, until efficient avoidance emerges.

Seligman altered this pattern by strapping dogs in harnesses and giving them shocks from which they had no means of escape. When he then placed these dogs in a shuttlebox he found that:

> such a dog reacts *initially* to shock in the shuttlebox in the same manner as the naive dog. However in dramatic contrast to the naive dog it soon stops running and remains silent until shock terminates. The dog does not cross the barrier and escape from shock. Rather it seems to "give up" and passively "accept" the shock. On succeeding trials the dog continues to fail to make escape movements and thus takes 50 seconds of severe, pulsating shock on each trial. . . . A dog previously exposed to inescapable shock . . . may take unlimited shock without escaping or avoiding at all.

After citing experiments Seligman and a colleague had done in 1967 in support of these observations, and similar results reported on rats by C. P. Richter of the Johns

Hopkins Medical School, Seligman, Maier, and Geer describe further experiments in which they again produced the state of helplessness in which the dogs accepted shock. This time the experimenters attempted to teach the dogs how to avoid shock. In this experiment the duration of actual shock experienced by the dogs on various occasions totaled more than twelve minutes. As a conclusion the experimenters said that "one might speculate" that traumatic events which the individual can do nothing to prevent result in a passive response to further "aversive events."[16]

Two years later Seligman reported on further experiments that he performed with Denis Groves at Cornell University which established that cage-raised beagles, kept isolated from other dogs and humans, are more susceptible to inescapable shock than ordinary mongrel dogs.[17]

At Tulane University in New Orleans, Gordon Gallup and Jack Maser have studied the effects of inescapable shock on chickens. They found that they could produce a state of frozen immobility in chickens by giving "intense" inescapable electric shock. They concluded that inescapable shock is "more aversive, or more aptly, more 'distressing' than escapable shock."[18]

The methods used by university teachers are, naturally enough, adopted by their students, and it is possible to gain a doctorate in psychology by shocking animals. At Pennsylvania State University, for instance, J. Barrett's work toward his PhD included placing twenty-five ducklings in isolated boxes and punishing them with shock for natural actions like pecking a pole or following a moving object. It proved possible to halt these actions by consistent punishment.[19]

Sometimes an experimenter will want to make sure that an animal really wants to do something very much, so that he can observe the effects of punishment on this desire. The simplest way to do this is to deprive the animal of food or water, since the animal can then be presumed to have a strong desire for the food or water. The following experiments illustrate the use of this technique:

Eward Deaux of Antioch College (in an experiment that also was part of a PhD dissertation) deprived sixty-six rats of water. He then permitted the rats to obtain water through a tube, but each rat received an electric shock every time it licked the tube. One group of rats, called "Group high," received larger water droplets from their tubes in a shorter period of time than another group, named "Group low." Deaux reported that the "Group high" rats licked their tubes less often than "Group low" rats. He concluded that the rate at which rats are allowed water is an "effective" variable in training and rewarding rats, and said that "the implications of this finding are great."[20]

At the University of North Carolina at Chapel Hill, D. E. McMillan starved four pigeons to 80 percent of their normal weight and implanted electrodes around their pubis bone (near the genitals) for delivering electric shock. The birds were trained to peck a key to obtain food, and they were then "punished" with a shock for pecking. Various drugs were injected into the birds to test their effects on the number of pecks the birds made while being punished. The experimenter warned, however, that "because so many factors may influence the effects of drugs on punished behavior, any simple description of the effects of a drug on punished behavior is probably an oversimplification."[21]

The use of the pubic regions for the delivery of electric shock, as in the preceding experiment, is a fairly standard procedure for experiments on birds; so much so that an article appeared recently in one of the scientific journals advising researchers that instead of using gold wire for the electrodes, which can be expensive, stainless steel wire should be used. According to Richard Coughlin, Jr., the author of the article, this can be used for as long as six months and "will allow for implantation of 200 to 300 pigeons at considerably less cost than if gold wire were used."[22]

In another "conflict" experiment W. Sawrey, J. Conger, and E. Turrell designed an apparatus which prevented rats from obtaining food and water unless they crossed an electrified grid. Other groups of rats underwent similar food and water deprivation, but without the opportunity of crossing the grid, while still others merely received electric shock without food and water deprivation. At the end of the experiment the animals were killed and their stomachs examined for ulcers. It was found that those who experienced the conflict between deprivation and shock had the most ulcers.[23]

Experimental psychologists have found other reasons for starving animals. Luci Paul of Temple University starved thirty-one rats for seven days and then offered them live mice and infant rats. The hungry rats killed and ate the infant rats as often as they did mice. Paul concluded that hunger was a powerful influence on the killing behavior of rats.[24]

H. Ziegler, H. Green, and R. Lehrer of the City University of New York's City College starved pigeons to 70 percent of their normal weight. They reported that as the birds lost weight they ate more and more food when allowed to do so in test sessions. They concluded that "prolonged periods of food deprivation are typically followed by an increased responsiveness to food which may be measured in a variety of ways." They added, however, that the relationship between food deprivation and eating is an "exceedingly complex" problem.[25]

At Princeton University William Moorcroft, Loy Lytle, and Byron Campbell "terminally deprived" 256 young rats of food and water. They then watched the rats die from thirst and starvation. They concluded that under conditions of fatal thirst and starvation young rats are much more active than normal adult rats given food and water.[26]

What is so disturbing about many of the preceding experiments is that despite the suffering the animals have gone through, the results obtained are very often trivial and obvious—even though these experiments were more significant, apparently, than others that did not get published. The conclusions of some of the experiments cited show, clearly enough, that experimental psychologists have put a lot of effort into telling us in scientific jargon what we knew all along, and what we could have confirmed in more harmless ways with a little thought.

So far we have seen psychology experiments on dogs, birds, and rats and mice. Apes and monkeys are also widely used because their behavior more closely resembles that of humans. One long and well-known series of experiments on monkeys has been performed under the guidance of Harry F. Harlow at the Primate Research Center, Madison, Wisconsin. In a paper written in 1965 with R. Dodsworth and M. Harlow, Harry Harlow describes his work as follows:

> For the past ten years we have studied the effects of partial social isolation by raising monkeys from birth onwards in bare wire cages. . . . These monkeys suffer total maternal deprivation. . . . More recently we have initiated a series of studies on the effects of *total* social isolation by rearing monkeys from a few hours after birth until 3, 6 or 12 months of age in [a] stainless steel chamber. During the prescribed sentence in this apparatus the monkey has no contact with any animal, human or sub-human.

These studies, Harlow continues, found that:

> sufficiently severe and enduring early isolation reduces these animals to a social-emotional level in which the primary social responsiveness is fear.[27]

In another article Harlow and associate Stephen Suomi describe how they were trying to induce psychopathology in infant monkeys by a technique that appeared not to be working. They were then visited by John Bowlby, a British psychiatrist. According to Harlow and Suomi's account Bowlby listened to the story of their troubles, and then toured the laboratory. After he had seen the monkeys individually housed in bare wire cages he asked: "Why are you trying to produce psychopathology in monkeys? You already have more psychopathological monkeys in the laboratory than have ever been seen on the face of the earth."

In this article Harlow and Suomi describe how they had the "fascinating idea" of inducing depression by "allowing baby monkeys to attach to cloth surrogate mothers who could become monsters":

> The first of these monsters was a cloth monkey mother who, upon schedule or demand, would eject high-pressure compressed air. It would blow the animal's skin practically off its body. What did the baby monkey do? It simply clung tighter and tighter to the mother, because a frightened infant clings to its mother at all costs. We did not achieve any psychopathology.
>
> However, we did not give up. We built another surrogate monster mother that would rock so violently that the baby's head and teeth would rattle. All the baby did was cling tighter and tighter to the surrogate. The third monster we built had an embedded wire frame within its body which would spring forward and eject the infant from its ventral surface. The infant would subsequently pick itself off the floor, wait for the frame to return into the cloth body, and then cling again to the surrogate. Finally, we built our porcupine mother. On command, this mother would eject sharp brass spikes over all of the ventral surface of its body. Although the infants were distressed by these pointed rebuffs, they simply waited until the spikes receded and then returned and clung to the mother.

These results, the experimenters remark, were not so surprising, since the only recourse of an injured child is to cling to its mother.

Eventually, Harlow and Suomi gave up on the artificial monster mothers because they found something better: a real monkey mother that was a monster. To produce such mothers, they reared female monkeys in isolation, and then tried to make them pregnant. Unfortunately the females did not have normal sexual relations with male monkeys, so they had to be made pregnant by a technique that Harlow and Suomi refer to as "a rape rack." When the babies were born the researchers observed the monkeys. They found that some simply ignored the infants, failing to cuddle the crying baby to the breast as normal monkeys do when they hear their baby cry. The other pattern of behavior observed was different:

> The other monkeys were brutal or lethal. One of their favorite tricks was to crush the infant's skull with their teeth. But the really sickening behavior pattern was that of smashing the infant's face to the floor, then rubbing it back and forth.[28]

More recent reports show that Harlow and his colleagues are still at it, thinking up endless new variations of their old theme. In a 1972 paper Harlow and Suomi say that because depression in humans has been characterized as embodying a state of "helplessness and hopelessness, sunken in a well of despair," they designed a device "on an intuitive basis" (that is, acting on a hunch) to reproduce such a "well" both physically and psychologically. They built a vertical chamber with stainless steel sides sloping inwards to form a rounded bottom and placed young monkeys in it for periods up to forty-five days. They found that after a few days of this confinement the monkeys "spend most of their time huddled in a corner of the chamber." The confinement produced "severe and persistent psychopathological behavior of a depressive nature." Even nine months after release the monkeys would sit clasping their arms around their bodies instead of moving around and exploring as normal monkeys do. But the report ends inconclusively, and ominously:

> whether [the results] can be traced specifically to variables such as chamber shape, chamber size, duration of confinement, age at time of confinement, prior and/or subsequent social environment or, more likely, to a combination of these and other variables remains the subject of further research.[29]

Another paper explains how, in addition to the "well of despair," Harlow and his colleagues created a "tunnel of terror" to produce terrified monkeys,[30] and in yet another report Harlow and colleagues P. Plubell and C. Baysinger describe how they were able to "induce psychological death in rhesus monkeys" by providing them with terrycloth-covered "mother surrogates" which were normally kept at a temperature of 99°F, but could be rapidly chilled to 35°F to simulate a kind of maternal rejection.[81]

The practices of the Wisconsin Primate Center are now spreading around the country. For example C. Baysinger, who collaborated with Harlow to produce "psychological death" in monkeys, teamed with E. Brandt and G. Mitchell at the National Center for Primate Biology, Davis, California, to deprive still more newborn monkeys of contact with their mothers and other monkeys. They observed "an incredible array of abnormal behaviors" including "bizarre movement, abnormal postures, stereotyped movements, self-biting, self-grasping the body, self-grasping the head, self-rubbing, self-threatening and autoeroticism." They noted that abnormal movements appeared in the first month, but each individual isolated monkey did not "settle down to his own favorite type of weirdness until well after seven months of age." The experimenters admitted, however, that previous researchers (they listed similar studies in 1960, 1963, 1964, 1965, 1966 and 1970) had witnessed "many or even most of the same isolate symptoms."[82]

I have only been able to list a few of the tens of thousands of experiments performed annually in the field of psychology; but perhaps these are enough to show that experiments involving animals can cause great pain with no prospect of yielding really momentous or vital new knowledge. Unfortunately animals have become, for the psychologist and for other researchers, mere tools. A laboratory may consider the cost of these "tools," but a certain callousness toward them becomes apparent, not only in the experiments performed but also in the wording of the reports. Consider, for instance, the description "his own favorite type of weirdness" in the report of the preceding experiment on isolated monkeys: can one imagine a scientist using such a phrase in a description of the behavior of neurotic children?

Another instance comes from Britain. In a report published in *New Scientist* under the title "Seeing and Nothingness" (apparently some kind of pun on Sartre's famous work *Being and Nothingness* was intended), Nicholas Humphrey described how he removed the visual cortex of a female monkey, which meant that although she could see, she could not recognize anything that she saw, and behaved more like a blind person than like one with normal sight. Some time after the operation, however, Humphrey says:

> At this stage our work was interrupted when we moved from Cambridge to the Oxford Laboratory. Helen [the monkey] moved with us, *but I had a thesis to finish, and she was left to her own devices for about ten months—such devices, that is, as she could manage in a small cage.*[33]

No doubt this kind of interruption happens fairly often in the busy life of researchers; it is merely unusual to find a researcher admitting in print that the completion of his thesis takes priority over the suffering of one of his experimental subjects.

Detachment is made easier by the use of a technical jargon that disguises the real nature of what is going on. Psychologists, under the influence of the behaviorist doctrine that only what can be observed should be mentioned, have developed a whole collection of terms that refer to pain without appearing to do so. Alice Heim, one of the few psychologists who has spoken out against the pointless animal experimentation of her colleagues, describes it this way:

> The work on "animal behavior" is always expressed in scientific, hygienic sounding terminology, which enables the indoctrination of the normal, non-sadistic young psychology student to proceed without his anxiety being aroused. Thus techniques of "extinction"

are used for what is in fact torturing by thirst or near-starvation or electric-shocking; "partial reinforcement" is the term for frustrating an animal by only occasionally fulfilling the expectations which the experimenter has aroused in the animal by previous training; "negative stimulus" is the term used for subjecting an animal to a stimulus which he avoids, if possible. The term "avoidance" is O.K. because it is an observable activity. The terms "painful" or "frightening" stimulus are less O.K. since they are anthropomorphic, they imply that the animal has feelings—and that these may be similar to human feelings. This is not allowable because it is non-behavioristic and unscientific (and also because this might deter the younger and less hard-boiled researcher from pursuing certain ingenious experiments. He might allow a little play to his imagination.) The cardinal sin for the experimental psychologist working in the field of "animal behavior" is anthropomorphism. Yet if he did not believe in the analogue of the human being and the lower animal even he, presumably, would find his work largely unjustified.[34]

We can see the kind of jargon to which Heim refers in the reports of experiments already given. Note that even when researchers like Seligman or Gallup and Maser feel compelled to say that the subjects of their experiments "gave up" trying to escape shock. or found inescapable shock "distressing," these experimenters find it necessary to place these terms, which imply the existence of feelings, in quotation marks, as if to say that they are not *really* imputing feelings to the animals, although the animals do behave as if they had the feelings in question.

Of course, the logical consequence of this view of "scientific method" is that experiments on animals cannot teach us anything about humans. Amazing as it may seem, some psychologists have been so concerned to avoid anthropomorphism that they have accepted this conclusion! This attitude is illustrated by the following autobiographical statement, which appeared in *New Scientist*:

When fifteen years ago I applied to do a degree course in psychology, a steely-eyed interviewer, himself a psychologist, questioned me closely on my motives and asked me what I believed psychology to be and what was its principal subject matter? Poor naive simpleton that I was, I replied that it was the study of the mind and that human beings were its raw material. With a glad cry at being able to deflate me so effectively, the interviewer declared that psychologists were not interested in the mind, that rats were the golden focus of study, not people, and that he advised me strongly to trot around to the philosophy department next door. . . .[35]

Perhaps not many psychologists would now proudly state that their work has nothing to do with the human mind. Nevertheless many of the experiments that are performed on rats can only be explained by assuming that the experimenters really are interested in the behavior of the rat for its own sake, without any thought of learning anything about humans. In that case, though, what possible justification can there be for the infliction of so much suffering? It is certainly not for the benefit of the rat.

So the researcher's central dilemma exists in an especially acute form in psychology: either the animal is not like us, in which case there is no reason for performing the experiment; or else the animal is like us, in which case we ought not to perform an experiment on the animal which would be considered outrageous if performed on one of us.

Another major field of experimentation involves the poisoning of millions of animals annually. Often this too is done for trivial reasons. In Britain it is known that over 23 percent of the 5 million experiments performed annually are mandatory tests of drugs and other materials required by law. In the United States no figures are available, but the Food and Drug Administration requires extensive animal testing of new substances before they are released. While it may be thought justifiable to require animal tests of potentially life-saving drugs, the same tests are done for products like cosmetics, food colorings, and floor polishes.

Should hundreds of animals suffer so that a new kind of lipstick or mouthwash can be put on the market? Don't we already have enough of these products? Who benefits from their introduction, except the companies that hope to make a profit from their new gimmick?

To appreciate what is involved in introducing these new products it is necessary to know something about the standard methods of testing. The standard test for toxicity, or the extent to which a substance is poisonous, is the "Lethal Dosage 50" test, commonly abbreviated to LD_{50}. The aim of this test is to determine the dosage level at which 50 percent of the test animals will die. Usually this means that all of the animals will become very sick before half finally succumb and the other half survive. In the case of fairly harmless substances it is still considered good procedure to find the concentration that will make half the animals die; consequently enormous quantities have to be force-fed to the animals, and death may be caused merely by the large volume or high concentration given to the animals—this has no relevance to the circumstances in which humans will use the product.[36] It is also normal to let the process of poisoning take its full course, until death occurs. To put dying animals out of their misery might give a slightly inaccurate result.

Cosmetics and other substances are also tested for eye damage and skin damage. Here the standard methods, used by the US Food and Drug Administration and in other countries, is the Draize test, named after J. H. Draize.[37] Rabbits are the animals most often used. Concentrated solutions of the product to be tested are dripped into the rabbits' eyes, sometimes repeatedly over a period of several days. The damage is then measured according to the size of the area injured, the degree of swelling and redness, and other types of injury. One researcher employed by a large chemical company has described the highest level of reaction as follows:

Total loss of vision due to serious internal injury to cornea or internal structure. Animal holds eye shut urgently. May squeal, claw at eye, jump and try to escape.[38]

By shutting or clawing at the eye, however, the rabbit may succeed in dislodging the substance. To prevent this the animals are now usually immobilized in holding devices from which only their heads protrude. In addition their eyes may be held permanently open by the use of metal clips which keep the eyelids apart. Thus the animals can obtain no relief at all from the burning irritation of substances placed in their eyes.

Skin testing on animals requires that hair be removed first. This can be done by applying a strong adhesive tape and then rapidly removing it. Repeated applications of the tape on the bare skin may be used to remove additional layers of skin. After the skin has been prepared the irritants are applied and covered with a patch of adhesive plaster. After one or two days the patch is removed and the skin examined. If a test of repeated applications of the substance is wanted, however, the patch is not used. Instead the animal is restrained in a device that prevents it from scratching or licking off the irritant. In this way applications can be repeated at frequent intervals for a year or so.[39]

These are the standard procedures, and the following example—a group of tests performed on a nasal decongestant known as "Amidephrine Mesylate"—is an ordinary example of these procedures in practice:

J. Weikel, Jr., and K. Harper, of the Mead Johnson Research Center at Evansville, Indiana, and the Huntingdon Research Center, Huntingdon, England, studied the acute toxicity of Amidephrine Mesylate in ninety-six rabbits, sixteen rhesus monkeys, eight squirrel monkeys, five cats, 376 rats, and an unstated number of dogs and mice. The substance was administered to the animals by mouth, by injection, into the nostrils, and tested for irritancy on the eyes and penises of rabbits. Rats and mice, regardless of the mode of administration, lost the power of muscular coordination, their eyes watered and their eyeballs protruded. Lethal doses caused, in addition, salivation, convulsions, and hemorrhage about the nose and mouth. Rabbits showed similar symptoms. Cats had a profuse watery discharge from the nose, diarrhea and vomiting. Dogs lost muscular coordination, salivated, and had diarrhea. The LD_{50} values were determined for all species.[40]

It must be remembered that this example is one of many thousands. In Britain almost 100 new cosmetics and toiletries come onto the market every *week*, and it has been estimated that up to a million animals die annually in research connected with cosmetics alone.[41] The figure for the United States is not known, but could well be much higher. To this must be added the enormous numbers of animals used to test inessential foodstuffs—new coloring agents, new sweeteners or other flavoring agents, new preservatives, and so on. Any company that wants permission to market such a new substance must lodge with the Food and Drug Administration evidence of the product's safety. This evidence consists of a thick file full of reports of the experimental poisoning of animals.

It is not only products intended for consumption that are tested. All kinds of industrial and household goods are fed to animals and tested on their eyes. A reference book, *Clinical Toxicology of Commercial Products,* provides data, mostly from animal experiments, on how poisonous hundreds of commercial products are. The products include: insecticides, antifreeze, brake fluids, bleaches, Christmas-tree sprays, church candles, oven-cleaners, deodorants, skin fresheners, bubble baths, depilatories, eye make-up, fire extinguishers, inks, suntan oils, nail polish, mascara, hair sprays, paints, and zipper lubricants.[42]

Whenever the testing on animals of products intended for human use is criticized, someone brings up the tragic "thalidomide babies" in support of the claim that thorough testing is needed to protect the general public. This example is worth investigating. The lesson to be learned from it is not what most people expect.

The first thing to remember is that thalidomide was not an essential, life-saving substance. It was a new kind of sleeping tablet, and while sleeping tablets may be more important than cosmetics, the animal suffering involved in testing a substance is in any case a high price to pay for the avoidance of sleeplessness. So doing without animal testing would not mean releasing substances like thalidomide untested; it would mean doing without it, and trying to become less dependent on drugs.

Second, and more important, is the fact that thalidomide *was* extensively tested on animals before it was released. These tests failed to show any abnormalities. Indeed, as the editor of a recent book on toxicology has stated: "the toxicity tests that had been carefully carried out on thalidomide without exception had demonstrated it to be an almost uniquely safe compound."[43] Even after the drug was suspected of causing deformities in human babies, tests on pregnant laboratory dogs, cats, rats, monkeys, hamsters, and chickens all failed to produce deformities. Only when a particular strain of rabbit was tried were deformities produced.[44]

The thalidomide story underlines something that toxicologists have known for a long time: species vary. Extrapolation from one species to another is a highly risky venture. Thalidomide is harmless to most animals. Insulin, on the other hand, can produce deformities in infant rabbits and mice, but not in humans.[45] And as another toxicologist has said: "If penicillin had been judged by its toxicity on guinea pigs it might never have been used on man."[46]

What we should learn from thalidomide, then, is not that animal testing is necessary, but that it is unreliable; not that we need to poison more animals, but that we need to find alternative methods of testing, and until then we should make do without new nonessential drugs.

When experiments can be brought under the heading "medical" we are inclined to think that any suffering they involve must be justifiable because the research is contributing to the alleviation of suffering. But the general label "medical research" can be used to cover research which is not directed toward the reduction of suffering, but is motivated by a general goalless curiosity that may be acceptable as part of a basic search for knowledge when it involves no suffering, but should not be tolerated if it causes pain. Very often this research has been going on for decades and much of it, in the long run, turns out to have been quite pointless. As an illustration, consider the following series of experiments, stretching back nearly a century, on the effects of heat on animals:

In 1880 H. C. Wood placed a number of animals in boxes with glass lids, and placed the boxes on a brick pavement on a hot day. He used rabbits, pigeons, and cats. His observations on a rabbit are typical. At a temperature of 109.5°F the rabbit jumps and "kicks hind legs with great fury." It then has a convulsive attack. At 112°F it lies on its side slobbering. At 120°F it is gasping and squealing weakly. Soon after it dies.[47]

In 1881 a report appeared in *The Lancet* on dogs and rabbits whose temperatures had been raised to 113°F. It was found that death could be prevented by cool air currents, and the results were said to indicate "the importance of keeping down the temperature in those cases in which it exhibits a tendency to rise to [an] extreme height. . . ."[48]

In 1927 W. W. Hall and E. G. Wakefield of the US Naval Medical School placed ten dogs in a hot humid chamber to produce experimental heatstroke. The animals first showed restlessness, breathing difficulties, swelling and congestion of eyes, and thirst. Some had convulsions. Some died early in the experiment. Those that did not had severe diarrhea and died after removal from the chamber.[49]

In 1954 at the Yale University School of Medicine M. Lennox, W. Sibley, and H. Zimmerman placed thirty-two kittens in a "radiant-heating" chamber. The kittens were "subjected to a total of 49 heating periods . . . struggling was common, particularly as the temperature rose." Convulsions occurred on nine occasions. "Repeated convulsions were the rule." As many as thirty convulsions occurred in rapid sequence. Five kittens died during convulsions, and six without convulsions. The other kittens were killed by the experimenters for autopsies. The experimenters reported that: "The findings in artificially induced fever in kittens conform to the clinical and EEG findings in human beings and previous clinical findings in kittens."[50]

(The following experiment, which was performed at the K. G. Medical College, Lucknow, India, is included as an example of the triumph of Western methods of research and attitudes to animals over the ancient tradition of Hinduism, which has more respect for nonhuman animals than the Judeo-Christian tradition.) In 1968 K. Wahal, A. Kumar, and P. Nath exposed forty-six rats to high temperature for four hours. The rats became restless, breathed with difficulty, and salivated profusely. One animal died during the experiment and the others were killed by the experimenters because "they could not survive anyway."[51]

S. Michaelson, a veterinarian at the University of Rochester, exposed dogs and rabbits to heat-producing microwaves until their temperatures reached the critical level of 107°F or greater. He observed that dogs start panting shortly after microwave exposure begins. Most "display increased activity varying from restlessness to extreme agitation." Near the point of death, weakness and prostration occur. In the case of rabbits, "Within 5 minutes, desperate attempts are made to escape from the cage . . ." and the rabbits die within forty minutes. Michaelson concluded that an increase in heat from microwaves produces damage "indistinguishable from fever in general."[52]

At the Heller Institute of Medical Research, Tel-Aviv, Israel, in experiments published in 1971 and paid for by the United States Public Health Service, T. Rosenthal, Y. Shapiro, U. Seligsohn, and B. Ramot placed thirty-three dogs "randomly procured from the local dog pound" in a temperature-controlled chamber and forced them to exercise on a treadmill in temperatures as high as 113°F until "they collapsed in heatstroke or reached a predetermined rectal temperature." Twenty-five of the dogs died. Nine more dogs were then subjected to a temperature of 122°F, without treadmill exercise. Only two of these dogs survived longer than 24 hours, and autopsies showed that all had hemorrhaged. The experimenters concluded: "The findings are in accordance with what is reported in the literature on humans."[53] In a further report published in 1973 Rosenthal and Shapiro, with E. Sohar, describe experiments on 53 dogs, involving various combinations of heat and treadmill exercise. Six of the dogs vomited, eight had diarrhea, four went into convulsions, twelve lost muscle coordination, and all salivated excessively. Of ten dogs whose rectal temperatures reached 113.2°F, five died "at the moment of maximum rectal temperature" and the other five died between 30 minutes and 11 hours after the end of the experiment. The experimenters concluded that "the sooner the heatstroke victim's temperature is brought down, the greater are the chances of recovery."[54]

Here we have a series of experiments going back into the nineteenth century—and I have had space sufficient to include only a fraction of the published literature. The experiments obviously cause great suffering; and at the end of these experiments, we are offered the advice that heatstroke victims should be cooled!—something that had been shown experimentally in 1881, seems in any case to be fairly elementary common sense, and must have already been borne out by observations of humans who have suffered natural heatstroke.

Similar series of experiments are to be found in many other areas of medicine. In the New York City offices of United Action for Animals (to the best of my knowledge the only American animal welfare organization that has performed the essential task of thoroughly researching the scientific journals) there are filing cabinets full of photocopies of experiments reported in the journals. Each thick file contains reports on numerous experiments, often fifty or more, and the labels on the files tell their own story: "Acceleration," "Aggression (Induced)," "Asphyxiation," "Blinding," "Burning," "Centrifuge," "Compression," "Concussion," "Crowding," "Crushing," "Decompression," "Drug Tests," "Experimental Neurosis," "Freezing," "Heating," "Hemorrhage," "Hindlimb Beating," "Immobilization," "Isolation," "Multiple Injuries," "Prey Killing," "Protein Deprivation," "Punishment," "Radiation," "Starvation," "Shock," "Spinal Cord Injuries," "Stress," "Thirst," and many more. While some of the experiments may have led to advances in medical knowledge, many of them appear trivial or misconceived, and some of them were not even designed to yield important benefits.

Consider, as another example of the way in which endless variations of the same or similar experiments are carried out, these experiments relating to the experimental production of shock in animals (by which is meant not electric shock but the mental and physical state of shock that often occurs after a severe injury). As long ago as 1946 a researcher in the field, Magnus Gregersen of Columbia University, surveyed the literature and found over 800 published papers dealing with experimental studies of shock. He describes the methods used:

> The use of a tourniquet on one or more extremities, crush, compression, muscle trauma by contusion with light hammer blows, Noble-Collip drum [a device in which animals are placed and the drum rotated; the animals tumble repeatedly to the bottom of the drum and injure themselves], gunshot wounds, strangulation of intestinal loops, freezing, and burns.

Gregersen also notes that hemorrhage has been "widely employed" and "an increasing number of these studies has been done without the complicating factor of anesthesia." He is not, however, pleased by all this diversity, and complains that the variety of methods makes it "exceedingly difficult" to evaluate the results of different researchers; there is, he says, a "crying need" for standardized procedures which will invariably produce a state of shock.[55]

Eight years later the situation had not changed much. S. M. Rosenthal and R. C. Millican wrote that "animal investigations in the field of traumatic shock have yielded diversified and often contradictory results." Nevertheless they looked forward to "future experimentation in this field" and like Gregersen they discouraged the use of anesthesia: "The influence of anesthesia is controversial . . . in the reviewers' opinion prolonged anesthesia is best avoided. . . ." They also recommended that "adequate numbers of animals must be employed to overcome biological variations."[56]

And in 1974 researchers were still working on "animal models" of experimental shock, still carrying out *preliminary* experiments to determine what injuries might be inflicted to produce a satisfactory "standard" state of shock. After decades of experiments designed to produce shock in dogs by causing them to hemorrhage, more recent studies now indicate that hemorrhage-induced shock in dogs is not like shock in humans. Noting these studies, researchers at the University of Rochester have caused hemorrhage in pigs, which they think may be more like humans in this respect, to determine what volume of blood loss might be suitable for the production of an experimental shock.[57]

Another medical field in which experiments on animals might be thought to be both simple and necessary is the field of nutrition. Perhaps it was once true that straightforward experiments told us a good deal about what kinds of food humans need to remain healthy—although, even then, there was a great deal to be learned from observing humans in various parts of the world who were badly nourished anyway, and this information may be more applicable to human nutrition than information derived from inducing malnutrition in other species. In any case, more recent experiments are no longer directed toward such simple and important goals as knowledge of the nutrients essential to human health. Experiments are now being performed over and over again in which animals are deprived of nutrients which have long been known to be necessary for humans. Moreover the experiments are carried on long past the point at which symptoms of malnutrition appear. Some samples:

Eight researchers from departments of Animal Husbandry, Veterinary Pathology, and Biochemistry at Michigan State University, East Lansing, studied the vitamin D_2 requirements of baby pigs by giving forty-five pigs varying levels of the vitamin. During the fourth week of each trial pigs receiving no vitamin D had convulsions and sudden deaths occurred. Other pigs survived to the end of the trial, but "exhibited classical symptoms of rickets, including deformed limbs and great difficulty in walking."[58]

At the National Institute of Health research center in Bethesda, Maryland, G. McKhan, O. Mickelson, and D. Taylor raised kittens on a diet deficient in pyridoxine (more widely known as vitamin B_6). They reported difficulties in conducting their study because although "approximately twenty-five kittens were started on the deficient diet," there were "only eleven available for final study." The other "approximately" fourteen had died from infections, after seizures, and from injuries "resulting from falling in the cage." The effects of the diet were described as "quite striking." They included below normal weight, thinning hair, and progressive loss of muscular coordination. "Ultimately the deficient animals became progressively weaker, developed generalized seizures and, if left on the diet, died." The experimenters noted that the seizures they observed had been demonstrated on pyridoxine-deficient diets in "a wide variety of experimental animals and man." They claimed, however, that in the cat this particular deficiency had been "rarely studied" and that for this species their experiment was "to our knowledge only the third report of the full-blown deficiency associated with seizures."[59]

In a preface to a report of a further study of pyridoxine deficiency, this time on chickens, C. Gries and M. Scott of Cornell University list some of the features that previous studies have shown to be associated with the deficiency. (In the following quotation I omit the citations of studies—often more than one—after each species is mentioned.)

Pyridoxine deficiency is associated with skin lesions in the rat, mouse and hamster, with a micrytic anemia in rats, dogs and swine, and with epileptiform seizures in rats, puppies, swine and calves. Rhesus monkeys on chronic pyridoxine-deficient diets show edema [swelling], weight loss, skin lesions, arteriosclerosis and dental caries . . . Human deficiency reports have described convulsions and anemia in infants and dermatitis and anemia in adults. As for poultry, previous studies were reported on chicks, turkeys and ducklings.[60]

This list gives an indication of how, once one particular type of experiment has been done for one species, other experimenters then go on to repeat it on as many other species as possible, and often more than once on the same species. In this way we may learn something new about rats or ducklings, but it is difficult to see what we learn that could help prevent malnutrition in humans. Incidentally we can see that even this extensive list of studies of pyridoxine deficiency is not complete—it omits the previous study of the deficiency in kittens, and the two earlier studies on cats referred to in that report. Clearly the literature has grown to such an extent that even in a quite specialized field it is difficult for one scientist to keep up with everything that his colleagues have been doing.

In this chapter I have been able to describe briefly only some of the variety of forms of suffering that may be inflicted on animals in the name of "medical research." Here, finally, are some isolated instances of types of research that I do not have the space to cover in more detail:

Observing that "it is well-known that pressure or trauma [injury] to the testes of man causes severe pain," D. F. Peterson and A. M. Brown of the University of Texas Medical School and the University of Utah Medical School "decided to investigate this problem in animals." They used "lightly anesthetized" male cats, immobilizing the left testicle of each cat in a cup-shaped device. The testicle was then compressed with a rod. The animals produced what was interpreted by the experimenters as "a painlike response."[61]

The cat, apparently, has an "almost legendary reputation as a difficult behavioral subject." But M. Loop and M. Berkley of Florida State University, Tallahassee, consider the cat "an extremely interesting organism for sensory experiments" and so they devised an "improved responding apparatus" for cats. The apparatus was tested on an unstated number of cats "obtained from the local animal shelter" and starved to 80 percent of their normal weight. The cats were then stood on a grid floor which could be electrified. Their heads were placed in a plexiglass cylinder at the back of which was a key that they had to press to obtain food. Each animal was trained to press the key between 1,500 and 2,000 times per hour. Although this seems an astonishingly high frequency, Loop and Berkley asserted: "We have not encountered a cat that could not be brought to this acceptable level of performance."

Electric shock was then used to teach the cats not to press the key whenever a white light was turned on. This training continued for three months, during which period a certain percentage of "unsignaled" shocks were also given, so that the cats were shocked whatever they did. The light was then dimmed to see what intensity the cats could detect. The results obtained were very similar to those obtained by other investigators in 1952 and 1970. The report concludes: "In conclusion we would like to put to rest the myth that the cat is a difficult behavioral S [subject] and offer this technique as a solution."[62]

At the University of Michigan Medical School G. Deneau, M. Seevers, and T. Yanagita confined sixty-four monkeys in small cubicles. The monkeys were then given unlimited access to a variety of drugs through tubes implanted in their arms. They could control the intake by pressing a lever. In some cases, after the monkeys had become addicted, supplies were abruptly cut off. Of the monkeys that had become addicted to morphine, three were "observed to die in convulsions" while others found dead in the morning were "presumed to have died in convulsions." Monkeys that had taken large amounts of cocaine inflicted severe wounds upon themselves, including biting off their fingers and toes, before dying convulsive deaths. Amphetamines caused one monkey to "pluck all of the hair off his arms and abdomen." In general, the experimenters found that "the manifestations of toxicity . . . were similar to the well-known toxicities of these drugs in man." They noted that experiments on animals with addictive drugs had been going on in their laboratory for "the last twenty years." (See photograph no. 12.)[63]

The following reports illustrate the nature of long-term studies on primates:

At the Walter Reed Army Institute of Research in Washington, J. V. Brady investigated the emotional behavior of monkeys over a period of years. Monkeys were kept in restraining chairs in which they could move their head and limbs but not their bodies. (See photograph no. 11.) This, coupled with various "conditioning procedures," "seemed to impose considerable emotional stress on the animals," and the physiological reactions of the monkeys to this stress were studied; however, one study involving nineteen monkeys "was brought to a halt when many of them died."

Since some of the dead monkeys were found to have had ulcers, Brady decided to investigate what had caused these ulcers. He set up an experiment using two monkeys in similar restraining chairs. Both monkeys received electric shocks, but one of the monkeys could prevent the shocks if it pressed a lever every twenty seconds. After twenty-three days in which the monkey was liable to receive shock for twelve hours a day, the monkey that had the power to prevent shock died and was found to have had an ulcer. A second experiment, identical to the first, was carried out with similar results, and then a "series of follow-up experiments" began in which the conditions were varied: some monkeys had to press a lever to avoid shock eighteen hours out of every twenty-four; others had the shocks programmed to come every two seconds, instead of every twenty, and their rest periods were never longer than thirty minutes. These other schedules, however, did not produce ulcers.[64]

J. Findley, W. Robinson, and W. Gilliam of the Johns Hopkins University Medical School have reported on a restraining chair they have developed for long-term studies on baboons. Noting that "the difficulties of restraint increase markedly with the use of electric shock" they "anchor" the baboons' arms so as not to allow the animal to straighten them. At the same time they allow room for the "considerable growth" to be expected in a long-term study. For the delivery of electric shock the baboon is fitted with an electrode around the waist, and other metal parts, including the seat itself, serve as a second electrode for the delivery of electric current. The report states that twenty-two baboons and rhesus monkeys have been restrained in this manner for "lengthy periods," "several" of them for one-and-one-half years of "continuous experimentation."[65]

The same experimenters, joined by J. Brady, then carried out an experiment in which two baboons were placed in the restraining chairs and subjected to "continuously programmed behavioral events" twenty-four hours a day for over a year. The events included pressing levers to obtain food and to avoid electric shock, as well as rest and sleep periods. The baboons, in their chairs, lived in a soundproof box, four feet by four feet by three feet, which served as an "experimental chamber." For two periods of six hours each in every twenty-four hours, a red light signaled the onset of electric shocks every two and one half minutes. If the baboon learned to press a lever 150 times the red light and electric shock would be turned off for a period of variable duration, averaging five minutes. Sometimes the shocks would occur before the baboons could complete their lever pressing, but eventually they learned to avoid "all but a few shocks" every day. The experimenters concluded that the study showed "the adequacy of the animal restraint . . . systems for continuous long-term observation." They also measured increases in blood pressure and heart rate which they said related to the fact that the baboons had had to perform tasks involving "aversive contingencies." (That is, the electric shocks.) They noted that previous studies had been done on the blood pressure and heartbeat of monkeys under stress.[66]

At the University of California Medical Center, San Francisco, Ralph Forsyth and Robert Harris studied the effects of severe stress over long periods of time on the blood pressure of twenty-three monkeys. After tubes were surgically implanted in their arteries the monkeys were placed in restraining chairs inside isolation booths. Electrodes were taped to their tails to deliver shock. Four monkeys were used as controls, "sitting in their chairs from 5–14 months after their training without any programmed stimuli." The other monkeys were trained to press a lever to avoid shock. Five had to press the lever every twenty seconds, twelve hours a day, for up to a year. Two others had to press levers every five or seven seconds, sixteen hours a day, and one was forced to press the lever when a signal came on, at any time of the day or night. Another had to respond only during the last ten seconds of each period of twenty seconds, responses made earlier being punished with a shock. All the experimental monkeys "became increasingly emotional and hyperactive." Their blood pressures rose. The changes observed were "similar to previous measurements both in humans and lower animals during acute stress." After the experiment ended all the monkeys were killed and autopsied, but "no consistent major pathological abnormality was found."[67]

How can these things happen? How can a man who is not a sadist spend his working day heating an unanesthetized dog to death, or driving a monkey into a lifelong depression, and then remove his white coat, wash his hands, and go home to dinner with his wife and children? How can taxpayers allow their money to be used to support experiments of this kind? And how can students go through a turbulent era of protest against injustice, discrimination, and oppression of all kinds, no matter how far from home, while ignoring the cruelties that are being carried out on their own campuses?

The answers to these questions stem from the unquestioned acceptance of speciesism. We tolerate cruelties inflicted on members of other species that would outrage us if performed on members of our own species. Speciesism allows researchers to regard the animals they experiment on as items of equipment, laboratory tools rather than living, suffering creatures. Sometimes they even refer to the animals in this way. Robert White of the Cleveland Metropolitan General Hospital, who has performed numerous experiments involving the transplanting of heads of monkeys, and the keeping alive of monkey brains in fluid, outside the body, has said in an interview that:

Our main purpose here is to offer a living laboratory tool: a monkey "model" in which and by which we can design new operative techniques for the brain.

And the reporter who conducted the interview and observed White's experiments found his experience

a rare and chilling glimpse into the cold, clinical world of the scientist, where the life of an animal has no meaning beyond the immediate purpose of experimentation.[68]

This "scientific" attitude to animals was exhibited to a large audience in December 1974 when the American public television network brought together Harvard philosopher Robert Nozick and three scientists whose work involves animals. The program was a follow-up to Fred Wiseman's controversial film *Primate*, which had taken viewers inside the Yerkes Primate Center, a research center in Atlanta, Georgia. Nozick asked the scientists whether the fact that an experiment will kill hundreds of animals is ever regarded, by scientists, as a reason for not performing it. One of the scientists answered: "Not that I know of." Nozick pressed his question: "Don't the animals count at all?" Dr. A. Perachio, of the Yerkes Center, replied: "Why should they?" while Dr. D. Baltimore, of the Massachusetts Institute of Technology, added that he did not think that experimenting on animals raised a moral issue at all.[69]

As well as the general attitude of speciesism which researchers share with other citizens there are some special factors operating to make possible the experiments I have described. Foremost among these is the immense respect that we still have for scientists. Although the advent of nuclear weapons and environmental pollution have made us realize that science and technology need to be controlled to some extent, we still tend to be in awe of anyone who

wears a white coat and has a PhD. In a well-known series
of experiments Stanley Milgram, a Harvard psychologist,
has demonstrated that ordinary people will obey the directions of a white-coated research worker to administer
what appears to be (but in fact is not) electric shock to
a human subject as "punishment" for failing to answer
questions correctly; and they will continue to do this even
when the human subject cries out and pretends to be in
great pain.[70] If this can happen when the participant be-
lieves he is inflicting pain on a human, how much easier
is it for a student to push aside his initial qualms when
his professor instructs him to perform experiments on animals? What Alice Heim has rightly called the "indoctrina-
tion" of the student is a gradual process, beginning with
the dissection of frogs in school biology classes. When
the budding medical student, or psychology student, or
veterinarian, reaches the university and finds that to complete the course of studies on which he has set his heart
he must experiment on living animals, it is difficult for him
to refuse to do so, especially since he knows that what he
is being asked to do is standard practice in the field.

Individual students will often admit feeling uneasy about
what they are asked to do, but public protests are very
rare. An organized protest did occur in Britain recently,
however, when students at the Welsh National School of
Medicine in Cardiff complained publicly that a dog was
unnecessarily injected with drugs more than 30 times to
demonstrate a point during a lecture. The dog was then
killed. One student said: "We learned nothing new. It
could all have been looked up in textbooks. A film could
be made so that only one dog dies and all this unnecessary
suffering is stopped."[71] The student's comment was true;
but such things happen routinely in every medical school.
Why are protests so rare?

The pressure to conform does not let up when the student receives his degree. If he goes on to a graduate degree
in fields in which experiments on animals are usual, he
will be encouraged to devise his own experiments and
write them up for his PhD dissertation. We have already
seen examples of work by PhD students—one student was
a member of the team that irradiated beagles at the Uni-

versity of Rochester in the experiment described on pages 28–29, the electric shocking of ducklings described on page 38 was work toward a PhD; and so was the experiment involving thirst and electric shock on the following page. Naturally, if this is how students are educated they will tend to continue in the same manner when they become professors, and they will, in turn, train their own students in the same manner.

It is not always easy for people outside the universities to understand the rationale for the research carried out under university auspices. Originally, perhaps, scholars and researchers just set out to solve the most important problems and did not allow themselves to be influenced by other considerations. Perhaps some are still motivated by these concerns. Too often, though, academic research gets bogged down in petty and insignificant details because the big questions have been studied already, and have either been solved or proven too difficult. So the researcher turns away from the well-ploughed fertile fields in search of virgin territory where whatever he learns will be new, although the connection with a major problem may be more remote. So we find articles in the scientific journals with introductions like the following:

> Although swelling from trauma and inflammatory agents has been the subject of investigation for years, meager information exists on the quantitative changes that occur over a period of time. . . . In the present study a simple method was developed for measuring the volume of the rodent tail, and the changes which occur after standardized trauma have been reported.[72]

The "simple method" involves severely injuring the tails of seventy-three unanesthetized mice; and it is difficult to see how measuring the swelling of the tail of a mouse can tell us much about anything—except the amount a mouse's tail swells. Here is another example: While "the effects of controlled hemorrhage resulting in reversible and irreversible shock have been studied in detail" there are "relatively few articles concerned with the controlled study of exsanguinating hemorrhage"—that is, hemorrhage that drains the body of all its blood, or at least until death occurs. Noting that patterns of dying from suffocation, drowning, and other causes have been studied in detail but that studies of the general pattern of death from exsanguinating hemorrhage have been "based on experiments performed on very few animals," experimenters gave sixty-five dogs an anesthetic that permitted "quick recovery . . . and study of the dying process without the influence of deep anesthesia." They then opened the aortic cannula in each dog and watched them go through a period they termed "the agonal state" which took up to ten minutes and was terminated by death. The experimenters describe their report as "merely a description of observations" and not an attempt to elucidate the mechanisms of the changes observed.[73]

When we read reports of experiments that cause pain and are apparently not even intended to produce results of real significance we are at first inclined to think that there must be more to what is being done than we can understand—that the scientist must have some better reason for doing what he is doing than his report indicates. Yet as we go more deeply into the subject we find that what appears trivial on the surface very often really *is* trivial. Experimenters themselves often unofficially admit this. H. F. Harlow, whose experiments on monkeys I described earlier, was for twelve years editor of the *Journal of Comparative and Physiological Psychology*, a journal which publishes more reports of painful experiments on animals than almost any other. At the end of this period, in which Harlow estimates he reviewed about 2,500 manuscripts submitted for publication, he wrote, in a semihumorous farewell note, that "most experiments are not worth doing and the data attained are not worth publishing."[74]

On reflection, perhaps this is not so surprising. Researchers, even those in psychology, medicine, and the biological sciences, are human beings and are susceptible to the same influences as any other human beings. They like to get on in their careers, to be promoted, and to have their work read and discussed by their colleagues. Publishing papers in the appropriate journals is an important element in the rise up the ladder of promotion and increased prestige. This happens in every field, in philosophy or history as much as in psychology or medicine, and it is entirely understandable and in itself hardly worth criticizing. The philosopher or historian who publishes to improve his career prospects does little harm beyond wasting paper and boring his colleagues; the psychologist or medical researcher, or anyone else whose work involves experimenting on animals, however, can cause severe pain or prolonged suffering. His work should therefore be subject to much stricter standards of necessity.

Once a pattern of animal experimentation becomes the accepted mode of research in a particular field, the process is self-reinforcing and difficult to break out of. Not only publications and promotions but also the awards and grants that finance research become geared to animal experiments. A proposal for a new experiment with animals is something that the administrators of research funds will be ready to support, if they have in the past supported other experiments on animals. New nonanimal-using methods will seem less familiar and will be less likely to receive support.

Those government agencies in the United States, Britain, and elsewhere that promote research in the biological sciences have become the major backers of experiments on animals. Indeed, public funds, derived from taxation, have paid for the vast majority of the experiments described in this chapter. Many of these agencies are paying for experiments that have only the remotest connection with the purposes for which the agencies were set up. Consider the following partial list of experiments that have been described in the preceding pages, with the agencies that paid for them:

PAGE	EXPERIMENT	PAID FOR BY
28	Strontium-90 poisoning; beagles	Atomic Energy Commission
28-29	X-ray irradiation; beagles	Atomic Energy Commission

PAGE	EXPERIMENT	PAID FOR BY
34-35	Variable current electric shock; rats	National Institute of Mental Health and US Public Health Service
35	Electric shock, with warning; rats	National Science Foundation
35-36	Electric shock, delayed response required; dogs	National Institutes of Health and US Public Health Service
36	Electric shock, inescapable; dogs	National Science Foundation and National Institute of Mental Health
38	Electric shock; ducklings	National Institute of Mental Health
40	Terminal deprivation of food and water; rats	US Public Health Service and National Institute of Mental Health
41-44	Maternal deprivation, designing of "well of despair" and "tunnel of terror," isolation in well of despair, inducing of psychological death; monkeys	National Institutes of Health
53-54	Heatstroke; dogs	US Public Health Service
57	Malnutrition; kittens	National Institutes of Health
58	Pain in testes; cats	US Public Health Service and General Research Support grant

PAGE	EXPERIMENT	PAID FOR BY
58-59	Development of apparatus for testing cats	National Institutes of Health and US Public Health Service
60-61	Development of restraining chair for baboons and long-term study of baboons in chairs	National Institutes of Health and US Army

In addition to the agencies listed here, experiments on animals are paid for by many other government bodies, for example the National Aeronautics and Space Administration, and the Veterans Administration. The Department of Defense is a major experimenter, testing new weapons on animals and using them for other purposes too. Exactly how many animals the Defense Department uses is not known. In Britain, where statistics are available, official figures show that 131,994 experiments on animals were carried out at Ministry of Defence research establishments during 1972. Since the US defense establishment is far larger than that in Britain, the corresponding figure is probably far higher.

Since these experiments are paid for by government bodies, it is hardly necessary to add that there is no law that prevents the scientist from carrying them out. There are laws that prevent ordinary people from beating their dogs to death, but a scientist can do the same thing with impunity, and with no one to check whether his doing so is likely to lead to benefits that would not occur from an ordinary beating. The reason for this is that the strength and prestige of the scientific establishment, supported by the various interest groups—including those who breed animals for sale to laboratories—have been sufficient to stop all attempts at effective legal control.

In the United States the only federal law on the matter is the Animal Welfare Act of 1970, which amended a 1966 act. The law sets standards for the transportation, housing, and handling of animals sold as pets, exhibited, or intended for use in research. So far as actual experimentation is concerned, however, it effectively allows the researcher to do exactly as he pleases. One section of the law requires that those facilities which register under the act (and neither government agencies doing research nor many smaller facilities have to register) must lodge a report stating that when painful experiments were performed without the use of pain-relieving drugs this was necessary to achieve the objectives of the research project. No attempt is made to assess whether these "objectives" are sufficiently important to justify the infliction of pain. Under these circumstances the requirement does no more than make additional paperwork. You can't, of course, electric shock a dog into a state of helplessness if you anesthetize him at the same time; nor can you produce depression in a monkey while keeping him happy with drugs. So you can truthfully state that the objectives of the experiment cannot be achieved if pain-relieving drugs are used, and then go on with the experiment as you would have done before the act came into existence.

An interesting feature of the act is that the statement justifying the infliction of pain must be signed by a veterinarian. Perhaps this requirement testifies to the prevalence of the myth that all vets are people devoted to the welfare of animals, people who go into the field because they care about animals and would never let them suffer unnecessarily. It does seem to be true that, as the *Journal of the American Veterinary Medical Association* said recently, "More than ever before, people look to the veterinary profession for protection of animals."[75] Regrettably, this confidence is not fully justified. No doubt many vets did go into the field because they cared about animals, and obviously many practicing vets still do care about animals; but it is difficult for someone who really cares about animals to go through a course of study in veterinary medicine without having his sensitivity to animal suffering blunted. Those most sensitive to animal suffering may not be able to complete their studies. One ex-veterinary student wrote to an animal welfare organization:

My life-long dream and ambition to become a veterinarian dissipated following several traumatic experiences involving standard experimental procedures utilized by the dispassionate instructors of the Pre-Vet school at my state university. They felt it was perfectly acceptable to experiment with and then terminate the lives of all the animals they utilized, which I found revoltingly unacceptable to my own moral code. After numerous confrontations with these heartless vivisectionists, I painfully decided to pursue a different career.[76]

What has happened to the veterinary profession? The basic trouble is that too many vets have accepted the attitude to animals that is dominant in our society. In 1966, when moves were being made to pass legislation to protect laboratory animals, the American Veterinary Medical Association testified to congressional committees that while it favored legislation to stop the stealing of pets for subsequent sale to laboratories, it was opposed to the licensing and regulation of research facilities, since this could interfere with research; and in its own journal, the Association supported this position by saying: "The decision made half a century ago was that animals should be used for scientific experimentation benefiting man and other animals."[77] Soon after another veterinarian advised his colleagues that "animals used in biomedical research should not be considered as mere animals but rather as standardized biological research tools."[78] More recently an article in the same journal—which a few months earlier had noted how the public looks to the veterinary profession for protection of animals—asked: "What is the role of the veterinarian?" and answered: "First of all, the *raison d'être* of the veterinary profession is the over-all well-being of man—not lower animals."[79]

Once the implications of this fine example of speciesism have been understood, it should surprise no one to learn that the teams of experimenters who designed and carried out the first three experiments described in this chapter—those on pages 28–29—all included veterinarians, and a vet also performed the heating experiment on dogs and rabbits described on page 53.

The moral of all this is that veterinarians are not necessarily the people to whom authority to assess cruelty should be given. Many vets do have the genuine interests of animals at heart; but others, especially research veterinarians, may not.

A final irony about the operation of the Animal Welfare Act is that the major lobby groups concerned to promote and defend experiments on animals have issued standards for experimenters to comply with, intended to help the experimenters satisfy a requirement in the act that "professionally acceptable standards" be followed. One of these groups is the National Society for Medical Research. To assess the adequacy of its standards, glance back at the report of the experiment at the University of Rochester in which beagles were killed by exposure to a high level of X-ray irradiation (pages 28–29). After describing the various forms of agony the dogs went through before dying, the experimenters' report calmly observes that in these experiments "the principles of animal care laid down by the National Society for Medical Research were observed." Principles laid down by other interested bodies, including the American Medical Association, the American Association of Laboratory Animal Care, and the National Academy of Sciences are equally compatible with the experiments described in this chapter. It should by now be obvious that standards laid down by those who participate in experiments on animals, or work closely with those who do so, will never protect animals against painful experiments performed for trivial reasons.

Britain is sometimes thought of as a nation more advanced than most in concern for animal welfare; but in Britain, although the law on experimenting on animals is more complex than that in the United States, it is not, in practice, much more effective. The British law was passed in 1876, when fewer than 800 experiments were conducted annually. It has never been amended, although the annual number of experiments has passed 5 million. The act requires experimenters to obtain a license, and has other provisions designed to reduce the amount of pain caused; but in practice any researcher can obtain a license, and the other provisions can be dispensed with by means of certificates issued by the appropriate official. Richard Ryder, a British psychologist who once experimented on animals himself but is now a leading campaigner against unnecessary and painful experiments, has written:

> There is no record of the Home Office refusing a licence on the grounds that a proposed experiment is pointless, badly designed, repetitive, or wasteful. . . . In other words, the principal loophole in this law, as in all equivalent laws in other countries, is simply that, although painful experiments are technically only allowed if they are "necessary," *the necessity itself is rarely, if ever, questioned.* . . . It is often argued that the British law is so much better than its equivalents in other countries that it needs no improvement. This is a patently false argument. It is rather like arguing that the concentration camp at Belsen was more humane than the one at Dachau.[80]

That Ryder's assertion is hardly an exaggeration is easily shown by looking at the experiments which are permitted and carried out in Britain under this allegedly advanced law. I have already referred to the testing of cosmetic and industrial products in Britain, and given an instance of the poisoning of animals carried out by a researcher at the Huntingdon Research Center in England (page 49). Radiation experiments, similar to those cited at the beginning of this chapter, are also being performed in England by the Medical Research Council's Radiobiology Unit, at the Harwell Research Complex near Didcot in Berkshire. So far, experiments on goats, guinea pigs, and rabbits have been reported, and experiments on "other species" are in progress.[81] We have seen that well over 100,000 experiments on animals are carried out by the Ministry of Defence each year. The following experiment on lead poisoning is another example of the kind of experiment allowed by the "advanced" British law—and incidentally this, like many others, was carried out with the assistance of public funds supplied through a Medical Research Council grant:

Anthony Hopkins of the Institute of Neurology, London, poisoned twelve adult and three infant baboons by injecting them with lead in varying doses for periods up to one year. Because earlier experiments on cats had shown that absorption of lead is more complete through the lungs, the doses were injected directly into the trachea, or windpipe, of each baboon, which was then held in an upright position so that the poison could "trickle" into its lungs. Before death occurred, loss of weight was "striking," five of the twelve adults losing 40 percent or more of their initial weight. Eight baboons had convulsive fits, thirty-four convulsive fits being observed, although "it is likely that others occurred when no observer was present."

In one baboon, seizures began with "twitching around the right eye, spreading to the rest of the right side of the face. During the next fifteen seconds the right arm became involved, and then seizures became generalized." Seizures were "occasionally preceded by a cry" and were sometimes "precipitated by a sudden movement of the animal as it tried to avoid transfer from one cage to another or whilst reaching up to take a banana." Other symptoms included bloody diarrhea, pneumonia, inflamed and bloody intestines, and liver degeneration. One baboon became so weak it could not stand up, and its left fingers could not grasp orange segments. For three weeks before it died this baboon was partially blind; it "groped for proffered fruit and on occasions appeared not to see it." Five of the baboons died in seizures; seven were found dead in their cages; the remaining three were "sacrificed."[82]

When are experiments on animals justifiable? Upon learning of the nature of many contemporary experiments, many people react by saying that all experiments on animals should be prohibited immediately. But if we make our demands as absolute as this, the experimenters have a ready reply: Would we be prepared to let thousands of humans die if they could be saved by a single experiment on a single animal?

This question is, of course, purely hypothetical. There never has been and there never could be a single experiment that saves thousands of lives. The way to reply to this hypothetical question is to pose another: Would the experimenter be prepared to carry out his experiment on

a human orphan under six months old if that were the
only way to save thousands of lives?

If the experimenter would not be prepared to use a
human infant then his readiness to use nonhuman animals
reveals an unjustifiable form of discrimination on the basis
of species, since adult apes, monkeys, dogs, cats, rats, and
other mammals are more aware of what is happening to
them, more self-directing, and, so far as we can tell, at
least as sensitive to pain as a human infant. (I specified
that the human infant be an orphan to avoid the complications of the feelings of parents, although in so doing I
am being overfair to the experimenter, since the nonhuman animals used in experiments are not orphans and in
many species the separation of mother and young clearly
causes distress for both.)

There is no characteristic that human infants possess to
a higher degree than adult nonhuman animals, unless we
are to count the infant's potential as a characteristic that
makes it wrong to experiment on him. Whether this characteristic should count is controversial—if we count it,
we shall have to condemn abortion along with experiments
on infants, since the potential of the infant and the fetus
is the same. To avoid the complexities of this issue, however, we can alter our original question a little and assume
that the infant is one with severe and irreversible brain
damage that makes it impossible for him ever to develop
beyond the level of a six-month-old infant. There are, unfortunately, many such human beings, locked away in
special wards throughout the country, many of them long
since abandoned by their parents. Despite their mental de-
ficiencies, their anatomy and physiology is in nearly all
respects identical with that of normal humans. If, therefore, we were to force-feed them with large quantities of
floor polish, or drip concentrated solutions of cosmetics
into their eyes, we would have a much more reliable indication of the safety of these products for other humans
than we now get by attempting to extrapolate the results
of tests on a variety of other species. The radiation experiments, the heatstroke experiments, and many other experiments described earlier in this chapter could also have told
us more about human reactions to the experimental situa-

tion if they had been carried out on retarded humans instead of dogs and rabbits.

So whenever an experimenter claims that his experiment is important enough to justify the use of an animal, we should ask him whether he would be prepared to use a retarded human at a similar mental level to the animal he is planning to use. If his reply is negative, we can assume that he is willing to use a nonhuman animal only because he gives less consideration to the interests of members of other species than he gives to members of his own—and this bias is no more defensible than racism or any other form of arbitrary discrimination.

Of course, no one would seriously propose carrying out the experiments described in this chapter on retarded humans. Occasionally it has become known that some medical experiments have been performed on humans without their consent, and sometimes on retarded humans; but the consequences of these experiments for the human subjects are almost always trivial by comparison with what is standard practice for nonhuman animals. Still, these experiments on humans usually lead to an outcry against the experimenters, and rightly so. They are, very often, a further example of the arrogance of the research worker who justifies everything on the grounds of increasing knowledge. If experimenting on retarded, orphaned humans would be wrong, why isn't experimenting on nonhuman animals wrong? What difference is there between the two, except for the mere fact that, biologically, one is a member of our species and the other is not? But *that*, surely, is not a morally relevant difference, any more than the fact that a being is not a member of our race is a morally relevant difference.

Actually the analogy between speciesism and racism applies in practice as well as in theory in the area of experimentation. Blatant speciesism leads to painful experiments on other species, defended on the grounds of its contribution to knowledge and possible usefulness for our species. Blatant racism has led to painful experiments on other races, defended on the grounds of its contribution to knowledge and possible usefulness for the experimenting race. Under the Nazi regime in Germany, nearly 200 doctors, some of them eminent in the world of medicine, took part in experiments on Jews and Russian and Polish prisoners. Thousands of other physicians knew of these experiments, some of which were the subject of lectures at medical academies. Yet the records show that the doctors sat through medical reports of the infliction of horrible injuries on these "lesser races" and then proceeded to discuss the medical lessons to be learned from them without anyone making even a mild protest about the nature of the experiments. The parallels between this attitude and that of experimenters today toward animals are striking. Then, as now, the subjects were frozen, heated, and put in decompression chambers. Then, as now, these events were written up in a dispassionate scientific jargon. The following paragraph is taken from a report by a Nazi scientist of an experiment on a human being, placed in a decompression chamber; it could equally have been taken from accounts of recent experiments in this country on animals:

> After five minutes spasms appeared; between the sixth and tenth minute respiration increased in frequency, the TP [test person] losing consciousness. From the eleventh to the thirtieth minute respiration slowed down to three inhalations per minute, only to cease entirely at the end of that period . . . about half an hour after breathing had ceased, an autopsy was begun.[83]

Then, as now, the ethic of pursuing knowledge was considered sufficient justification for inflicting agony on those who are placed beyond the limits of genuine moral concern. Our sphere of moral concern is far wider than that of the Nazis; but so long as there are sentient beings outside it, it is not wide enough.

To return to the question of when an experiment might be justifiable. It will not do to say: "Never!" In extreme circumstances, absolutist answers always break down. Torturing a human being is almost always wrong, but it is not absolutely wrong. If torture were the only way in which we could discover the location of a nuclear time bomb hidden in a New York City basement, then torture would be justifiable. Similarly, if a single experiment could cure a major disease, that experiment would be justifiable. But in actual life the benefits are always much, much more remote, and more often than not they are nonexistent. So how do we decide when an experiment is justifiable?

We have seen that the experimenter reveals a bias in favor of his own species whenever he carries out an experiment on a nonhuman for a purpose that he would not think justified him in using a human being, even a retarded human being. This principle gives us a guide toward an answer to our question. Since a speciesist bias, like a racist bias, is unjustifiable, an experiment cannot be justifiable unless the experiment is so important that the use of a retarded human being would also be justifiable.

This is not an absolutist principle. I do not believe that it could *never* be justifiable to experiment on a retarded human. If it really were possible to save many lives by an experiment that would take just one life, and there were *no other way* those lives could be saved, it might be right to do the experiment. But this would be an extremely rare case. Not one tenth of one percent of the experiments now being performed on animals would fall into this category. Certainly none of the experiments described in this chapter could pass this test.

It should not be thought that medical research would grind to a halt if the test I have proposed were applied, or that a flood of untested products would come onto the market. So far as new products are concerned it is true that, as I have already said, we would have to make do with fewer of them, using ingredients already known to be safe. That does not seem to be any great loss. But for testing really essential products, as well as for other areas of research, alternative methods not requiring animals can be and would be found. Some alternatives exist already and others would develop more rapidly if the energy and resources now applied to experimenting on animals were redirected into the search for alternatives.

At present scientists do not look for alternatives *simply because they do not care enough about the animals they are using.* I make this assertion on the best possible authority, since it has been more or less admitted by Britain's Research Defence Society, a group which exists to defend researchers from criticism by animal welfare organizations. A recent article in the *Bulletin* of the National Society for Medical Research (the American equivalent of the Research Defence Society) described how the British group successfully fought off a proposed amendment to the British law regulating experiments that would have prohibited any experiment using live animals if the purpose of that experiment could be achieved by alternative means not involving animals. The main objections lodged by the Research Defence Society to this very mild attempt at reform were, first, that in some cases it may be cheaper to use animals than other methods, and secondly, that:

> in some cases alternatives may exist but they may be unknown to an investigator. With the vast amount of scientific literature coming out of even a very narrow field of study it is possible that an investigator may not know all that is now known about techniques or results in a particular area. . . .

(This ignorance would make the experimenter liable to prosecution under the proposed amendment.)

What do these objections amount to? The first can mean only one thing: that economic considerations are more important than the suffering of animals; as for the second, it is a strong argument for a total moratorium on animal experiments until every experimenter has had time to read up on the existing reports of alternatives available in his field and results already obtained. Is it not shocking that experimenters may be inflicting agony on animals only because they have not kept up with the literature in their field—literature that may contain reports of methods of achieving the same results without using animals? Or even reports of similar experiments that have been done already and are being endlessly repeated?

The objections of the Research Defence Society to the British amendment can be summed up in one sentence: the prevention of animal suffering is not worth the expenditure of extra money or of the time the experimenter would need to read the literature in his field. And of this "defense," incidentally, the National Society for Medical Research has said:

> The Research Defence Society of Great Britain deserves the plaudits of the world's scientific community for the manner in which it expressed its opposition to this sticky measure.[84]

It would not be appropriate here to go into the alternatives to animal experiments that are already available. The subject is a highly technical one, more suited for researchers than for the general reader. But we already have the means to reduce greatly the number of animals experimented upon, in techniques like tissue culture (the culture of cells or groups of cells in an artificial environment); mathematical or computer models of biological systems; gas chromatography and mass spectrometry; and the use of films and models in educational instruction. Considering how little effort has been put into this field, the early results promise much greater progress if the effort is stepped up.[85]

In some important areas improvements can easily be made without using animals. Although thousands of animals have been forced to inhale tobacco smoke for months and even years, the proof of the connection between tobacco usage and lung cancer was based on data from clinical observations of humans.[86]

The US government is pouring billions of dollars into research on cancer. Much of it goes toward animal experiments, many of them only remotely connected with fighting cancer—experimenters have been known to relabel their work "cancer research" when they found they could get more money for it that way than under some other label. Of all cancers, lung cancer is the biggest killer. We know that smoking causes 80–85 percent of all lung cancer —in fact this is a "conservative" estimate, according to the director of the National Cancer Institute.[87] In a case like this we must ask ourselves: can we justify inflicting lung cancer on thousands of animals when we know that we could virtually wipe out the disease by eliminating the use of tobacco? And if people are not prepared to give up tobacco, can it be right to make animals suffer the cost of their decision to continue smoking?

Of course, it must be admitted that there are some fields of scientific research that will be hampered by any genuine consideration of the interests of animals used in experimentation. No doubt there have been genuine advances in knowledge which would not have been attained as easily or as rapidly without the infliction of pain on animals. The ethical principle of equal consideration of interests does rule out some means of obtaining knowledge, and other means may be slower or more expensive. But we already accept such restrictions on scientific enterprise. We do not believe that our scientists have a general right to perform painful or lethal experiments on human beings without their consent, although there are cases in which such experiments would advance knowledge far more rapidly than any alternative method. My proposal does no more than broaden the scope of this existing restriction on scientific research.

Finally, it is important to realize that the major health problems of the world largely continue to exist, not because we do not know how to prevent disease and keep people healthy, but because no one is putting the manpower and money into doing what we already know how to do. The diseases that ravage Asia, Africa, Latin America, and the pockets of poverty in the industrialized West are diseases that, by and large, we know how to cure. They have been eliminated in communities which have adequate nutrition, sanitation, and health care. Those who are genuinely concerned about improving health and have medical qualifications would probably make a more effective contribution to human health if they left the laboratories and saw to it that our existing stock of medical knowledge reaches those who need it most.

When all this has been said, there still remains the practical question: what can be done to change the widespread practice of experimenting on animals? Undoubtedly some action at the government level is needed, but what action precisely? And how can we succeed now when previous efforts failed? What can the ordinary citizen do to help bring about a change?

Unlike many other much needed reforms, this one does not lack popular support. We have already seen that in the United States a larger number of people wrote to the Defense Department about the beagle experiments than about the bombing of North Vietnam. In Britain, too, members of Parliament have reported receiving more mail from constituents concerned about the use of animals in laboratories than about the nation's entry into the European Common Market.[88] A British opinion poll conducted in 1973 found that 73 percent of the electors disapproved of the use of animals in the testing of weapons, toiletries, and cosmetics. Barely one in ten actually approved of these practices; however, only about one in four knew that animals actually were being used to test weapons and cosmetics.[89]

So the problem is not so much one of altering the views of the public. There is a huge amount of ignorance to be dispelled, but once the public knows what goes on there is little doubt that the public will disapprove, and disapprove strongly. The problem is one of channeling the attitudes of the public through the machinery of politics into effective action. On this topic the *Bulletin* of the National Society for Medical Research has again had some revealing things to say, this time about how the democratic process was frustrated by the British Parliament when the mild amendment I referred to earlier was brought up:

Parliament spent so much time discussing the proposed amendment that it eventually died without a vote being taken. The utmost delicacy was used in avoiding any stand on the bill . . . The bill died, yet no-one can be accused of voting against it. Therefore each member of Parliament is able to face the animal lobby in his home district.[90]

Why do legislators try so hard to fool their constituents, instead of working to remedy the situation against which their constituents' anger is rightly directed? In part, no doubt, it is because they are overly influenced by scientific, medical, and veterinary groups. In the United States, these groups maintain registered political lobbies in Washington, and they lobby hard against proposals to restrict experimentation. In any case, since legislators do not have the time to acquire expertise in these fields, they rely on what the "experts" tell them. But this is a moral question, not a scientific one, and the "experts" usually have an interest in the continuation of experimentation, or else are so imbued with the ethic of furthering knowledge that they cannot detach themselves from this stance and make a critical examination of what their colleagues do. Legislators must learn that when discussing animal experimentation they have to treat the medical, veterinary, psychological, and biological associations as they would treat General Motors and Ford when discussing air pollution. These groups should be given an opportunity to state their case, but they cannot be regarded as impartial authorities, and above all they cannot be entrusted with setting or enforcing standards of animal care.

Nor is the task of reform made any easier by the fact that there are now large companies involved in the profitable business of breeding or trapping animals and selling them to research laboratories. As a research veterinarian has said in testimony before the US House of Representatives House Appropriations Committee: "An entire new industry has been developed . . . with several of the larger companies having obtained international status with stock traded regularly on the major exchanges of the world."[91] The veterinarian was testifying in favor of more federal dollars to pay for more housing, equipment, technicians, and so on; but for those interested in curtailing animal experimentation, the existence of this industry is another obstacle, both because large companies are prepared to spend money to oppose legislation which will deprive them of their profitable markets, and because they use all the sophisticated selling techniques of other companies to increase the use of their products and expand their markets.

In journals like *Lab Animal*, a publication of United Business Publications, Inc., the breeding and trapping companies promote their wares as if they were new cars or another brand of cigarettes. "Demand our '74 model, the CD2F1 hybrid mouse," Charles River Breeding Laboratories, Inc., of Wilmington, Massachusetts, tells its potential customers in full-page advertisements; and in another issue it announces that, having taken over Primate Imports Corporation of Port Washington, New York, it can now supply, "Direct from trapping," "almost any species of monkey you desire. Squirrels, Baboons, Rhesus, Capuchins, Stumptails, Pigtails, African Greens, Chimpanzees and others." Meanwhile salesmen from companies of this sort, and those that sell cages and other equipment used with laboratory animals, visit educational institutions around the world, encouraging the use of animals in experimentation.

Whatever reforms are proposed, therefore, the most pressing need is that they include in a central, decision-making role a group of people totally free of any personal stake in the use of animals for research. Only in this way could effective control become a reality. United Action for Animals has proposed a "Public Science Council," consisting of nonanimal-using scientists, which would have authority to regulate the sums of public money that go into research in fields in which animals are used. By insisting on the replacement of animal-using methods by alternative methods not involving animals it would be possible for such a council to foster the growth of a new and more humane approach to scientific inquiry. This approach might not even require legislation, so far as the United States is concerned. All that would be necessary is that the research grants, public contracts, training grants, fellowships, and other awards now given to animal-using scientists be redirected toward other methods. A council of this sort might also contain representatives of the general public. The public provides the money for most scientific research; and the public has the right to direct the way in which its funds are used.

Until some major change in national policy has been effected, citizens can work on a more local level to make known what is happening all around the country, and quite possibly at universities and commercial laboratories in their own community. Students should refuse to carry out experiments required for their courses. Students and the animal welfare organizations should study the academic journals to find out where painful experiments are being carried out. They should then demonstrate against those university departments that abuse animals. Pressure should be put on universities to cut off funds to departments that have a bad record in this respect, and if the universities do not do so this should be publicized. Since universities are dependent on public good will for financial support, this method of protest should be effective. No doubt the cry will be raised that such demands are a restriction of "scientific freedom," but as there is no freedom to inflict agony on humans in the name of science, why should there be any freedom to inflict agony on other animals? Especially where public funds are involved, no one has a right to the freedom to use these funds to inflict pain.

The vital role played by public funds in the use of animals for experimentation suggests another political tactic. During the American involvement in Vietnam, opponents of that war withheld a portion of their taxes, roughly the proportion of the national revenues that went toward the war, as a way of emphasizing their opposition to the war. Such tactics should only be used in extreme cases; but perhaps this case is sufficiently extreme. Obviously experimenting on animals only uses a tiny fraction of the funds that went toward the war in Vietnam, although no figures are available to show how much is spent on animal experiments. A token tax withholding, say 1 percent of the tax payable, would cover the amount actually spent, and serve as a symbolic form of protest that would enable every taxpayer to express his opposition to the use made of his taxes.

By publicly exposing what is happening behind closed laboratory doors, protesting against these things, writing letters to those legislators who provide the funds for them, withholding taxes, and publicizing the records of candidates for public office before elections, it may be possible to bring about a reform. But the problem is part of the larger problem of speciesism and it is unlikely to be eliminated altogether until speciesism itself is eliminated. Surely one day, though, our children's children, reading about what was done in laboratories in the twentieth century, will feel the same sense of horror and incredulity at what otherwise civilized people can do that we now feel when we read about the atrocities of the Roman gladiatorial arenas or the eighteenth-century slave trade.

NOTES

1. *Air Force Times,* 28 November 1973; *New York Times,* 14 November 1973.

2. From a paper by R. Maclellan, B. Boecher, and others in M. Goldman and L. Bustad, eds., *Biomedical Implications of Radio-Strontium Exposure,* Atomic Energy Commission Symposium, Series #25, CONF-710201 (April 1972). The source for the starting date of these experiments is *Laboratory Animal Care,* 20 (1) p. 61 (1970).

3. K. Woodward, S. Michaelson, T. Noonan, and J. Howland, *International Journal of Radiation Biology,* 12 (3) p. 265 (1967).

4. A. Tegeris, F. Earl, H. Smalley, and J. Curtis, *Archives of Environmental Health,* 13, p. 776 (1966).

5. *Animal Welfare Enforcement, 1973.* Report of the Secretary of Agriculture to the President of the Senate and the Speaker of the House of Representatives (US Department of Agriculture, June 1974), pp. 19-21.

6. Personal communication to the author, 8 October 1974.

7. Hearings before the Subcommittee on Livestock and Feed Grains of the Committee on Agriculture (US House of Representatives, 1966), p. 63.

8. *Christian Science Monitor,* 18 July 1973.

9. Report of the Littlewood Committee, pp. 53, 166; quoted by Richard Ryder, "Experiments on Animals," in Stanley and Roslind Godlovitch and John Harris, eds., *Animals, Men and Morals* (New York: Taplinger Publishing Co., 1972), p. 43.

10. Ryder, "Experiments on Animals," p. 43.

11. *Journal of Comparative and Physiological Psychology,* 75 (1) p. 73 (April 1971).

12. *Journal of the Experimental Analysis of Behavior,* 19 (1) p. 25 (January 1973).

13. *Journal of Comparative and Physiological Psychology,* 67 (1) p. 110 (April 1969).

14. *Journal of the Experimental Analysis of Behavior,* 13 (1) p. 41 (January 1970).

15. *Journal of Abnormal and Social Psychology,* 48 (2) p. 291 (April 1953).

16. *Journal of Abnormal Psychology,* 73 (3) p. 256 (June 1968).

17. *Psychonomic Science* 19 (3) p. 191 (May 1970).

18. *Journal of Comparative and Physiological Psychology,* 78 (1)

p. 22 (January 1972); see also *Psychosomatic Medicine*, 36 (3) p. 199 (May-June 1974).

19. *Journal of the Experimental Analysis of Behavior*, 18 (2) p. 305 (September 1972).

20. *Journal of Comparative and Physiological Psychology*, 82 (2) p. 308 (February 1973).

21. *Journal of the Experimental Analysis of Behavior*, 19 (1) p. 133 (January 1973).

22. *Journal of the Experimental Analysis of Behavior*, 13 (3) p. 368 (May 1972).

23. *Journal of Comparative and Physiological Psychology*, 49 (5) p. 457 (1956).

24. *Journal of Comparative and Physiological Psychology*, 78 (1) p. 69 (January 1972).

25. *Journal of Comparative and Physiological Psychology*, 76 (3) p. 468 (September 1971).

26. *Journal of Comparative and Physiological Psychology*, 78 (2) p. 202 (February 1972).

27. *Proceedings of the National Academy of Science*, 54, p. 90 (1965).

28. *Engineering and Science*, 33 (6) p. 8 (April 1970).

29. *Journal of Comparative and Physiological Psychology*, 80 (1) p. 11 (July 1972).

30. *Behavior Research Methods and Instrumentation*, 1, p. 247 (1969).

31. *Journal of Autism and Childhood Schizophrenia*, 3 (3) p. 299 (July-September 1973).

32. *Primates*, 13 (3) p. 257 (September 1972).

33. *New Scientist*, 30 March 1972. (My italics.)

34. A. Heim, *Intelligence and Personality* (Baltimore: Penguin Books, 1971), p. 150.

35. *New Scientist*, 31 August 1972, from a book review by Chris Evans.

36. A. C. Frazer, quoted by Richard Ryder, *Victims of Science* (London: Davis-Poynter, 1975), p. 40.

37. See J. H. Draize, "Dermal Toxicity," in *Appraisal of the Safety of Chemicals in Foods, Drugs and Cosmetics*, Association of Food and Drug Officials, Austin, Texas, 1959, pp. 45-59; see also "Testing Procedures for Hazardous Substances," *Federal Register*, 17 September 1964. I owe this information, and many other references in this section, to material supplied to me by Richard Ryder.

38. *Journal of the Society of Cosmetic Chemists*, 13 (9) (1962).

39. A. Lansdown, "An Appraisal of Methods for Detecting Primary Skin Irritants," *Journal of the Society of Cosmetic Chemists*, 23, pp. 739-772 (1972).

40. *Toxicology and Applied Pharmacology*, 23 (4) p. 589 (December 1972).

41. *Sunday Mirror* (London), 24 February 1974, p. 10.

42. M. N. Gleason et al., eds., *Clinical Toxicology of Commercial Products* (Baltimore: Williams and Wilkins, 1969).

43. S. F. Paget, ed., *Methods in Toxicology* (Blackwell Scientific Publications, 1970), p. 4.

44. Ibid., pp. 134-139.

45. Ibid., p. 132.

46. G. F. Somers, *Quantitative Method in Human Pharmacology and Therapeutics* (Elmsford, New York: Pergamon Press, 1959); quoted by Richard Ryder, *Victims of Science*, p. 153.

47. H. C. Wood, *Fever: A Study in Morbid and Normal Physiology*, Smithsonian Contributions to Knowledge No. 357 (Philadelphia: Lippincott and Co., 1880).

48. *Lancet*, 17 September 1881, p. 515.

49. *Journal of the American Medical Association*, 89 (3) p. 177 (1927).

50. *Journal of Pediatrics*, 45, p. 179 (1954).

51. *Indian Journal of Medical Research*, 56 (1) p. 12 (January 1968).

52. S. Cleary, ed., *Biological Effects and Health Implications of Microwave Radiations*, US Public Health Service Publication PB 193 898 (1969).

53. *Thrombosis et Diathesis Haemorphagica*, 26 (3) p. 417 (1971).

54. *Archives of Internal Medicine*, 131, p. 688 (May 1973).

55. *Annual Review of Physiology*, 8, p. 335 (1946).

56. *Pharmacological Review*, 6 (4) p. 489 (1954).

57. K. Hobler and R. Napodano, *Journal of Trauma*, 14 (8) p. 716 (August 1974).

58. *Journal of Nutrition*, 83, p. 140 (1964).

59. *American Journal of Physiology*, 200, p. 34 (1961).

60. *Journal of Nutrition*, 102 (10) p. 1259 (October 1972).

61. *Journal of Neurophysiology*, 36 (3) p. 425 (May 1972).

62. *Behavior Research Methods and Instrumentation*, 4 (3) p. 121 (1972).

63. *Psychopharmacologia*, 16, p. 30 (1969).

64. *Scientific American*, 199 (4) p. 95 (1958).

65. *Journal of the Experimental Analysis of Behavior* 15 (1) p. 69 (Jan. 1971).

66. *Communications in Behavioral Biology*, 6, p. 49 (1971).

67. *Circulation Research*, 27, Supplement 1, pp. 1-13 (1970).

68. *Scope* (Durban, South Africa), 30 March 1973.

69. "The Price of Knowledge," broadcast in New York, 12 December 1974, WNET/13; transcript supplied courtesy WNET/13 and Henry Spira.

70. S. Milgram, *Obedience to Authority* (New York: Harper & Row, 1974). Incidentally, these experiments were widely criticized on ethical grounds because they involved human beings without their consent. It is indeed questionable whether Milgram should have deceived participants in his experiments as he did; but when we compare what was done to them with what is commonly done to nonhuman animals, we can appreciate the double standard with which critics of the experiment operate.

71. *South Wales Echo*, 21 January 1974.

72. S. Rosenthal, "Production and Measurement of Traumatic Swelling," *American Journal of Physiology*, 216 (3) p. 630 (March 1969).

73. R. Kirimli, S. Kampschulte, P. Safar, "Patterns of dying from exsanguinating hemorrhage in dogs," *Journal of Trauma*, 10 (5) p. 393 (May 1970).

74. *Journal of Comparative and Physiological Psychology*, 55, p. 896 (1962).

75. *Journal of the American Veterinary Medical Association*, 161 (11) 1 December 1972.

76. United Action for Animals Report, *The Death Sciences in Veterinary Research and Education*, p. iii.

77. *Journal of the American Veterinary Medical Association*, 147 (10) 5 November 1965; see also the statement of the Association to the Subcommittee on Livestock and Feed Grains of the Committee on Agriculture, US House of Representatives, 1966.

78. *Journal of the American Veterinary Medical Association*, 147 (10) 15 November 1965.

79. *Journal of the American Veterinary Medical Association*, 163 (9) 1 November 1973.

80. Ryder, "Experiments on Animals," in *Animals, Men and Morals*, pp. 69-70, 74.

81. *International Journal of Radiation Biology*, 25 (1) p. 61 (January 1974).

82. *British Journal of Industrial Medicine*, 27, p. 130 (1970); for further experiments in the lead poisoning of baboons by the same experimenter, see A. P. Hopkins and A. D. Dayan, *British Journal of Industrial Medicine*, 31, p. 128 (1974).

83. From the transcript of the "Doctors Trial," Case I, *United States v. Brandt et al.* Quoted by W. L. Shirer, *The Rise and Fall of the Third Reich* (New York: Simon & Schuster, 1960), p. 985. A brief account of the Nazi experiments can be found in this book, pp. 979-991; for a fuller account, see A. Mitscherlich and F. Mielke, *Doctors of Infamy* (New York, 1949).

84. *Bulletin of the National Society for Medical Research*, 24 (10) October 1973.

85. For further details see Terrence Hegarty, "Alternatives," in *Animals, Men and Morals;* Mr. Hegarty is an adviser to the Fund for the Replacement of Animals in Medical Experiments (for address, see Appendix 3). United Action for Animals, New York, has also published a series of reports on alternative methods, under titles like: "How Isolated Organs Can Be Used in Research, Testing and Teaching"; "Alternatives in Car Crash Research"; "Mathematical Modelling in Biomedical Research"; and "Abstracts Regarding Testing of Environmental Chemicals."

86. E. Wynder and D. Hoffman, in *Advances in Cancer Research*, 8, 1964; see also the Royal College of Physicians of London report, *Smoking and Health* (1962) and studies by the US Health Department. I owe these references to Richard Ryder, "Experiments on Animals," in *Animals, Men and Morals*, p. 78.

87. Hearings before the Committee on Appropriations, Subcommittee on Departments of Labor and Health, Education and Welfare Appropriations, House of Representatives, 1974, Pt. 4, National Institutes of Health, pp. 83, 87.

88. *Bulletin of the National Society for Medical Research*, 24 (10) October 1973.

89. From an address by Richard Ryder, reported in *RSPCA Today*, Summer 1974. The poll was conducted by N.O.P. Market Research Ltd.

90. *Bulletin of the National Society for Medical Research*, 24 (10) October 1973.

91. *Journal of the American Veterinary Medical Association*, 160, p. 1568 (1972).

3

Down on the Factory Farm ...

or what happened to your
dinner when it was still an
animal.

For most humans, especially those in modern urban and
suburban communities, the most direct form of contact
with nonhuman animals is at meal time: we eat them. This
simple fact is the key to our attitudes to other animals, and
also the key to what each one of us can do about changing these attitudes. The use and abuse of animals raised
for food far exceeds, in sheer numbers of animals affected,
any other kind of mistreatment. Hundreds of millions of
cattle, pigs, and sheep are raised and slaughtered in the
United States alone each year; and for poultry the figure
is a staggering three *billion*. (That means that about 5,000
birds—mostly chickens—will have been slaughtered in the
time it takes you to read this page.) It is here, on our
dinner table and in our neighborhood supermarket or
butcher's shop, that we are brought into direct touch with
the most extensive exploitation of other species that has
ever existed.

In general, we are ignorant of the abuse of living creatures that lies behind the food we eat. Our purchase is the
culmination of a long process, of which all but the end

product is delicately screened from our eyes. We generally
buy our meat and poultry in neat plastic packages. It
hardly bleeds. There is no reason to associate this package
with a living, breathing, walking, suffering animal. The
very words we use to describe it conceal its origin: we eat
beef, not bull, steer, or cow, and pork, not pig—although
for some reason we seem to find it easier to face the true
nature of a leg of lamb. The term "meat" is itself decep-
tive. It originally meant any solid food, not necessarily the
flesh of animals. This usage still lingers in an expression
like "nut-meat" which seems to imply a substitute for
"flesh-meat" but actually has an equally good claim to
be called "meat" in its own right. By using the more
general "meat" we avoid facing the fact that what we are
eating is really flesh.

These verbal disguises are merely the top layer of a
much deeper ignorance of the origin of our food. Consider
the images conjured up by the word "farm": a house, a
barn, a flock of hens, overseen by a strutting rooster,
scratching around the farmyard, a herd of cows being
brought in from the fields for milking, and perhaps a sow
rooting around in the orchard with a litter of squealing
piglets running excitedly behind her.

Very few farms were ever as idyllic as that traditional
image would have us believe. Yet we still think of a farm
as a pleasant place, far removed from our own industrial,
profit-conscious city life. Of those few who think about
the lives of animals on farms, not many know much of
modern methods of animal raising. Some people wonder
whether animals are slaughtered painlessly, and anyone
who has followed a truckload of cattle must know that
farm animals are transported in very crowded conditions;
but few suspect that transportation and slaughter are anything more than the brief and inevitable conclusion of a
life of ease and contentment, a life that contains the natural pleasures of animal existence without the hardships
that wild animals must endure in the struggle for survival.

These comfortable assumptions bear little relation to the
realities of modern farming. For a start, farming is no
longer controlled by simple country folk. It is a business,
and big business at that. In the last thirty years the entry

of large corporations and assembly line methods of production have turned farming into "agribusiness." This process began when big companies gained control of poultry production, once the preserve of every farmer's wife. Today twenty large corporations control poultry production in the United States. In the field of egg production, single plants contain a million or more laying hens. The remaining small producers have had to adopt the methods of the giants, or else go out of business. Companies that had no connection with agriculture have become farmers on a huge scale in order to gain tax concessions or to diversify profits. Greyhound Corporation now produces turkeys; the ham you last ate might have come from IT&T, and your roast beef from John Hancock Mutual Life Insurance, or from one of a dozen oil companies that have invested in cattle feeding, building feedlots that hold 100,000 or more cattle.[1]

For the big corporations, and for those who must compete with them or leave the land, there is no place for sentiment or for a sense of harmony with plants, animals, and nature. Farming is competitive and the methods which are adopted are those which cut costs and increase production. So farming is now "factory farming." Animals are treated like machines that convert low-priced fodder into high-priced flesh, and any innovation that results in a cheaper "conversion-ratio" is liable to be adopted. Most of this chapter is simply a description of these methods, and of what they mean for the animals to whom they are applied. I shall show that under these methods most animals lead miserable lives from birth to slaughter. Once again, however, my point is not that the people who do these things to the animals are cruel, wicked people. On the contrary, the attitudes of the consumers and the producers are not fundamentally different. The farming methods I am about to describe are merely the logical extension and application of the attitudes and prejudices that are discussed elsewhere in this book. Once we place nonhuman animals outside our sphere of equal consideration and treat them as things we use to satisfy our own desires, the outcome is predictable.

There are three different ways in which farm animals

may be made to suffer: in slaughter, in transportation, and in the general process of rearing. Although we have to look at all three of these to obtain a complete picture of what happened to our dinner when it was still an animal, I shall concentrate on the rearing process, since the suffering involved in modern methods of rearing animals is the most prolonged for the animals, and at the same time it is the aspect of farming about which the average consumer knows least.

As in the previous chapter, in order to make my account as objective as possible I have not based the descriptions that follow on my own personal observations of farms and the conditions in them, nor have I relied on reports from others especially sympathetic to animal welfare. Had I done so I could have been charged with having written a selective, biased account, based on a few visits to unusually bad farms. Instead the account is drawn largely from the source that can be expected to be most favorable to the farming industry: the magazines and trade journals of the farm industry itself.

Naturally, articles directly exposing the sufferings of farm animals are not to be found in farm magazines. In fact the farm magazines are not interested in the question of animal suffering in itself. Time and again farmers are advised to avoid practices that would make their animals suffer because the animals will gain less weight under these conditions; and they are urged to handle their animals less roughly when they send them to slaughter because a bruised carcass fetches a lower price; but the idea that we should avoid confining animals in uncomfortable conditions simply because this is in itself a bad thing is not mentioned. Ruth Harrison, the author of an exposé of intensive farming methods in Britain entitled *Animal Machines*, concluded that "cruelty is acknowledged only where profitability ceases."[2] That, certainly, is the attitude exhibited in the pages of the farming magazines, in the United States as well as in Britain.

Still, we can learn a great deal about the conditions of farm animals from the farm magazines. We learn of the attitudes of some of the farmers to the animals under their absolute and unrestricted rule, and we learn also of the new methods and techniques that are being adopted, and of the problems that arise with these techniques. Provided we know a little about the requirements of farm animals, this information is enough to give us a picture of animal farming in the United States today.

The first animal to be removed from the relatively natural conditions of the traditional farms and subjected to the full stress of modern intensive farming was the chicken. Chickens have the misfortune of being useful to humans in two ways: for their flesh and for their eggs. There are now standard mass production techniques for obtaining both of these products.

Agribusiness enthusiasts consider the rise of the chicken industry to be one of the great success stories of farming. At the end of World War II chicken for the table was still relatively rare. It came mainly from small independent farmers or from the unwanted males produced by egg-laying flocks. Today "broilers"—as table chickens are now usually called—are produced literally by the million from the highly automated factorylike plants of the large corporations that own or control 98 percent of all broiler production in the United States.[3] A dozen of these corporations account for around 40 percent of the nearly three billion birds reared and slaughtered annually. Some of these big producers are feed companies that originally sold the feed to the farmer, and then gradually took over successive stages of production; others, like Textron, Inc., a manufacturer of items ranging from pencils to helicopters (and now chickens), had no agricultural connection and went into the business simply because it looked like a profitable investment.[4]

The essential step in turning the chicken from a farm-yard bird into a manufactured item was confining it indoors. A broiler producer today gets a load of 10,000, 50,000, or even more day-old chicks from the hatcheries, and puts them straight into a long, windowless shed—usually on the floor, although some producers use tiers of cages in order to get more birds into the same size shed. Inside the shed, every aspect of the birds' environment is controlled to make them grow faster on less feed. Food and water are fed automatically from hoppers suspended from the roof. The lighting is adjusted according to advice from agricultural researchers: for instance, there may be bright light twenty-four hours a day for the first week or two, to encourage the chicks to gain quickly; then the lights may be dimmed slightly and made to go off and on every two hours, in the belief that the chickens are readier to eat after a period of sleep; finally there comes a point, around six weeks of age, when the birds have grown so much that they are becoming crowded, and the lights will then be made very dim at all times. The point of this dim lighting is to reduce the effects of crowding.

Toward the end of the eight- or nine-week life of the chicken, there may be as little as half of a square foot of space per chicken—or less than the area of a sheet of quarto paper for a three-and-one-half-pound bird. Under these conditions with normal lighting the stress of crowding and the absence of natural outlets for the birds' energies lead to outbreaks of fighting, with birds pecking at each other's feathers and sometimes killing and eating one another. Very dim lighting has been found to reduce this and so the birds are likely to live out their last weeks in near-darkness.

Feather-pecking and cannibalism are, in the broiler producer's language, "vices." They are not natural vices, however—they are the result of the stress and crowding to which the modern broilerman subjects his birds. Chickens are highly social animals, and in the farmyard they develop a hierarchy, sometimes called a "pecking order." Every bird yields, at the food trough or elsewhere, to those above it in rank, and takes precedence over those below. There may be a few confrontations before the order is firmly established but more often than not a show of force, rather than actual physical contact, is enough to put a chicken in its place. As Konrad Lorenz, a renowned figure in the field of animal behavior, wrote in the days when flocks were still small:

Do animals thus know each other among themselves? They certainly do. . . . Every poultry farmer knows that . . . there exists a very definite order, in which each bird is afraid of those that are above her in rank. After some few disputes, which need not necessarily come to blows, each bird knows which of the others she has to fear and which must show respect to her. Not only physical strength, but also personal courage, energy, and even the self-assurance of every individual bird are decisive in the maintenance of the pecking order.[5]

Other studies have shown that a flock of up to ninety chickens can maintain a stable social order, each bird knowing its place; but 10,000 birds crowded together in a single shed is obviously a different matter.[6] The birds cannot establish a social order, and as a result they fight frequently with each other. Quite apart from the inability of the individual bird to recognize so many other birds, the mere fact of extreme crowding probably contributes to irritability and excitability in chickens, as it does in humans and other animals. This is something that the farming magazines are aware of, and they frequently warn their readers:

Feather-pecking and cannibalism easily become serious vices among birds kept under intensive conditions. They mean lower productivity and lost profits. Birds become bored and peck at some outstanding part of another bird's plumage. . . . While idleness and boredom are predisposing causes of the vices, cramped, stuffy and overheated housing are contributory causes.[7]

Feather-pecking and cannibalism have increased to a formidable extent of late years, due, no doubt, to the changes in technique and the swing towards completely intensive management of laying flocks and table poultry. . . . The most common faults in management which may lead to vice are boredom, overcrowding in badly ventilated houses . . . lack of feeding space, unbalanced food or shortage of water, and heavy infestation with insect pests.[8]

Clearly the farmer must stop "vices," since they cost him money; but although he may know that overcrowding is the root cause, he cannot do anything about this, since in the competitive state of the industry eliminating overcrowding could mean eliminating his profit margin at the same time—he would have fewer birds to sell, but would have had to pay the same outlay for his building, for the automatic feeding equipment, for the fuel used to heat and ventilate the building, and for labor. So the farmer limits his efforts to reducing the consequences of the stress that costs him money. The unnatural way in which he keeps his birds causes the vices; but to control them the poultryman must make the conditions still more unnatural. Very dim lighting is one way of doing this. A more drastic step, though one now almost universally used in the industry, is "de-beaking." This involves inserting the chick's head in a guillotinelike device which cuts off part of its beak. Alternatively the operation may be done with a hot knife. Some poultrymen claim that this operation is painless, but an expert British government committee under zoologist Professor F. W. Rogers Brambell appointed to look into aspects of intensive farming found otherwise:

> . . . between the horn and the bone is a thin layer of highly sensitive soft tissue, resembling the "quick" of the human nail. The hot knife used in de-beaking cuts through this complex of horn, bone and sensitive tissue, causing severe pain.[9]

De-beaking, which is routinely performed in anticipation of cannibalism by most poultrymen, does greatly reduce the amount of damage a chicken can do to other chickens. It also, in the words of the Brambell committee, "deprives the bird of what is in effect its most versatile member" while it obviously does nothing to reduce the stress and overcrowding that lead to this unnatural cannibalism in the first place.

Once chickens were individuals; if a chicken bullied others (and this could happen, though it was not the general rule) that bird would be removed from the flock. Similarly if a bird became sick or was injured it could be attended to, or if necessary quickly killed. Now one man looks after tens of thousands of birds. A United States secretary of agriculture has written enthusiastically in the preface of a Department of Agriculture Yearbook that "using a modern feeding system for broilers, one man can take care of 60,000 to 75,000 broilers."[10] "Take care of" cannot mean what it used to mean, since if the poultry- man were to spend no more than one second a day inspect- ing each bird, it would take him twenty hours a day merely to complete his inspection, let alone do the other chores. In fact, all the modern poultryman does is remove dead birds. It is cheaper to lose a few extra birds in this way than to pay for the extra labor needed to watch the health of individual birds.

In order to allow total control of light and some con- trol of temperature (there is usually heating, but rarely cooling) the broiler sheds have solid, windowless walls and rely on artificial ventilation. The birds never see daylight, until the day they are taken out to be killed; nor do they breathe air which is not heavy with the ammonia from their own droppings. The ventilation is adequate to keep the birds alive in normal circumstances but if there should be a mechanical failure the birds soon suffocate. Even as obvious a possibility as a power failure can be disastrous, since not all broiler producers have their own auxiliary power units. When electricity workers went on strike in England in the winter of 1971 and power had to be cut off in certain areas, several producers returned to their sheds to find an unnatural quiet. The birds had suffocated when the fans stopped.

There are other ways in which birds can suffocate in a broiler house. There is the phenomenon known as "piling." Chickens kept in the broiler sheds become nervous, jittery creatures. Unused to strong light, loud noise, or other in- trusions, they may panic at a sudden disturbance and flee to one corner of the shed. In their terrified rush to safety they pile on top of each other so that, as one poultryman describes it, they "smother each other in a pitiful heap of bodies in one corner of the rearing area."[11]

The piling problem can be eliminated by a further de- gree of constraint: putting the chickens in cages. Caging laying hens in long rows of wire cages, three or four tiers high (called "battery cages" or "hen batteries"), is now standard in the egg industry, but has not been widely adopted for table chickens. One reason for this is that birds kept on wire develop sores or abscesses on their breasts, which reduces the value of the broiler bird, but does not matter to the egg producer whose birds are only suitable for chicken soup anyway. Another disadvantage of cages is the labor involved in putting the birds into cages at the beginning of their lives and taking them out again when they are ready to be killed; this cost is acceptable in the case of a layer, who will stay in the cage a year or more, but not for a broiler with a life span of eight or nine weeks.

Researchers at the University of Delaware, however, are now trying out a new technique which eliminates the labor problem and could make caged broilers more popular. In this system (already in use in Europe) the birds are reared in the crates in which they are trucked to the slaughter-house. The crates, which hold thirteen to fifteen chickens, can be slotted in and out of a 4-tier stand. When the birds are ready to be eaten the crates are slid out onto a truck. At the processing plant the crates are emptied, sterilized, and returned to the farm for another set of chicks. The system promises four times as many birds to a given area of shed, because the birds are stacked up one on top of another, but it is based on a degree of crowding in the last weeks of the birds' lives that is even more severe than that which prevails on the floor. The crates are stocked at a density of three birds to every square foot. This barely gives them room to move; but if the density were lower the return on capital invested would not be so high, and the trucks would have to make more trips from farm to slaughterhouse.[12]

If growing chickens in shipping crates will increase crowding, it may at least lessen slightly the terror that the birds go through when they are ready to be killed, since they will have one less novelty to adjust to. At present the first change the birds notice is that their food is suddenly cut off—there is no profit in undigested food. Perhaps twelve hours later the doors will be flung open and the birds, accustomed now to semidarkness, are grabbed by the legs, carried out upside down for their first and only exposure to sunlight, and summarily stuffed into crates which are piled on the back of a truck.

Since catching the broilers by hand and packing them in crates requires a good deal of labor, other methods are being looked into. An article in the British trade journal *Poultry World* has described a system of sucking the birds through suction pipes up to 200 feet long and then sliding them down into the crates.[13] At the 1972 International Poultry Show, in London, Anglian Livestock Appliances, an equipment manufacturer, was given a silver medal for designing broiler cages featuring a cage floor which is pulled out at catching time, allowing the birds to drop onto a conveyor belt which carries them to the crating point at the end of the cage block. At this point suction pipes can be used to bring them up to the height of the truck.[14]

Whatever method of packing is used, the birds in their crates are driven to the "processing" plant, where the chickens are to be killed, cleaned, and turned into neat plastic packages. At the plant they are taken off the truck and stacked, still in crates, to await their turn. That may take several hours, during which time they remain without food or water. Finally they are taken out of the crates and hung upside down on the conveyor belt that leads to the knife that will end their joyless existence.

The plucked and dressed bodies of the chickens will then be sold to millions of families who will gnaw on their bones without pausing for an instant to think that they are eating the dead body of a living creature, or to ask what was done to that creature in order to enable them to buy and eat its body. And if they did stop to ask, where would they find the answer? If they hear Frank Perdue, president of Perdue, Inc., one of the largest broiler producers in the country, telling them in radio advertisements that his chickens live in "a house that's just chicken heaven," how are ordinary people to find out that Perdue, like every other major broiler producer, has to cut the beaks off his chickens in order to prevent them from becoming cannibals under the stress of life in a huge, crowded broiler house with thousands of other chickens whom they cannot learn to recognize?[15]

Paramount chickens, another large broiler producer, has television commercials in which Pearl Bailey tells the audience that Paramount looks after their chickens "just like a mother hen"; another grotesque fantasy. Assuming that no one really cares about a chicken, the broiler producers tell blatant lies to the public, and since neither the press and television nor the animal welfare societies are interested in the welfare of farm animals, the lies pass unchallenged.

The reader who, after reading this section, is contemplating buying turkey instead of chicken should be warned that this traditional centerpiece of the family's Thanksgiving dinner is now reared by the same methods as broiler chickens, and that de-beaking is the general rule among turkeys too.

"A hen," Samuel Butler once wrote, "is only an egg's way of making another egg." Butler, no doubt, was being humorous; but when Fred C. Haley, president of a Georgia poultry firm that controls the lives of 225,000 laying hens, describes the hen as "an egg producing machine" his words have more serious implications. To emphasize his businesslike attitude Haley adds: "The object of producing eggs is to make money. When we forget this objective, we have forgotten what it is all about."[16]

Nor is this only an American attitude. A British farming magazine has told its readers:

The modern layer is, after all, only a very efficient converting machine, changing the raw material—feedingstuffs—into the finished product—the egg—less, of course, maintenance requirements.[17]

Remarks of this kind can regularly be found in the egg industry trade journals throughout the United States and Europe, and they express an attitude that is common in the industry. As may be anticipated, its consequences for the laying hens are not good.

Laying hens go through many of the same procedures as

broilers, but there are some differences. Like broilers, layers have to be de-beaked, to prevent the cannibalism that would otherwise occur in their crowded conditions; but because they live much longer than broilers, they often go through this operation twice. So we find a poultry specialist at the New Jersey College of Agriculture advising poultrymen to de-beak their chicks when they are between one and two weeks old because there is, he says, less stress on the chicks at this time than if the operation is done earlier, and in addition "there are fewer culls in the laying flock as a result of improper de-beaking." In either case, the article continues, the birds must be de-beaked again when they are ready to begin laying, at around twenty weeks of age.[18]

Laying hens get no more individual attention than broilers. Alan Hainsworth, owner of a poultry farm in upstate New York, told an inquiring local reporter that four hours a day is all he needs for the care of his 36,000 laying hens, while his wife looks after the 20,000 pullets (as the younger birds not yet ready to lay are called): "It takes her about 15 minutes a day. All she checks is their automatic feeders, water cups and any deaths during the night."

This kind of care does not make for a happy flock, as the reporter's description shows:

Walk into the pullet house and the reaction is immediate—complete pandemonium. The squawking is loud and intense as some 20,000 birds shove to the farthest side of their cages in fear of the human intruders.[19]

Julius Goldman's Egg City, fifty miles northwest of Los Angeles, is one of the world's largest egg producing units, consisting of two million hens divided into block-long buildings containing 90,000 hens each, five birds to a 16-by-18-inch cage. When the *National Geographic Magazine* did an enthusiastic survey of new farming methods Ben Shames, Egg City's executive vice president, explained to their reporter the methods used to look after so many birds:

We keep track of the food eaten and the eggs collected in 2 rows of cages among the 110 rows in each building. When production drops to the uneconomic point, all 90,000 birds are sold to processors for potpies or chicken soup. It doesn't pay to keep track of every row in the house, let alone individual hens; with 2 million birds on hand you have to rely on statistical samplings.[20]

Pullets used to be reared outdoors, in the belief that this made them stronger laying birds, better able to withstand life in the cage. Now they have been moved inside, and in many cases are placed in cages almost from birth, since with tiers of cages more birds can be accommodated in each shed and overheads per bird are correspondingly lower. Since the birds grow rapidly, however, they have to be moved to larger cages and this is a disadvantage, since "mortality may be a little higher. . . . Broken legs and bruised heads are bound to occur when you move birds."[21]

Whatever the method of rearing used, nearly all the big egg producers now keep their laying hens in cages. Originally there would be only one bird to a cage, and the idea was that the farmer could then tell which birds were not laying enough eggs to give an economic return on their food. Those birds would then be killed. Then it was found that more birds could be housed, and costs per bird reduced if two birds were put in each cage. That was only the first step, and as we have seen there is no longer any question of keeping a tally of each bird's eggs. The advantages of cages for the egg producer now consist in the greater number of birds that can be housed, warmed, fed, and watered in one building, and in the greater use that can be made of labor-saving automatic equipment.

The cages are stacked in tiers, with food and water troughs running along the rows, filled automatically from a central supply. They have sloping wire floors. The slope —usually a gradient of one in five—makes it more difficult for the birds to stand comfortably, but it causes the eggs to roll to the front of the cage where they can easily be collected by hand or, in the more modern plants, carried by conveyor belt to a packing plant.

The wire floor also has an economic justification. The excrement drops through and can be allowed to pile up for many months until it is all removed in a single operation. Unfortunately the claws of a hen are not well adapted to living on wire, and reports of damage to hens' feet are common whenever anyone bothers to make an examination. Without any solid ground to wear down the birds' toenails, these nails become very long and may get permanently entangled in the wire. An ex-president of a national poultry organization reminisced in an industry magazine recently about the occasions when, on removing a batch of hens whose productivity had started to decline:

> we have discovered chickens literally grown fast to the cages. It seems that the chickens' toes got caught in the wire mesh in some manner and would not loosen. So, in time, the flesh of the toes grew completely around the wire. Fortunately for the birds, they were caught near the front of the cages where food and water were easily available to them.[22]

Next we must consider the amount of living space available to laying hens in cages. There is, in Britain, a law entitled the Protection of Birds Act, passed in 1954 and intended to prevent cruelty to birds. Clause 8, subsection 1, of this law runs as follows:

> If any person keeps or confines any bird whatsoever in any cage or other receptacle which is not sufficient in height, length or breadth to permit the bird to stretch its wings freely, he shall be guilty of an offence against the Act and be liable to a special penalty.

While any caging is objectionable, the principle that a cage should be large enough to allow a bird to stretch its wings freely seems an absolute minimum necessary to protect birds from an intolerable degree of confinement that frustrates a very basic urge. So, one might assume, poultry cages in Britain must at least be large enough to give the birds this minimal freedom.

The assumption would be wrong. The subsection quoted above has a short but significant proviso attached to it:

Provided that this subsection shall not apply to poultry. . . .

This amazing proviso testifies to the relative strength of desires that emanate from the stomach and those that are based on compassion in a country that has a reputation for kindness to animals. There is nothing in the nature of those birds we call "poultry" that makes them less desirous of stretching their wings than other birds. The only conclusion we can draw is that the members of the British Parliament are against cruelty except when it might affect their dinner.

Curiously, there is a close parallel to this in America. Under the Animal Welfare Act of 1970 standards have been set which require that cages for animals shall "provide sufficient space to allow each animal to make normal postural and social adjustments with adequate freedom of movement." This act applies to zoos, circuses, wholesale pet dealers, and laboratories, but not to animals being reared for food.[23]

So how do cages for laying hens measure up by these standards? To answer this question we should know that the wingspan of a light hybrid layer averages around thirty inches. Cage sizes vary, but one of the common sizes has a floor area twenty inches wide and eighteen inches deep. Obviously this size is too small for even one bird to stretch her wings fully in. Consider, then, the fact that the "Codes of Practice" issued by the British Ministry of Agriculture allow *five* light hybrid laying hens to be kept in one such cage throughout their adult lives. Had the Ministry allowed only three birds to be kept in a cage this size—a density that Professor Brambell's government-appointed expert committee considered the absolute maximum tolerable—it would have been possible for *one* bird to stretch *one* wing at a time. Under the Ministry's Code—which is merely a "recommendation" to farmers and does not have the force of law—even this ridiculously modest freedom is denied.[24]

It may help to make these figures meaningful if the reader measures out an area 20 by 18 inches—or as an approximation, take a single page of a large format newspaper, like *The New York Times* or the London *Times*. Now imagine five birds, each weighing four pounds, living on that space for a year or more.

The reader who has performed this exercise now has an idea of the living conditions of British hens. Having grasped that, he will find what follows difficult to believe, but it is nevertheless true: *in the United States birds are usually more crowded still.* Take as an example the huge farm in Southern California I have already mentioned, Egg City. Here two million hens are housed five to each 16-by-18-inch cage. That is 20 percent less space than recommended under the British Ministry of Agriculture's Code.[25] When a reporter from the New York *Daily News* wanted to see a typical modern egg farm he visited Frenchtown Poultry Farm, in New Jersey, where he found:

> Each 18 by 24 inch cage on the Frenchtown farm contains nine hens who seemed jammed into them by some unseen hand. They barely have enough room to turn around in the cages.
> "Really, you should have no more than eight birds in a cage that size," conceded Oscar Grossman, the farm's lessor. "But sometimes you have to do things to get the most out of your stock."[26]

Actually, if Mr. Grossman had put only eight birds in his cages they would still have been grossly overcrowded, even by the miserly British standards; at nine to a cage they have only one-third square foot per bird, or 33 percent less than is required in Britain.

In 1968 the farm magazine *American Agriculturist* advised its readers in an article headed "Bird Squeezing" that it had been found possible to stock at one-third square foot per bird by putting four birds in a 12-by-16-inch cage. This was apparently a novel step at the time; the steady increase in densities over the years is indicated by the fact that a

1974 issue of the same magazine describing the Lannsdale Poultry Farm, near Rochester, New York, mentions the same housing density without any suggestion that it is unusual.[27] In reading egg industry magazines I have found numerous reports of similar high densities, and scarcely any that are substantially lower. My own visits to poultry farms in the United States have shown the same pattern. The highest reported density that I have read about is at the Hainsworth farm in Mt. Morris, New York, where four hens are squeezed into cages 12 inches by 12 inches, or just one square foot—and the reporter adds: "Some hold five birds when Hainsworth has more birds than room."[28] This means one-fourth and sometimes one-fifth square foot per bird—twice, and sometimes more than twice, the maximum density recommended in Britain. At this stocking rate a single sheet of quarto paper represents the living area of two to three hens.

Under the conditions standard on modern egg farms in the United States and other "developed nations" every natural instinct the birds have is frustrated. They cannot walk around, scratch the ground, dust-bathe, build a nest, or stretch their wings. They are not part of a flock. They cannot keep out of each other's way and weaker birds have no escape from the attacks of stronger ones, already maddened by the unnatural conditions. The extraordinary degree of crowding results in a condition that scientists call "stress," which really does appear to resemble the stress that occurs in humans subject to extreme crowding, confinement, and frustration of basic activities. I have already mentioned, when discussing broilers, one of the symptoms of this stress—aggressive pecking, leading to cannibalism. The Texas naturalist Roy Bedichek observed other signs:

> I have looked attentively at chickens raised in this fashion and to me they seem to be unhappy and in poor health. Their combs are dull and lifeless except for glaring and unnatural patches of color that appear occasionally; . . . the battery chickens I have observed seem to lose their minds about the time they would normally be weaned by their mothers and off in the weeds chasing grasshoppers on their own account.

Yes, literally, actually, the battery becomes a gallinaceous madhouse.[29]

Noise is another indication of distress. Hens scratching in a field are generally quiet, making only an occasional cluck. Caged hens tend to be very noisy. I have already quoted the reporter who visited the pullet house on the Hainsworth farm and found "complete pandemonium." Here is the same reporter's account of the laying house:

> The birds in the laying house are hysterical. The uproar of the pullet house was no preparation for this. Birds squawk, cackle and cluck as they scramble over one another for a peck at the automatically controlled grain trough or a drink of water. This is how the hens spend their short life of ceaseless production.[30]

My own observations show that these reports are not at all exaggerated; indeed they do not even convey an adequate impression of the constant and acute frustration of the lives of hens in modern egg factories. To appreciate this it is necessary to watch a cage full of hens for a short period. They seem unable to stand or perch comfortably, and are constantly restless. Even if one or two birds were content with their positions, so long as other birds in the cage are moving, they must move too. Watching the hens is like watching three people trying to spend a comfortable night in a single bed—except that the hens are condemned to this fruitless struggle for a whole year rather than a single night. An added irritation is that after a few months in the cages the birds start to lose their feathers, whether from rubbing against the wire, from feather-pecking by other birds, or because of the general diet and sunless conditions I do not know. The result is that their skin begins to rub against the wire, and it is common to see birds that have been in the cages for some time with skin rubbed bright red and raw, especially around the tail.

Finally, in most cages there is one bird—maybe more than one in larger cages—that has lost the will to resist being shoved aside and pushed underfoot by other birds. Perhaps these are the birds that, in a normal farmyard, would be low in the pecking order; but under normal conditions this would not matter so much. In the cage, however, these birds can do nothing but huddle in a corner of the cage, usually near the bottom of the sloping floor, where their fellow-inmates trample over them as they try to get to the food or water troughs.

Ultimately the most convincing way a bird can indicate that its conditions are inadequate is by dying. A high rate of mortality will occur only under the most extreme conditions, since the normal life span of a chicken is far longer than the eighteen months to two years that laying hens are allowed to live. Hens, like humans in slave-labor camps, will cling tenaciously to life under the most miserable conditions. Yet it is commonplace for an egg farm to lose 10–15 percent of its hens in one year, and many of these clearly die of stress from overcrowding and related problems. Here is one example:

> According to the manager of a 50,000 bird egg ranch near Cucamonga, California, five to ten of his hens succumb daily to confinement stress. (That's between two and four thousand per year.) "These birds," he says, "don't die of any disease. They just can't take the stress of crowded living."[31]

A carefully controlled study by members of the Department of Poultry Science at Cornell University confirmed that crowding increases death rates. Over a period of less than a year, mortality among layers housed three to a 12-by-18-inch cage was 9.6 percent; when four birds were put in the same cage, it jumped to 16.4 percent; with five birds in the cage, 23 percent died. Despite these findings the researchers advised that "under most conditions Leghorn layers should be housed at four birds per 12-by-18-inch cage" since the greater total number of eggs obtained made for a larger return on capital and labor, which more than compensated for the higher costs in respect of what the researchers termed "bird depreciation."[32] Indeed, if egg prices are exceptionally high, the report concluded, "five layers per cage make a greater profit."

So the hens that produce our eggs live and die. Perhaps

those that die early are the lucky ones, since their hardier companions have nothing in store for them except another few months of crowded discomfort. They lay until their productivity declines, and then they are sent off to be slaughtered and made into chicken pies or soups, which by then is all that they can be used for.

There is only one likely alternative to this routine, and that not a pleasant one. When egg production begins to drop off it is possible to restore the hens' reproductive powers by a procedure known as "force-molting." The object of force-molting is to make the hen go through the physiological processes associated, under natural conditions, with the seasonal loss of old plumage and growth of fresh feathers. After a molt, whether natural or artificial, the hen lays eggs more frequently. To induce a hen to molt when she is living in a controlled-environment shed without seasonal changes in the temperature or length of light requires a considerable shock to her system. Typically the hens will find that their food and water, which has been freely available to them until this time, is suddenly cut off. For two days they will have neither water nor food. At the same time the lighting, which has been on about seventeen hours a day to stimulate laying, is abruptly cut back to perhaps four hours, leaving the birds in darkness for the remaining twenty. After two days water will be restored, and food after another day. Over the next few weeks the lighting will be returned to normal and those hens that have survived—some succumb from the shock— may be expected to be sufficiently productive to be worth keeping for another six months or so. Most poultrymen, however, do not consider this procedure worth the trouble; hens are cheap, so they prefer to get a new flock as soon as the present one is past its peak.[83]

To the very end the poultryman allows no sentiment to affect his attitudes to the birds who have laid so many eggs for him. In contrast to the prisoner who gets a special meal before being hanged, the condemned hens may get no food at all. "Take Feed Away From Spent Hens" advises a headline in *Poultry Tribune,* and the article below tells poultrymen that food given to hens in the thirty hours

prior to slaughter is wasted, since the processors pay no
more for food that remains in the digestive system.[34]

Of all the animals commonly eaten in the Western
world, the pig is without doubt the most intelligent. The
natural intelligence of the pig is comparable to that of a
dog; it is possible to rear a pig as a pet and train it to
respond to simple commands much as a dog would. When
George Orwell put the pigs in charge of Animal Farm his
choice was defensible on scientific as well as literary
grounds.

The high intelligence of pigs must be borne in mind
when we consider whether the conditions in which they
are reared are satisfactory. While any sentient being, intelligent or not, should be given equal consideration, animals of different capacities have different requirements.
Common to all is a need for physical comfort. We have
seen that this elementary requirement is denied to hens;
and as we shall see, it is sometimes denied to pigs too,
though not with the same frequency or to the same degree.
In addition to physical comfort, a hen requires the structured social setting of the normal flock; it may also miss
the warmth and reassuring clucks of the mother hen immediately after hatching; and recent research has provided
evidence that even a chicken can suffer from simple boredom.[35] To whatever extent this is true of chickens, it is
certainly true, and to a greater extent, of pigs.

A pig may be physically comfortable in some of the confinement systems that exist today. Unlike the hen, the pig
can usually lie down in peace. But with nothing to do but
stand up and lie down, the pig may still be a bored and
unhappy pig. Unfortunately this boredom may not be reflected in a reduction of weight gain, and so it may not
worry the farmer at all. With nothing at all to do except
eat and sleep, a pig can hardly fail to put on weight, but
this should not be taken as evidence that his living conditions are satisfactory from the point of view of the pig's
welfare.

Farmers do occasionally notice that their pigs like stimulation. One British farmer wrote to *Farmer's Weekly* describing how he had housed pigs in a derelict farmhouse

and found that they played all around the building, chasing each other up and down the stairs. He concluded that:

> our stock need variety of surroundings . . . gadgets of different make, shape and size should be provided . . . like human beings, they dislike monotony and boredom.[36]

When kept in unsuitable, overcrowded conditions pigs are prone to "vice," as hens are. Instead of feather-pecking and cannibalism pigs take to biting each others' tails. This leads to fighting in the pig pen and reduces weight gains. Since pigs do not have beaks farmers cannot de-beak them to prevent this, but they have found another way of eliminating the symptoms without altering the conditions that cause the trouble: they cut off the pigs' tails. The expert British committee under Professor Brambell that described de-beaking as a painful and unnecessary mutilation reported in similar terms about tail-docking, and recommended that it be prohibited except under certain special circumstances. Nevertheless tail-docking as a routine precautionary measure continues to be widespread both in Britain and the United States.

The need to deprive a pig of its tail is an indication that the pigs are being kept in unsuitable and insufficiently stimulating conditions. Giving the pigs more room would reduce tail-biting, and other surprisingly simple devices can have the same effect. One American farmer has reported that a chain hung from the rafters of a building in which the pigs are kept will soon become a plaything, and tail-biting will be correspondingly reduced.[37]

Another respect in which confined pigs resemble confined hens is that they suffer from stress, and in many cases they die from it. Because in pig farming the individual pig makes a much larger contribution to total profits than the individual hen does, the pig farmer has to take this problem more seriously than the poultry farmer. There is a name for this condition—the "Porcine Stress Syndrome" —and the symptoms have been described in one farming journal as: "extreme stress . . . rigidity, blotchy skin, panting, anxiety, and often—sudden death." The condition is especially upsetting to producers because, as the same article says: "Painfully, you often lose PSS hogs when they near market weight, with a full investment of feed." The deaths can occur on any occasion when the pigs are under stress—when they are weaned, moved to new housing, mixed with strange pigs from a different pen, or when they are being sorted and loaded for market.

Confined pigs are so delicate that any disturbance can bring on the symptoms, including a strange noise, sudden bright lights, or the farmer's dog. A 1971 survey showed that more than a third of pig producers had experienced these sudden deaths; moreover these were the larger producers, responsible for 44 percent of all pigs marketed.[38] Nevertheless, if one were to suggest reducing stress by eliminating confinement methods of production, the reaction would almost certainly be that expressed in *Farmer and Stockbreeder* some years ago when confinement was still fairly new and stress-related deaths were just beginning to be noticed:

These deaths in no way nullify the extra return obtained from the higher total output.[39]

The conditions in which pigs are kept vary greatly. Pork production is not yet dominated by huge indoor units to the same extent that poultry and egg production are. It is still possible to allow pigs to graze on pasture land and compete in price with the big producers; but the trend is toward intensive units and perhaps half of all pigs slaughtered today never lived outside. Farmers are urged on by advertisements that tell them "How to make $12,000 profit sitting down"—and the way to do it is to buy the "Bacon Bin," which is "not just a confinement house. . . . It is a profit producing, pork production system."[40]

In fact the "Bacon Bin" is an automated confinement house in which 500 pigs get seven square feet of living space each. One of the reasons for the large profit it allegedly produces is that one man is said to be able to handle the entire system, thanks to automated feeding and slatted floors which allow the manure to drop through for easy disposal. Another saving, with this as with all other confinement systems, is that with less room to move about the pig will burn up less of its food in "useless" exercise, and so can be expected to put on more weight for each pound of food. Finally, for the big producers with thousands of pigs it is important to systematize management so that precise records can be kept, gains calculated, and instructions given accordingly. So pigs can be factory-produced almost as predictably and routinely as a manufactured item. This consideration is so important that nearly all the big producers now confine their animals indoors.

A typical new operation was described in *Farm Journal* under the heading "Pork Factory Swings into Production." The article began: "Hogs never see daylight in this half-million dollar farrowing-to-finish complex near Worthington, Minnesota." The complex comprises seventeen "Bacon Bins" and turns out 13,000 pigs each year.[41]

By the standards of the traditional farm, 13,000 pigs a year is a huge operation; yet in the accelerating trend to large, automated plants it has already been dwarfed. The indications are that what happened to the poultry and egg industries twenty years ago is about to happen in pig farming. At present the largest pig units in the world are in Eastern Europe, and they produce about 250,000 pigs a year; but in 1974 a start was made on a North Carolina unit that, when completed, will turn out one million pigs a year; and in Missouri an unsuccessful attempt was made to raise capital to develop a pig unit with a capacity of 2.5 million pigs annually. One study of the entry of corporations into pig confinement units has said it could signal "the removal of feeder pig production from the farm to the factory in relatively few years."[42] Meanwhile in England John Eastwood, head of a company that already has 3.5 million laying hens in cages and produces 60 million chickens for the table annually, has announced plans to become a major pig farmer as well.[43]

In addition to the problems of stress, boredom, and crowding that occur in modern confinement units for pigs, there is also a problem of physical comfort because the floors of these buildings are designed for ease of maintenance and the elimination of chores like manure disposal, rather than for the comfort of the animals. In most units the floors are either slatted or solid concrete. Neither is satisfactory; both damage the feet and legs of the pigs. One recent study showed that 65 percent of all market-weight hogs had foot damage, and a Nebraska survey put the incidence very near 100 percent for pigs raised on concrete or metal slats. On old-style dirt runs the problem was quite minor. A University of Nebraska swine special-ist, Bob Fritschen, advises that plenty of bedding—straw or something similar—can reduce the problem, but admits "even with good management and facilities you'll have some lameness with confined hogs."[44] In fact because straw costs money and requires labor to be replaced, bed-ding is rarely provided in modern systems for pigs destined for market, although it may be used for the sows and boars who breed generation after generation of market pigs, since these animals are more valuable and live longer. In a dis-cussion of slatted floors the editor of the magazine *Farmer and Stockbreeder* stated the producers' attitude to this question clearly:

> . . . the commonsense approach at this stage in our knowledge is that for expendable stock the slatted floor seems to have more merit than disadvantage. The animal will usually be slaughtered before serious de-formity sets in. On the other hand, breeding stock, with a longer working life before it, must grow and keep good legs; risk of damage here would seem to outweigh the advantages.[45]

While the fact that the animal will usually be slaughtered before serious deformity sets in may minimize the finan-cial loss to the farmer, it can hardly comfort the animal standing continuously on unsuitable flooring, acquiring a foot or leg deformity that would become serious, were he or she not to be slaughtered at an early age.

Given a choice, pigs will express their preference clearly enough. Breeders who avoid leg and foot troubles by pro-viding sand pits as well as slats find that the sows keep to the sand, except to eat or excrete. (Pigs, despite their rep-utation, are naturally clean animals and will never will-ingly soil their resting area.) "Sows really like it," says one breeder of his sand pit. "They like to 'bed.' This gives them a place."[46]

Very few pigs have the luxury of sand pits, and the way things are going those that have a hard concrete floor beneath them may be the lucky ones. Taking a lead from the poultry industry once again, pig farmers in Holland, Belgium, and England have begun rearing baby pigs in cages. The idea has not yet caught on in America, but some producers are trying it. Apart from the usual desire for faster gains on less feed and more tender meat because of the restricted opportunities for exercise, the main advantage of cages is that the pigs can be weaned from their mothers earlier. This means that the sow's lactation will cease, and within a few days she will become fertile. She will then be made pregnant again, either by a boar or by artificial insemination techniques—the latter are not as reliable for pigs as they are for cattle, and so natural mating is not obsolete yet. The result is that with early weaning a sow can produce an average of 2.6 litters a year, instead of the maximum of 2.0 that can be produced if the pigs are allowed to suckle for three months as they would naturally do.[47]

Most cage pig rearers do allow the piglets to nurse from their mothers for at least a week before moving them to cages. At least one large manufacturer of farm equipment, however, has made and is strongly promoting what it calls "Pig Mama"—a mechanical teat that replaces the natural one altogether, and allows weaning at six to twelve hours after birth. Reporting on this development, *Farm Journal* says that "it looks as if the 1970s could bring an end to the nursing phase of pig production" and expects "a tremendous jump in the number of pigs a sow could produce in a year." J. G. Leece, a researcher at North Carolina State University, agrees: "Automated pig production is a solid idea and the time is ripe." By the combination of mechanical nursing and other novel techniques like superovulation, which increases the number of fertile eggs the sow produces, researchers foresee highly automated systems of pig production producing as many as 45 pigs per sow per year, instead of the 16 that have been the average up to now. The report ends on a note of eager anticipation of the "exciting changes" in pig farming that the next decade will bring.[48]

For the pigs themselves, the decade could prove less than exciting. There are two aspects of these developments that are alarming. First there is the effect on the baby pigs, deprived of their mothers and confined in wire cages. In the previous chapter we saw that monkeys reared in similar conditions became depressed and showed many symptoms of psychopathological behavior; it is a reasonable supposition that the separation of mother and child also causes distress to young pigs. As for the cages themselves, an ordinary citizen who kept dogs in similar conditions for their entire lives would risk prosecution for cruelty. A farmer who keeps an animal of comparable intelligence in this manner, however, is more likely to be rewarded with a tax concession or, in some countries, a direct government subsidy.

The second alarming aspect of the new techniques is that the sow is being turned into a living reproduction machine. Under the best conditions there is little joy in an existence that consists of pregnancy, birth, having one's babies taken away, and becoming pregnant again so that the cycle can be repeated—and sows do not live under the best conditions. They are often closely confined for both pregnancy and birth. While pregnant they may be housed in stalls two feet wide and six feet long, or scarcely bigger than the sow herself; or they may be tethered by a collar around the neck; or they may be in stalls and tethered. In any of these systems the sow can stand up or lie down, but she cannot turn around or exercise in any other way.[49] Again, savings on feed and labor are the reasons for confinement. When the sow is ready to give birth she is moved to a farrowing pen, and here too she may be tightly restricted in her movements. A Scandinavian device, nicknamed "the iron maiden" and consisting of an iron frame that prevents free movement, has now been introduced in Britain and other countries. The ostensible purpose of this device is to stop the sow lying on and crushing her piglets, but this can be achieved by other methods that still allow the sow to move about.

When the sow is confined both while pregnant and while nursing—or when she is deprived of the opportunity to nurse—she is tightly restricted for almost the whole of her life. Under close confinement, sows show signs of stress, such as gnawing the bars of their stalls. This is, as a veterinarian has noted, "one of the few physical expressions available to her in her barren environment."[50] Only when the sow is placed with the boar does she have a short period of freedom in a larger pen—although this is still likely to be indoors. For at least ten months in every year, the pregnant and nursing sow will be unable to walk around. When artificial insemination is perfected, as one day it no doubt will be, this sensitive animal will be denied her last chance to exercise, as well as the only remaining natural contact she has with another member of her species, apart from her fleeting contact with her offspring.

In pig farming, as in the animal experimentation industry and in other areas of animal raising, new techniques that disregard animal welfare are being pioneered and promoted by two separate groups: commercial interests who want to sell equipment, feed, drugs, and services; and government-supported research institutions. From the first of these groups perhaps we should not expect anything other than a desire to make more money by selling new products; but do the latter have no role other than to maximize the exploitation of farm animals? J. G. Leece, North Carolina State University's enthusiastic promoter of mechanical nursing and other exciting innovations, has said: "It's up to research institutions that can afford the risk of experimentation to prove the economics. . . ."[51] Have the people who provide the taxes that support these institutions been asked whether economics is all they are interested in? Perhaps, if consulted, taxpayers would like research to be done into ways of restoring the simple pleasures of a more natural existence to farm animals.

Here, as in the area of animal experimentation, the colleges of veterinary medicine do not give first priority to animal welfare. In reporting on an annual Congress of the British Veterinary Association, *The Times* said of the relationship between the vets and the factory farms:

. . . before being admitted to the register of the Royal College of Veterinary Surgeons, new graduates promise to place before all other considerations the welfare of animals committed to their care . . . It soon became clear, however, that it was easier to define economic factors than to debate the ethical considerations that disturbed some people.[52]

Not all vets, however, are prepared to go along with intensive farming. In 1972, when cage rearing of pigs was being introduced in Britain, a Coventry vet wrote to the editor of *Farmer and Stockbreeder*:

May I dissociate myself completely from any implication that this is a tolerable form of husbandry? I hope many of my colleagues will join me in saying that we are already tolerating systems of husbandry which, to say the least of it, are doubtfully humane. This latest experiment is downright cruel. . . . Cost effectiveness and conversion ratios are all very well in a robot state; but if this is the future, then the sooner I give up both farming and farm veterinary work the better.[53]

So far as the practicing vet is concerned, the problem is that he receives his remuneration from the farmer, not the animal, and if there is a clash of interest between the two there will be a strong motivation to favor the one who pays the bills. Inherent in this situation is a real danger that those vets who care for animals more than they care for money will turn away from farm veterinary work, leaving it in the hands of insensitive technocrats who neglect their obligations to place the welfare of animals above economic considerations.

Of all the forms of intense farming now practiced, the quality veal industry ranks as the most morally repugnant, comparable only with barbarities like the force-feeding of geese through a funnel that produces the deformed livers made into *pâté de foie gras*. The essence of veal raising is the feeding of a high-protein food—which should be used to reduce malnutrition in poorer parts of the world—to confined, anemic calves in a manner that will produce a tender, pale-colored flesh that will be served to gourmets in expensive restaurants. Fortunately this industry does not compare in size with poultry, beef, or pig production; nevertheless it is worth our attention because it represents an extreme, both in the degree of exploitation to which it subjects its animals, and in its absurd inefficiency as a method of providing people with nourishment.

Veal is the flesh of a young calf, and the term was originally reserved for calves killed before they had been weaned from their mothers. The flesh of these very young animals was paler and more tender than that of a calf that had begun to eat grass; but there was not much of it, since calves begin to eat grass when they are a few weeks old and still very small. So there was little money in veal, and the small amount available came from the unwanted male calves produced by the dairy industry. These males were a nuisance to the dairy farmers, since the dairy breeds do not make good beef cattle. Therefore they were sold as quickly as possible. A day or two after being born they were trucked to market where, hungry and frightened by the strange surroundings and the absence of their mothers, they were sold for immediate delivery to the slaughterhouse.

Once this was the main source of veal in the United States. Now, using methods first developed in Holland, farmers have found a way to keep the calf longer without the flesh becoming darker in color or less tender. This means that the veal calf, when sold, may weigh as much as 325 pounds, instead of the ninety-odd pounds that newborn calves weigh; and as veal fetches a premium price, this has made rearing veal calves a profitable occupation.

The trick depends on keeping the calf in highly unnatural conditions. If the calf were left to grow up outside, its playful nature would lead it to romp around the fields. Soon it would begin to develop muscles, which would make its flesh tough. At the same time it would eat grass and its flesh would lose the pale color that the flesh of newborn calves has. So the specialist veal producer takes his calves straight from the auction ring to a confinement unit. Here, in a converted barn or purpose-built shed, he will have rows of wooden stalls. Each stall will be 1 foot 10 inches wide and 4 feet 6 inches long. It will have a slatted wooden floor, raised above the concrete floor of the shed. The calves will be tethered by a chain around the neck to prevent them turning around in their stalls. (The chain may be removed when the calves grow too big to turn around in such narrow stalls.) The stall will have no straw or other bedding, since the calf might eat it, spoiling the paleness of his flesh.

Here the calves will live for the next thirteen to fifteen weeks. They will leave their stalls only to be taken out to slaughter. They are fed a totally liquid diet, based on non-fat milk powder with added vitamins, minerals, and growth-promoting drugs.

This method of raising calves was introduced to the United States in 1962 by Provimi, Inc., of Watertown, Wisconsin. Provimi is a feed manufacturer. Its name comes from the "Proteins, Vitamins and Minerals" of which its feeds are composed—ingredients that, one might think, could be put to better use than veal raising. Provimi, according to its own boast, created this "new and complete concept of veal raising" and is still by far the largest organization in the business. Its interest in promoting veal production lies in developing a market for its feed. Accordingly, in conjunction with its distributor, Agway, Inc., of Syracuse, New York, it has put out the *Provimi Veal Raising Manual,* in which the methods I have described in the previous paragraphs are recommended to the producer. Provimi also has representatives wherever there is a potential for veal raising (mainly in dairying districts) who encourage farmers to start a veal unit and assist those who already have one. Provimi also publishes a newssheet under the supposedly humorous title *The Stall Street Journal.* From this publication we learn what Provimi considers "optimum veal production":

The dual aims of veal production are firstly, to produce a calf of the greatest weight in the shortest possible time and secondly, to keep its meat as light colored as possible to fulfill the consumer's requirement. All at a profit commensurate to the risk and investment involved.[54]

In Britain similar methods are used; here too, the Dutch example has been followed. Theoretically the Ministry of Agriculture's Codes of Practice would prevent veal raisers using stalls as narrow as those used elsewhere. The code for cattle states that the width of the pen should not be less than the height of the animal at the shoulder. The idea of this regulation is that the animal should be able to lie down in the pen with its legs stretched out. But allowing the calves this much room would sharply reduce the number of calves that can be accommodated in a given building, since a calf is about 3 feet 6 inches high at the shoulder, or almost twice as high as the pens are wide. Pens this wide would also allow the calves to turn around in their stalls. For the veal producer these are two good reasons for keeping the stalls narrow. One of Britain's biggest veal raisers, Frank Paton of Somerset, keeps his calves in stalls less than two feet wide and has said that he has no intention of observing the Code. He has been quoted as saying that "farming is about money production, not food production," and he doesn't think it will pay him to provide wider stalls. Since the Codes are merely recommendations, little can be done to force him to comply.[55]

The narrow stalls and their slatted wooden floors are a serious source of discomfort to the calves. The inability to turn around is frustrating. When he lies down, the calf must lie hunched up, sitting almost on top of his legs rather than having them out to one side as he might do if he had more room. (See photo no. 7.) A stall too narrow to turn around in is also too narrow to groom comfortably in; and calves have an innate desire to twist their heads around and groom themselves with their tongues. A wooden floor without any bedding is hard and uncomfortable; it is rough on the calves' knees as they get up and lie down. In addition, animals with hooves are uncomfortable on slatted floors. A slatted floor is like a cattle grid, which cattle will always avoid, except that the slats are closer together. The spaces, however, must still be large enough to allow manure to fall or be washed through, and this means that they are large enough to make the calves uncomfortable on them.[56]

The special nature of veal and the veal calf has other implications that make the industry incompatible with any genuine concern for the animals' welfare. Obviously the calves sorely miss their mothers. They also miss something to suck on. The urge to suck is strong in a baby calf, as it is in a baby human. These calves have no teat to suck on, nor do they have any substitute. From their first day in confinement—which may well be only the third or fourth day of their lives—they drink from a plastic bucket. Attempts have been made to feed calves through artificial teats, but the problems of keeping the teats clean and sterile are apparently not worth the farmer's trouble. It is common to see calves frantically trying to suck some part of their stalls, although there is usually nothing suitable; and if you offer a veal calf your finger you will find that the calf immediately begins to suck on it, as a human baby sucks its thumb.

Later on the calf develops a desire to ruminate—that is, to take in roughage and chew the cud. But roughage is strictly forbidden and so, again, the calf may resort to vain attempts to chew the sides of its stall. Digestive disorders, including stomach ulcers, are common in veal calves, as are chronically loose bowel movements.

As if this were not enough, there is the fact that the calf is deliberately kept anemic. As Provimi's *Stall Street Journal* has said:

> Color of veal is one of the primary factors involved
> in obtaining "top-dollar" returns from the fancy veal
> markets . . . "light color" veal is a premium item
> much in demand at better clubs, hotels and restaurants.
> "Light color" or pink veal is partly associated with
> the amount of iron in the muscle of the calves.[57]

So Provimi's feeds, like those of other manufacturers of veal feeds, are deliberately kept low in iron. A normal calf would obtain iron from grass or other forms of roughage, but since a veal calf is not allowed this he becomes anemic. Pale pink flesh is in fact anemic flesh. The demand for flesh of this color is a matter of snob appeal. The color does not affect the taste and it certainly does not make the flesh more nourishing—rather the opposite.

The anemia is, of course, controlled. Without any iron at all the calves would drop dead. With a normal intake their flesh will not fetch as much per pound. So a balance is struck which keeps the flesh pale and the calves—or most of them—on their feet long enough for them to reach market weight. The calves, however, are unhealthy and anemic animals. Kept deliberately short of iron they develop a craving for it and will lick any iron fittings in their stalls. This explains the use of wooden stalls. As Provimi tells its customers:

> The main reason for using hardwood instead of metal boxstalls is that metal may affect the light veal color. . . . Keep all iron out of reach of your calves.[58]

And again:

> It is also necessary that calves do not have access to a continuous source of iron. (Water supplies should be checked. If a high level of iron [excess of 0.5 ppm] is present an iron filter should be considered.) Calf crates should be constructed so calves have no access to rusty metal.[59]

The anemic calf's insatiable craving for iron is one of the reasons why the producer is anxious to prevent it from turning around in its stall. Although calves, like pigs, normally prefer not to go near their own urine or manure, urine does contain some iron. The desire for iron is strong enough to overcome the natural repugnance and the anemic calves will lick the slats that are impregnated with urine. The producer does not like this, because it gives the calves a little iron and because in licking the slats the calves may pick up infections from their manure, which falls on the same spot as their urine.

We have seen that in the view of Provimi, Inc., the twin aims of veal production are producing a calf of the greatest possible weight in the shortest possible time and keeping the meat as light in color as possible. We have seen what is done to achieve the second of these aims, but there is more to be said about the techniques used to achieve fast growth.

To make an animal grow quickly it must take in as much food as possible, and it must use up as little of this food as possible in its daily life. To see that the veal calf takes in as much as possible, the calves are given no water. Their only source of liquid is their food—the rich milk replacer based on powdered milk and added fat. Since the buildings in which they are housed are kept fairly warm, the thirsty animals take in more of their food than they would do if they could drink water. A common result of this overeating is that the calves break out in a sweat, rather like, it has been said, an executive who has had too much to eat too quickly.[60] In sweating the calf loses moisture, which makes him thirsty, so that he overeats again next time. By most standards this process is an unhealthy one, but by the standards of the veal producer aiming at producing the heaviest calf in the shortest possible time, the long-term health of the animal is irrelevant, so long as it survives to be taken to market; and so Provimi advises that sweating is a sign that "the calf is healthy and growing at capacity."[61]

Getting the calf to overeat is half the battle; the other half is ensuring that as much as possible of what has been eaten goes toward putting on weight. Confining the calf so that it cannot exercise is one requirement for achieving this aim. Keeping the barn warm also contributes to it, since a cold calf burns calories just to keep warm. Even warm calves in their stalls are apt to become restless, however, for they have nothing to do all day except for their two mealtimes. A Dutch researcher has written:

. . . veal calves suffer from the inability to do something. . . . The food-intake of a veal calf takes only 20 minutes a day! Besides that there is nothing the animal can do. . . . One can observe teeth grinding, tail waggling, tongue swaying and other stereotype behavior. . . . Such stereotype movements can be regarded as a reaction to a lack of occupation.[62]

To reduce the restlessness of their bored calves, many veal producers leave the animals in the dark at all times, except when they are being fed. Since the veal sheds are normally windowless, all that is necessary to do this is to turn off the lights. Thus the calves, already missing most of the affection, activity, and stimulation that their natures require, are deprived of visual stimulation and of contact with other calves for more than twenty-two hours out of every twenty-four. Illnesses in dark sheds have been found to be more persistent.[63]

Calves kept in this manner are unhappy and unhealthy animals. Despite the fact that the veal producer selects only the strongest, healthiest calves to begin with, uses a medicated feed as a routine measure, and gives additional injections at the slightest sign of illness, digestive, respiratory, and infectious diseases are widespread. It is common for a veal producer to find that one in ten of a batch of calves do not survive the fifteen weeks of confinement. Ten percent mortality over such a short period would be disastrous for anyone raising calves for beef, but the veal producer can tolerate this loss because of the high price restaurants are prepared to pay for his product. If the reader will recall that this whole laborious, wasteful, and painful process exists for the sole purpose of pandering to would-be gourmets who insist on pale, soft veal, no further comment should be needed.

Traditionally, cattle raised for beef in America have roamed freely over the vast open spaces that we see in cowboy movies. By comparison with chickens, pigs, and veal calves, beef cattle still see more of the great outdoors, but the duration of their freedom has diminished. Most of them roam freely for the first six months. Ten years ago they would have continued to graze for another year or two. Now after six months to a year cattle are rounded up to be "finished"—that is, to be brought quickly to market weight and condition by being fed a more concentrated form of nourishment than that obtainable from grass. For this purpose they are shipped long distances to feedlots. Here thousands of cattle are kept in small enclosures, on a surface that is either mud or packed dirt, depending on the weather. They are fed corn or other cereals. After six to eight months of this they are ready for market.

The growth of these large feedlots has been the dominant trend in the cattle industry over the past decade, although skyrocketing grain prices in 1974 have slowed the trend down and continued high prices may in time reverse it. Of the 27 million cattle slaughtered each year in the United States, 75 percent are now brought to market weight on feedlots. Large feedlots, producing more than 16,000 head of cattle a year, are now responsible for 30 percent of the nation's beef. These larger feedlots are substantial commercial undertakings, often financed by oil companies or Wall Street money looking for tax concessions.

Feedlots are economic, so long as grain prices do not go too high, because cattle fatten more quickly on grain than on grass. Yet cattle do not have stomachs suited for the rich, concentrated diet that they receive in feedlots. One farmer has termed it "a monstrously unnatural diet"[64] and another report puts it this way:

Feedlot cattle already live on the edge of indigestion because of the amount of feed they consume. It is as if you would sit down at the table three times a day for 150 days and eat a Christmas dinner each time.[65]

Cattle are ruminant animals. This means that their stomachs are designed for breaking down roughage by the process of "chewing the cud." A diet with little roughage frustrates rumination. In an effort to obtain more fiber, cattle on an all-cereal diet lick their own and each other's coats, and the large amount of hair that they take into the rumen in this way may cause abscesses.[66] Diluting the grain with the roughage that cattle need and crave, however, would slow down their weight gain.

Feedlots do not confine cattle as severely as cages confine hens, or stalls confine sows and veal calves. Stocking densities have been increasing, but even when they go as high as 900 animals to the acre (and this is still unusual in outdoor feedlots) each animal has fifty square feet of space and can wander around its compound, which may be an acre in area. Boredom from the barren, unchanging environment is more of a problem than restriction of movement.

Another problem is exposure to the elements. In summer the cattle may be out in the Texas sun without shade; in winter they may have no protection from conditions to which they are not naturally suited. In the winter of 1972–73, for instance, severe weather killed between 4 percent and 10 percent of all feedlot cattle in Texas, Kansas, Colorado, and Oklahoma. Many of the losses, one source reported, were of cattle recently shipped from the South and already under stress from the journey. The ice and snow, coupled with muddy, sometimes frozen feedlots, were more than the cattle could take.[67]

Confining beef cattle indoors is not unknown but it is still rare. It protects the animals from the weather, but always at the cost of much more crowding, since the cattleman wants the greatest possible return on the capital he has invested in the building. The University of Minnesota, in experimental trials with different systems of confinement, found that:

> returns to labor and management, the economic yardstick, show that the more animals per unit the better the return.

Accordingly this study suggests a stocking rate allowing each animal only fourteen square feet of space—despite the fact that the average daily gain each animal makes tends to drop off as densities reach this level. The diminishing gains suggest an increase in stress from crowding; but the greater number of animals produced in a more crowded unit compensates the farmer for this decline and yields a larger total profit.[68] The pattern is one that we have seen in other kinds of animal rearing, and should now be familiar. It is a pattern that conclusively refutes the claim sometimes heard that farmers put the welfare of their animals first because it pays them to do so. Unfortunately there is no such sweet harmony between economics and animal welfare, so far as the commercial rearing of animals is concerned. As we shall see in the next chapter, the

only way to harmonize economics and animal welfare is
to stop rearing animals for food.

Intensively confined beef cattle are generally kept together in groups, in pens rather than in single stalls.
Slatted floors are often used for ease of cleaning, although
beef cattle, like pigs and veal calves, are uncomfortable on
slats and can develop lameness and foot deformities. At
present high corn prices appear likely to halt the trend
toward ever more confinement of beef cattle; but if corn
prices should fall beef cattle could easily become subject
to the same degree of confinement that is now standard
in other areas of animal production.

No area of animal raising is safe from the inroads of
technology and the pressure to intensify and standardize
production. Baby lambs, those joyous symbols of spring-
time that now gambol in the fields, may be headed for the
dark interiors of confinement houses. The method would be
to use hormones to produce multiple births instead of the
normal single lamb per ewe, and then place the offspring
indoors immediately after birth. The lamb will then be
put into a stall and fed by a mechanical teat. This system
has been reported in use in Nebraska. Each lamb is allowed four feet of space. The Virginia Polytechnic Institute has also developed a confinement system for lambs,
reportedly in use on several Virginia farms, and similar
methods are at the experimental stage in Britain.[69]

Other animals already being reared intensively include
rabbits, turkeys, and many species of fur-bearing animals,
especially minks.

The dairy industry may be the last major area of animal
rearing to deprive its animals of all freedom of movement,
since it is necessary to bring the cows to the milking parlor
twice a day and then return them to pasture or, in winter,
to barns. There are already in use, however, semiconfine-
ment systems in which the cows spend most of the year
inside a barn; and Alfa-Laval, a Swedish agricultural company, has applied its ingenuity to the problem of getting
the cow to the milking parlor. It claims to have a solution
which eliminates the labor and time this operation normally requires. Each cow is placed in a contraption called

the "Unicar" which is a kind of cage on wheels that moves along a railway line. The cages, with cows in them, spend most of their time filed in rows in a storage barn. Two or three times a day the farmer pushes a button in the milking parlor. Rows of cows then move automatically up to the milking parlor like a long train. As they go their car wheels trip switches which feed, water, and clean the cars. After milking, the cows, still in the cages, roll back to the storage area. The cows live in their cages for ten months of the year, during which time they are unable to walk and turn around. Because the system requires a heavy capital investment and its productivity has still to be proven, it has not yet been introduced to either the United States or Britain. It could represent the future of the dairying industry, however, because it offers, according to *Farm Journal,* "substantial savings in feed, labor and barn space." Commercial plants using this system are reportedly being established in Germany.[70]

We have now surveyed the main areas of animal raising in which traditional methods have been transformed into factory farming. I think it is clear from the degree of confinement that these methods involve, the disruption of the finement that these methods involve the disruption of the forms of behavior or "vices" that are indications of stress or tension, that these methods are incompatible with any genuine concern for the welfare of the animals. There may, however, still be a few skeptical readers. Perhaps, they will say to themselves, an animal which has never known natural conditions does not suffer from confinement as an animal that had once been free to roam outside would. To settle this doubt we need to look at a more authoritative judgment on this topic.

I have already more than once in this chapter mentioned the report of the committee appointed by the British government under the chairmanship of F. W. Rogers Brambell. This committee was set up by the British Minister of Agriculture in 1964 as a result of revelations by the animal welfare campaigner Ruth Harrison about the new factory farming methods then being introduced into

Britain. Ruth Harrison wrote a book, entitled *Animal Machines*, on the subject, and *The Observer*, a leading Sunday newspaper, published long extracts from it. There was an immediate and widespread public reaction. The minister at first attempted to reassure the public that all was well, but the public wisely refused to accept his assurance, and he was forced to appoint an expert committee to investigate the situation. (In retrospect this tactic may be seen as a way of postponing action until public feeling had died down, but at the time it seemed a positive move.) The committee the minister appointed is undoubtedly the best qualified group of experts, in any country, ever to make a detailed study of the question of animal welfare on intensive farms. In addition to Brambell, himself a noted zoologist, the committee included W. H. Thorpe, the director of the department of animal behavior at Cambridge University, and other experts in veterinary science, animal husbandry, and agriculture. Though they in no way questioned the right of humans to raise animals for food, the members of the committee were able to draw on the most recent information about the nature of domestic animals, the conditions under which they are kept, and the extent to which these conditions are likely to cause them to suffer.

The committee received evidence from associations of farmers and livestock producers, manufacturers of cages, the Royal College of Veterinary Surgeons, animal welfare societies, and concerned individuals. They also visited fifty-four livestock establishments throughout Britain and, for comparative purposes, in Denmark and Holland. They set out their findings and recommendations in an eighty-five-page official report, published in December 1965. I shall now go through the most important of these findings and recommendations, comparing them with the conditions that exist today on farms in the United States, where no study comparable to the Brambell Report has as yet been made. This section will therefore serve both as a more authoritative statement of the effect on animals of the methods described earlier in this chapter, and as a brief summary and recapitulation of the main points of the discussion of these methods.

What Is Animal Welfare?

After deciding, on grounds similar to those given in the first chapter of this book, that animals are capable of suffering and capable of feeling "rage, fear, apprehension, frustration and pleasure," the committee considered the cumulative effect on animals of long-term conditions that might be tolerable in the short term. They rejected the argument, often used by farmers, that productivity is a satisfactory indication of the absence of suffering—the fact that an animal is putting on weight can, they said, be a "pathological condition." (Indeed, no one who finds that he or she eats more and puts on weight when depressed will be inclined to believe that weight gain is a sign of happiness.)

On the important issue of the extent to which domestic animals may suffer from the peculiarly unnatural and restrictive environment in which they are kept on intensive farms, the committee expressed general agreement with the views of W. H. Thorpe, who in a special appendix considered the most recent findings in the fields of physiology and ethology. In this appendix Thorpe says:

All the domestic animals which man farms are species which, in the wild, show a fairly highly organized social life either in flock, family, clan or herd. This means that their behavioral organization is also potentially on a high level, far higher than the ordinary man imagines. Even though a cow in a stall or a pig in a sty may appear stupid enough, this impression may be quite erroneous simply because we have never even begun to comprehend the social organization of the wild ancestor which in turn, despite the effects of domestication, still undoubtedly determines the sensory abilities and level of feeling and perception of the animal.

Though domestic animals have been selectively bred, Thorpe stresses that observation of their behavior has shown that they are "still essentially what they were in the prehistoric wild," with innate behavior patterns and needs which are still present *even if the animal has never known natural conditions*. While noting that there are still some aspects of these behavior patterns that we do not know enough about, Thorpe concludes:

> ... certain basic facts are clear enough to justify action. Whilst accepting the need for much restriction, we must draw the line at conditions which completely suppress all or nearly all the natural, instinctive urges and behavior patterns characteristic of actions appropriate to the high degree of social organization as found in the ancestral wild species and which have been little, if at all, bred out in the process of domestication. In particular it is clearly cruel so to restrain an animal for a large part of its life that it cannot use any of its normal locomotory behavior patterns. [Brambell Report, appendix, pp. 74, 76, 79]

Accepting this view, the committee enunciated the following modest, but fundamental, principle to govern the degree to which an animal may be confined:

> In principle we disapprove of a degree of confinement of an animal which necessarily frustrates most of the major activities which make up its natural behavior. ... An animal should at least have sufficient freedom of movement to be able without difficulty to turn around, groom itself, get up, lie down and stretch its limbs. [Brambell Report, par. 37]

The committee then went on to consider in turn each of the major areas of intensive farming.

Laying Hens

After describing the growing practice of placing egg-laying hens in batteries of cages, the committee said:

> First, it must be noted that the degree of confinement to which the battery hen is subjected is extremely close

and imposes strict limitation of the normal behavior
pattern of the bird. Cages containing two or three birds
and measuring 12–14 inches wide and 17 inches deep
are commonly used. Under such conditions the birds
cannot stretch their wings, move without touching one
another or stand fully upright at the rear of the
cage. . . .

Much of the ingrained behavior pattern is frustrated
by caging. The normal reproductive pattern of mating,
hatching and rearing young is prevented and the only
reproductive urge permitted is laying. They cannot fly,
scratch, perch or walk freely. Preening is difficult and
dust-bathing impossible. [Brambell Report, pars. 57–
58]

Reluctantly, the committee decided that it would be un-
realistic to recommend the immediate abolition of caging
for hens, and decided that caging should be permitted to
continue "for the time being" while an alternative commercially feasible system was developed. This continuance,
however, was to be "conditional on certain basic standards
being applied" to hens in cages. These conditions included:[71]

Not more than three birds to each cage. With larger numbers the committee found evidence of an increase in cannibalism, even if space were increased proportionately, and
under these circumstances "there is ample evidence to
show the existence of a peck order leading to stress and
injury."

In the United States, cages containing five, six, nine, or
more birds are common.

Minimum space allowances. Since "the welfare of the bird
in a cage is closely related to the amount of space which it
enjoys" the committee recommended that the three-bird
cage should measure no less than 20 by 17 inches, for two
birds 16 by 17 inches, and for one bird 12 by 17 inches.
These dimensions were calculated to allow a bird to stretch
one wing.

In the United States as many as *four* birds are sometimes

put into a cage that is *smaller* than the minimum size the Brambell committee would have allowed for *one* bird; the gigantic Egg City ranch in Southern California puts five birds in a cage smaller than that recommended as a minimum for three.

Prohibition of de-beaking. In a general remark about the practice of mutilating animals, the committee said:

> We dislike all such practices in principle. We dislike particularly mutilations which result in a permanent disability, affecting the normal behavior of the animal, and we do not regard such mutilations as permissible simply because they may be judged necessary to counter a defect in the system of husbandry. [Brambell Report, par. 34]

Of de-beaking specifically the committee said that the operation causes "severe pain" and that in addition it deprives the bird of its beak, which is "its most versatile member." Therefore:

> We recommend that de-beaking should be prohibited as soon as possible for all birds which are to be kept in battery cages and we are satisfied that the standards we advocate will obviate the need for this mutilation by removing the danger of cannibalism under this system of husbandry. [Brambell Report, pars. 97–98]

In the United States, de-beaking is practically universal in the egg industry, and many egg producers perform the operation twice, soon after birth and when the birds begin to lay.

Table Chickens (Broilers)

Minimum space allowances.

> We consider space per bird to be the most important factor in their welfare. This has been steadily reduced

since the industry began. We recommend that a minimum standard should be laid down and that for each bird above the age of six weeks there should be at least one square foot of floor space. [Brambell Report, par. 90]

In the United States there are, of course, no minimum standards and a higher degree of crowding can occur. The system of growing broilers in shipping crates pioneered by the University of Delaware is based on a stocking rate of *three* birds to every square foot.

Prohibition of de-beaking. The committee expressed confidence that "de-beaking is unnecessary for broilers," because "cannibalism is not a serious problem with young birds." They recommended that "de-beaking of all poultry to be kept as broilers be prohibited forthwith." (Of course, the "necessity" of de-beaking depends on how the birds are kept; the committee apparently had in mind birds kept in reasonable conditions, without severe overcrowding.)

In the United States de-beaking of broilers is almost universal. As we saw on page 102 de-beaking is a routine precaution even for a producer who advertises his conditions as "chicken heaven."

Collecting, packing, transport, and slaughter. Although this area was outside the committee's strict terms of reference, they went out of their way to express their opinion that "cruelty arises amongst broilers . . . in the collection, packing and transport of the birds to the slaughterhouse [and] . . . in the slaughterhouse." They recommended both legislation and effective action under existing legislation.[72]

In the United States there is no comprehensive legislation on this topic.

Pigs

Minimum space allowances.

A primary concern is the amount of living space available to the animal. This has tended to decline to a level at or near that at which the saving in capital costs of the buildings becomes offset by loss in production and is clearly well below that which is acceptable. We are of opinion that basic mandatory standards should be set in the general interest of the welfare of pigs and we recommend accordingly that the minimum floor space allowed per pig, between 150–210 lbs. liveweight, should be 8 square feet clear . . . and above 210 lb. liveweight it should be 10 square feet clear. [Brambell Report, par. 118]

In the United States, with no regulations, space has declined to the level the committee described.

Prohibition of routine tail-docking. Observing that "the vice of tail-biting is rare under good management in suitable houses that are not overstocked," the committee went on to say of the preventive measure of cutting off pigs' tails:

We disapprove of this mutilation in principle; it involves the destruction of sensitive tissue and bone, thus causing severe pain and we recommend that the docking of pigs should be prohibited, save when necessary as a remedial treatment by a veterinary surgeon. [Brambell Report, par. 124]

In the United States pigs commonly have their tails docked as a routine precaution against outbreaks of tail-biting.

Prohibition of confinement for sows.

A recently introduced practice is the keeping of pregnant sows in cubicles in which they cannot turn around. . . . We are unable to approve such close confinement continuously during pregnancy. . . . After weaning the breeding sow has at best only a few days of comparative freedom before the next service and repetition of the regime. She may spend, therefore, the greater part of her breeding life in very close confinement. We recommend that pregnant sows should not be kept without daily exercise in quarters which do not permit them to turn around freely and in any event they should not be tethered indoors. [Brambell Report, par. 125]

In the United States sows are kept continuously in stalls that do not permit them to turn around. They are not taken out for exercise. They are often tethered indoors.

Veal Calves

Calves to receive adequate iron. Having laid down the general principle that:

We do not consider a diet permissible that is known to be deficient in some component or components necessary to maintain the animal in full health, whether or not this leads to an overt pathological condition. . . . [Brambell Report, par. 39]

the committee then carried out a lengthy examination of the practice of withholding iron from veal calves to produce "white" veal and recommended that the diet be reinforced with iron in a suitable form "to ensure that on a normal intake the animal is in no wise deficient in this element" (Brambell Report, par. 145).

In the United States, all producers of "prime" veal deliberately keep their calves short of iron.

Calves to receive roughage.

A normal calf, raised with its dam, begins to nibble grass or other roughage at an early age, probably when it is not much more than a fortnight old. . . . The veal calf, deprived of fodder and fed exclusively on a liquid diet, cannot ruminate because it has no roughage. . . . We find it hard to believe that the urge to ruminate is not part of the satisfaction of feeding. It is true that suckling seems to suppress the urge to

"Farm fresh eggs" today come from "farms" like this one, near Monticello, New York. The filth and smell are indescribable. The birds' droppings, visible here on the top of the lower tier of cages, accumulate for months before being cleaned out. The cage floors slope, to allow the eggs to roll to the front for easy collection; and the birds' toes protrude through the unsuitable wire flooring. (Photo by Tom Ackerson)

As many as 9 hens are squeezed into the 18 by 24 inch cages shown here. The crowding declines only as the weaker birds die. One dead bird is visible on the right of the picture. It has been taken out of the cage and placed on top for later removal. To save labor, no attempt is made to care for sick birds. (Photo by Ede Rothaus)

Live chickens on their way to slaughter at the processing plant. (Photo by Pat Goudvis)

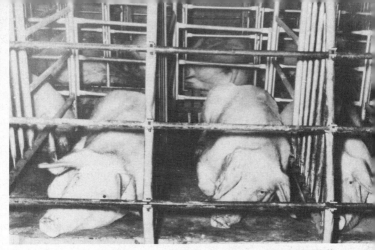

Above: Sows spend most of their lives pregnant, confined in stalls. Unable to move freely, they are plainly bored; but animals that do not move consume less food, and are more profitable. (Photo by John L. Jones) Below: After their confinement during pregnancy, sows are now often immobilized from the time they give birth until the piglets are weaned. This picture shows the "Protecta" holding frame, first developed in Sweden. (Photo courtesy Keystone Press)

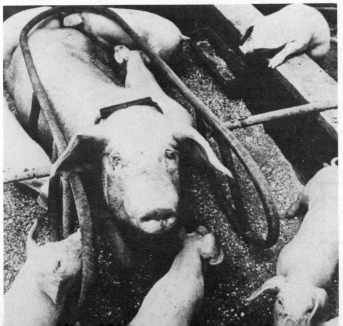

In this Connecticut veal unit, 400 calves spend their lives confined in stalls. For 22 hours out of every 24, they are in darkness. This photograph was taken at one of their two mealtimes, when the lights are turned on. (Photo by the author)

When the calves lie down, they must hunch up to fit their legs into the 22 inch wide stalls. (Photo by the author)

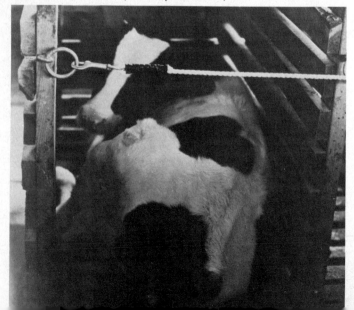

The original Associated Press caption for this picture read: "Rump Roast? You can tell by the smell of seared flesh in the air that it's branding time throughout the West. Two men hold down a calf on a ranch near Bothell, Washington, as a third sears the ranch's brand on her backside." (Photo courtesy Wide World Photos)

To test a detergent for possible eye irritation, a paste of the detergent is applied directly to the eyes of rabbits, and left bandaged. The immobilized rabbits are then stacked on shelves (visible in the background) for several hours. Since rabbits cannot cry and flush the material from the eye, their capacity for irritation is much greater than that of humans. (UPI photo)

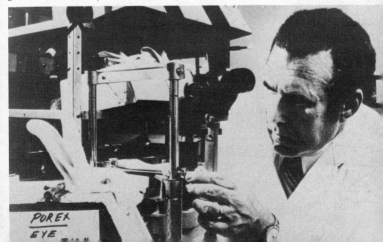

PORE X
EYE

These rabbits, at the Squibb Institute, New Brunswick, N.J., are part of a routine drug testing program. (Photo courtesy of Wide World Photos)

Monkeys and apes used in long term experiments may be kept for over a year in "restraining chairs" like these at the Walter Reed Army Institute of Research, Washington, D.C. This particular experiment, designed to test the effect of electric shock and anxiety on the growth of ulcers, is described in the text on page 60. (Photo courtesy Wide World Photos)

Researchers in the Pharmacology Department at the University of Michigan have addicted dozens of monkeys to various drugs. This one, suffering from morphine withdrawal, is about to be injected with another dose. For further details, see the text, p. 59. (Photo courtesy B.I.P.S.)

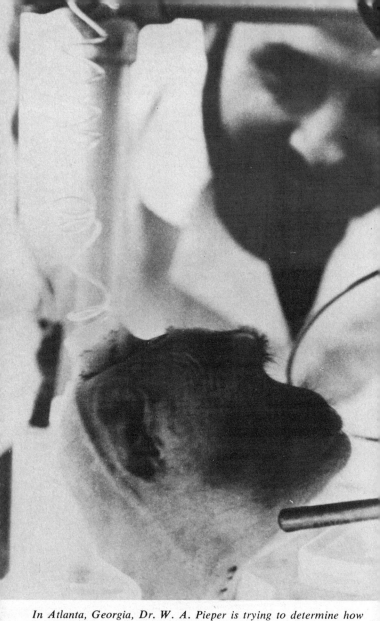

In Atlanta, Georgia, Dr. W. A. Pieper is trying to determine how long it takes this monkey to become dependent on alcohol. (Photo courtesy of Wide World Photos)

ruminate, but even the suckling calf will ruminate
when it has nibbled fodder, although it does not do so
to the extent of a calf removed from its mother and
given solid food. The "white" veal calf has not the satisfaction either of suckling or of rumination. Its habit
of nibbling the woodwork of its pen and anything else
it can reach suggests a desire for solid food. . . . We
recommend that all calves be provided with palatable
roughage daily at all ages from a week after birth.
[Brambell Report, pars. 144–145]

In the United States, calves raised for veal are never
given any roughage.

Calves to be free to move.

. . . Calves are normally active, playful animals. They
lick and groom themselves, show curiosity about their
environment and are sociable. Under unrestrained circumstances they display few of the objectionable
habits associated with close confinement. . . . We consider that calves should have sufficient room to be able
at all ages to turn around, to groom themselves, and to
move without discomfort. The size of the pen in common use at present for "white" veal production is, we
believe, too small to meet these requirements adequately. . . . We recommend that individual pens for
calves should be of a sufficient size to allow the calf
freedom of movement, including ability to turn around,
and that those for calves of 200–300 lbs. liveweight
should measure at least 5 feet by 3 feet 6 inches.
    We recommend that the yoking or close tethering of
calves, except for short periods and for specific purposes (e.g. feeding or veterinary treatment) should be
prohibited. [Brambell Report, pars. 147–149]

In the United States the standard width of a veal pen is
1 foot 10 inches. When young the calves are tethered;
the tethers are removed only when the calves become too
big to turn around in their stalls.
    The total effect of the implementation of the commit-

tee's recommendations concerning veal calves, incidentally, would be the abolition of the "white" or "prime" veal trade, since the flesh of animals kept as the committee recommends would be a natural red color instead of the pale pink of "white" veal. Obviously in the view of the committee the production of "white" veal is necessarily inhumane.

Beef Cattle

The committee did not consider the welfare of animals in American-style large outdoor feedlots, since these are not generally used in Britain. They did, however, recommend that cattle being fed on grain should be provided with roughage to enable them to ruminate. When cattle are kept indoors they recommended a minimum space allowance of twenty-five square feet per animal, and they thought totally slatted flooring should be prohibited because cattle are uncomfortable on slats, and the slats cause injury and lameness. They recommended the provision of straw or other forms of bedding for cattle kept on solid surfaces.[73]

In the United States most beef cattle are fattened on feedlots, not indoors. They are usually not given roughage, although they have more space than the committee's minimum. Some cattle are confined indoors, however, and in these systems they may have much less space. We saw on page 130 that a University of Minnesota study told farmers that they could make more money by reducing space to fourteen square feet per animal. Totally slatted floors may be used, and bedding is not provided.

Stockmanship

The committee stressed the importance of good stockmanship when intensive systems are used, saying that there should be:

proper routine inspection of all the animals ... preferably at least twice a day and never less than once. We are not prepared to tolerate any system where such in-

spection is likely to be ineffective in recognizing sick or
injured animals. . . . [Brambell Report, par. 44]

In the United States, the huge numbers of animals now
being entrusted to the care of a single stockman make
proper inspection impossible. Particularly in the poultry
industry, no attempt is made to recognize sick or injured
animals—only when they die are laying hens removed from
their cages. As we saw on page 100, these deplorable
standards of stockmanship have actually been endorsed by
a US Secretary of Agriculture, who has said that one man
can look after 60,000–75,000 chickens.

Throughout this section I have been contrasting the
recommendations of the Brambell committee with the conditions of animals in the United States. Readers in other
countries may be inclined to believe that conditions in their
own country are not so bad; but if they live in one of the
industrialized nations, there are no grounds for complacency. In Britain, for instance, conditions are much
closer to those in the United States than to those recommended by the committee. This is because the government,
under pressure from the agribusiness lobby, watered down
the recommendations of its own expert committee until they
became, in the words of a letter to *The Times*, signed by
Brambell, Thorpe, and other members of the committee:

> a compromise approximating to current practice; a
> compromise on a compromise for which no case other-
> wise than commercial expediency exists.[74]

and this verdict was described as a "justified condemnation"
in a further letter, signed by J. S. Huxley, Desmond
Morris, N. Tinbergen, and six other eminent zoologists,
who added:

> As scientists familiar with the behavior of animals we
> feel strongly, with the Brambell Committee, that every
> possible step must be taken to prevent "a degree of
> confinement of an animal which necessarily frustrates
> most of the major activities which make up its natural
> behavior."[75]

Despite these protests from those best qualified to assess the matter, the "Codes of Practice" later issued by the minister and accepted by Parliament allow the continuation of the "white" veal trade; allow both cattle and sows to be kept in stalls and tethered, allow entirely slatted floors for cattle, sharply reduce the space allowances for poultry, and permit de-beaking; moreover, even these weak codes were not made mandatory, and as we saw on page 124, it is possible for a major veal producer to state publicly that he does not intend to observe the code, and get away with it.

Finally, it is important to remember that although the implementation of the Brambell recommendations, in full, would be a major advance in Britain, the United States, or anywhere else where factory farming exists, the Brambell recommendations are very far from giving equal consideration to the interests of animals and humans. The committee represents an enlightened and humane form of speciesism, but it is speciesism nonetheless. The committee did not, and within its terms of reference could not, question the idea that animals may be used as means to human ends. Its members operated within the conventional assumptions about animals: humans may use animals for their own purposes, and they may raise and kill them to satisfy their preference for a diet containing animal flesh. It was because they were thinking within these assumptions that the committee members, in Thorpe's words, "accept[ed] the need for much restriction" and then decided what degree of restriction was excessive.

But since, as we shall see in the next chapter, methods of agriculture that do not involve animals are far more efficient in producing food than methods that do involve animals, there is really no "need" at all for restriction. Indeed, by describing the "Codes of Practice" as "a compromise on a compromise," the committee, in the letter I have quoted, admitted that its own recommendations were already a compromise between the requirements of animal welfare and what it considered practical within the context of a society used to eating large quantities of animal products.

I have concentrated on modern intensive farming methods in this chapter because the general public is largely ignorant of the suffering that these methods involve; but it is not only intensive farming that causes animals to suffer. Animals undergo numerous minor cruelties whether they are reared by modern or traditional methods. Some of these have been normal practice for centuries. This may lead us to disregard them, but it is no consolation to the animal on whom they are inflicted. Consider, for example, some of the routine operations that cattle are still subjected to.

Nearly all cattlemen de-horn, brand, and castrate their animals. All of these processes can cause severe physical pain. Horns are cut off because horned animals take up more space at a feeding trough or in transit, and can harm each other when packed tightly together. Bruised carcasses and damaged hides are costly. The horns are not merely insensitive bone. Arteries and other tissue have to be cut when the horn is removed, and bleeding results, especially if the calf is not de-horned shortly after birth.

Castration is practiced because steers are thought to put on weight better than bulls—although in fact they seem only to put on more fat—and because there is a fear of a taint developing in the flesh from the male hormones. Castrated animals are also easier to handle. Most farmers admit that the operation causes shock and pain to the animal. In Britain an anesthetic must be used, unless the animal is very young, but in America anesthetics are not in general use. The procedure is to pin the animal down, take a knife and slit the scrotum, exposing the testicles. You then grab each testicle in turn and pull on it, breaking the cord that attaches it; on older animals it may be necessary to cut the cord.[76]

Some farmers, to their credit, are troubled by this brutal surgery. In an article entitled "The Castration Knife Must Go," C. G. Scruggs, editor of *The Progressive Farmer*, refers to the "extreme stress of castration" and suggests that since lean meat is now in demand, male animals could be left unmutilated.[77] The same view has been expressed in the pig farming industry, where the practice is similar. Said an article in the British magazine *Pig Farming*:

Castration itself is a beastly business, even to the hardened commercial pig man. I'm only surprised that the anti-vivisection lobby have not made a determined attack on it.

And since research has now shown a way of detecting the taint that boar meat occasionally has, the article suggests that we "think about giving our castrating knives a rest."[78]

Branding cattle with a hot iron is widely practiced, as a protection against straying and cattle rustlers (who still exist) as well as to assist record-keeping. Although cattle have thicker skins than humans, their skins are not thick enough to protect them against a red-hot iron applied directly to the skin—the hair having been clipped away first —and held there for five seconds. To permit this operation to be done, the animal is thrown to the ground and pinned there (see photo no. 8). Alternatively it may be held in a contraption called a "squeeze chute" which is an adjustable crate that can be fitted tightly around it. Even so, as one guide notes, "the animal will usually jump when you apply the iron."[79]

As an additional mutilation, cattle are likely to have their ears cut with a sharp knife into special shapes. This is done so that, out on the range, they can be identified from a distance or when they are viewed from the front or rear, where the brand would not be visible.[80]

These, then, are some of the standard procedures of traditional methods of rearing cattle. Similar things are done to other animals when they are reared for food. And finally, in considering the welfare of animals under traditional systems, it is important to remember that almost all methods involve the separation of the mother and young at an early age, and that this causes considerable distress to both. No form of animal raising allows the animals to grow up and become part of a community of animals of varying ages, as they would be under natural conditions.

Although castration, branding, and the separation of mother and child have caused suffering to farm animals for centuries, it was the cruelty of transportation and slaughter that used to arouse the most anguished pleas from the humane movement in the days—back in the nineteenth century—when the humane movement cared about what happened to farm animals. Then animals were driven from pastures near the Rockies down to the railheads, and jammed into railway cars for several days without food until the train reached Chicago. There, in gigantic stockyards reeking of blood and putrefying flesh, those that had survived the journey would wait until their turn came to be dragged and goaded up the ramp at the top of which stood the man with the poleax. If they were lucky, his aim was good; but many were not lucky.

Since that time there have been some changes. In 1906 a federal law was passed limiting the time that animals could spend in a railway car without food or water to twenty-eight hours, or thirty-six hours in special cases. After that time the animals must be unloaded, fed, given water, and rested for at least five hours before the journey is resumed. Obviously, a period of twenty-eight to thirty-six hours in a lurching railway car without food or water is still long enough to cause distress, but it is an improvement. As for slaughter, there has been improvement here too. Most animals are stunned before slaughter now, which means they die painlessly—although as we shall see there are important exceptions to this statement. Because of these improvements transportation and slaughter are today lesser problems, I believe, than the factorylike methods of production which turn animals into machines for converting low-priced fodder into high-priced flesh. Nevertheless any account of what happens to your dinner while it is still an animal would be incomplete without some description of transportation and slaughter methods.

Transportation of animals includes more than the final trip to slaughter. When slaughtering was concentrated at major centers like Chicago this used to be the longest, and in many cases the only, trip the animals made. They grew to market weight on the open ranges on which they were born. When refrigeration techniques enabled slaughtering to become less centralized, the trip to slaughter became correspondingly shorter. Today, however, it is much less common for animals, especially cattle, to be born and raised to market weight in the same area. Young calves may be born in one state—say, Florida—and then trucked to pasture many hundreds of miles away—perhaps in West

Texas. Cattle who have spent a year out on the ranges in Utah or Wyoming may be rounded up and sent to feedlots in Iowa or Oklahoma. These animals face trips of up to 2,000 miles. For them, the journey to the feedlot is likely to be longer and more harrowing than the journey to the slaughterhouse.

The federal law of 1906 provided that animals transported by rail had to be rested, fed, and given water at least every thirty-six hours. It said nothing about animals being transported by truck. Trucks were not used for transporting animals in those days. Nearly seventy years later, the transportation of animals by truck is still unregulated. Repeated attempts have been made to bring the law about trucks into line with that about rail transport, but so far none has succeeded.* Accordingly cattle often spend not twenty-eight or thirty-six, but forty-eight or even seventy-two hours inside a truck without being unloaded.[81] Not all truckers would leave cattle this long without rest, food, or water, but some are more concerned with getting the job finished than with delivering their load in good condition.

Cattle placed in a truck for the first time in their lives are likely to be frightened, especially if they have been handled hastily and roughly by the men loading the truck. The motion of the truck is also a new experience, and one which may make them ill. After one or two days in the truck without food or water they are desperately thirsty and hungry. Normally cattle eat frequently throughout the day; their special stomachs require a constant intake of food if the rumen is to function properly. If the journey is in winter, subzero winds can result in severe chill; in summer the heat and sun may add to the dehydration caused by the lack of water. It is difficult for us to imagine what this combination of fear, travel sickness, thirst, near-starvation, exhaustion, and possibly severe chill feels like to the cattle. In the case of young calves which may have gone through the stress of weaning and castration only a few days earlier, the effect is still worse. Veterinary experts recommend that, simply in order to improve their

---

* As this book goes to press, yet another attempt to extend the law relating to rail transport to the trucking industry is before the House of Representatives.

prospects of surviving, young calves should be weaned, castrated, and vaccinated at least thirty days prior to being transported. This gives them a chance to recover from one stressful experience before being subjected to another. These recommendations, however, are not always followed.[82]

Although the animals cannot describe their experiences, the reactions of their bodies tell us something. There are two main reactions: "shrinkage" and "shipping fever."

All animals lose weight during transportation. Some of this weight loss is due to dehydration and the emptying of the intestinal tract. This loss is easily regained; but more lasting losses are also the rule. For an 800-lb. steer to lose seventy pounds, or 9 percent of his weight, on a single trip is not at all unusual; and it may take more than three weeks for the animal to recover the loss. This "shrink," as it is known in the trade, is regarded by researchers as an indication of the stress to which the animal has been subjected. Shrink is, of course, a worry to the meat industry, since animals are sold by the pound.

In an experimental study undertaken to investigate shrink, cattle in Texas were grouped in pairs of similar weight and shape. One animal of each pair was then slaughtered on the spot; the other animal was transported to Iowa and slaughtered there. In each case the various parts of the body were weighed. As expected, the transported cattle were consistently lighter. What surprised the researchers was that the difference existed, to a statistically significant degree, not only in the fleshy parts of the animal but also in parts consisting predominantly of bone and connecting tissue, like the heads and shanks. Said Dr. Self, of Iowa State University, who conducted the experiment: "It is evident that anything that can decrease the weight of something as non-muscular as a shank is exerting a severe amount of otherwise unmeasurable stress on those animals."[83] Other indications, no doubt, would have led us to the same conclusion, though with less precision. What would you have to go through to lose 9 percent of your weight in a day or two?

"Shipping fever," a form of pneumonia that strikes cattle after they have been transported, is the other major in-

dicator of stress in transportation. A survey carried out by
Livestock Conservation, Inc., an organization supported
mainly by farmers' associations and meat packers, indicated that 352,800 cattle, or more than one for every
100 to reach market, died from shipping fever in 1972,
making it the most costly (nonhuman) animal disease in
the United States. This takes no account of the many animals who become ill with the disease but recover. The
longer the distances the cattle had been hauled, the more
got the disease. Although shipping fever is associated with
a virus, healthy cattle have no difficulty in resisting it;
severe stress, however, weakens their resistance.[84]

Shrinkage and susceptibility to fever are indications that
the animals have been subjected to extreme stress; but the
animals that shrink and get shipping fever are the ones
that survive. Others die before reaching their destination,
or arrive with broken limbs or other injuries. Another
Livestock Conservation survey has estimated the losses
from "Bruises, Transit Cripples and Deads" as equivalent
to 391,000 pigs, 99,000 cattle, 34,000 calves, 56,000 sheep
or lambs—a total of 580,000 animals.[85]

The term "bruises" here refers to injuries received on
the trip to slaughter that subsequently cause the animal's
flesh to be condemned as unsuitable for consumption; and
the trade definition of a "cripple" is an animal that must
be carried or dragged from the vehicle. An animal that can
limp out on three legs is not a "cripple." Being dragged out
of the back of a truck, incidentally, is how an animal that
cannot move, perhaps because of broken limbs suffered
when others piled on top of it, is likely to be handled. Although some of the men who drive and handle farm animals at slaughteryards do their best to be humane under
the circumstances, most handlers are in a hurry and take
out their frustration at delays on the animals in their
charge. In the livestock business these men are often
known as "floggers"—a term that indicates clearly enough
what their job is thought to involve. A Livestock Conservation consultant, whose interest seems to be mainly in
the avoidance of lost profits caused by bruised meat, has
said of the way pigs are treated:

Hogs . . . are slow-moving and considered obstinate.
These characteristics often provoke the handler to the
point of undue violence vented through the toe of a
boot, closest club or even a rock or piece of concrete.[86]

Animals that die in transit do not die easy deaths. They
freeze to death in winter and collapse from thirst and heat
exhaustion in summer. They die, lying unattended in stockyards, from injuries sustained in falling off a slippery loading ramp. They suffocate when other animals pile on top
of them in an overcrowded, badly loaded truck. They die
from thirst or starve when careless stockmen forget to give
them water or food. And they die from the sheer stress of
the whole terrifying experience, for which nothing in their
lives has given them the slightest preparation.

The animal that you are having for dinner tonight did
not die in any of these ways; but these deaths are and always have been part of the over-all process that provides
you with your meat.

Killing an animal is in itself a troubling act. It has been
said that if we had to kill our own meat we would all be
vegetarians. There may be exceptions to that general rule,
but it is true that most people prefer not to inquire into
the killing of the animals they eat. Very few people ever
visit a slaughterhouse; and films of slaughterhouse operations are rarely shown on television. People may hope that
the meat they buy came from an animal that died without
pain, but they do not really want to know about it. Yet
those who, by their purchases, require animals to be killed
have no right to be shielded from this or any other aspect
of the production of the meat they buy. If it is distasteful
for humans to think about, what can it be like for the animals to experience it?

Killing, though never pleasant, need not be painful. To
many animals in the United States and other countries
with humane slaughter laws, death comes quickly and
painlessly. The animals are stunned by electric current or
a captive-bolt pistol and have their throats cut while still
unconscious. They probably felt terror shortly before their
death, when being goaded up the ramp to slaughter, smell-

ing the blood of those who had gone before; but the moment of death itself is as painless as it could be.

It might be thought, then, that short of not killing animals at all there is nothing more to be done for the welfare of animals being slaughtered; and this would be true if all animals were killed by these humane means; but that is not the case. Many countries, including Britain and the United States, have an exception for slaughter according to Jewish and Moslem rituals which require the animals to be fully conscious when slaughtered. A second important exception in the United States is that the Federal Humane Slaughter Act, passed in 1958, applies only to slaughterhouses selling meat to the United States government or its agencies. For the humane methods required in this act to become universal the states would have to enact parallel legislation. To date twenty-eight states have done so; but this leaves twenty-two states, including such major ones as New York, where slaughterers not selling to the federal government are under no compulsion to use humane methods.[87]

Let us consider this second loophole first. There are approximately 7,000 slaughterhouses in the United States. Nearly half of these are described as "large" or "medium" operations by the US Department of Agriculture, which means that they produce more than 300,000 pounds of meat each per year. Yet fewer than 700 plants were federally inspected for compliance with the humane slaughter law. Of plants not federally inspected many were not inspected by any other authority either, since they were in states without humane slaughter laws. In the state of New York, for instance, there are 139 slaughterhouses, of which thirty-six are federally inspected; the other 103, including fourteen large plants each producing more than two million pounds of meat annually, are under no inspection for humane slaughter, nor are they under any legal obligation to use humane methods. It is entirely legal for these slaughterhouses to use the ancient and brutal poleax; and this method is still in use in some American slaughterhouses.

The poleax is really a heavy sledgehammer rather than an ax. The man wielding the long-handled hammer stands above the animal and tries to knock it unconscious with a single blow. The problem is that he must aim his long over-head swing at a moving target; for to succeed the hammer must land at a precise point on the animal's head, and a frightened animal is quite likely to move its head. If the swing is a fraction astray the hammer can crash through the animal's eye or nose; then, as the animal thrashes around in agony and terror, several more blows may be needed to knock it unconscious. The most skilled poleax man cannot be expected to land the blow perfectly every time. As he may have to kill eighty or more animals an hour, if he misses in only one out of every hundred swings, he will still be inflicting terrible pain on several animals every day. It should also be remembered that to make a skilled poleax man it is necessary for an unskilled poleax man to get a lot of practice. The practice will be on live animals.

Why are such primitive methods, universally condemned as inhumane, still in use? The reason is the same as in other areas of animal raising: slaughtering is a competitive business, and if humane procedures cost more or reduce the number of animals that can be killed per hour, a firm cannot afford to adopt humane methods while its rivals continue to use the old methods. The cost of the charge used to fire the captive-bolt pistol, though only a cent or two per animal, is sufficient to deter slaughterhouses from using it. Electrical stunning is cheaper in the long run but installation is expensive. Unless these is a law forcing slaughterers to adopt one of these methods they are not likely to be used.

The second major loophole in the humane slaughter laws is that slaughter according to a religious ritual need not comply with the provision that the animal be stunned before being killed. Orthodox Jewish and Moslem dietary laws forbid the consumption of meat from an animal which is not "healthy and moving" when killed. The idea behind this requirement may have been to prohibit the eating of flesh from an animal that had been found sick or dead; as interpreted by the religiously orthodox today, however, the law also rules out making the animal unconscious a few seconds before it is killed. The killing is supposed to be carried out with a single blow of a sharp knife, aimed at the jugular vein and windpipe. At the time this method of slaughter was laid down in Jewish law it was probably more humane than any alternative; now, however, it is less humane, under the best circumstances, than more modern methods of stunning and killing an animal; moreover in the United States there are special circumstances which turn this method of slaughter into a grotesque travesty of any humane intentions that may once have lain behind it.

Whether the death that results from ritual slaughter under ideal conditions is painful is a controversial issue. The animals kick and thrash about for some time after the cut is made; but it is said by defenders of ritual slaughter that the animals lose consciousness almost instantly because of the loss of blood from the brain, and any later movements are not accompanied by pain. This claim has been challenged. A British veterinarian has said that the blood vessels around the brain can retract and reseal themselves, allowing consciousness to return for a time to some animals—an opinion which has, in turn, been denied by veterinary researchers in America. Using EEG readings, which measure brain waves, the American researchers report that the brain wave pattern indicates unconsciousness about fifteen seconds after the cut is made.[88] Assuming this to be correct, it still means that animals killed by this method may suffer up to fifteen seconds of acute pain before death.

Unfortunately animals subject to ritual slaughter in the United States suffer for much longer than fifteen seconds. This is due to a combination of the requirements of ritual slaughter and of the Pure Food and Drug Act of 1906, which for sanitary reasons stipulates that a slaughtered animal must not fall in the blood of a previously slaughtered animal. Effectively, this means that the animal must be killed while being suspended from a conveyor belt instead of when lying on the slaughterhouse floor. The requirement does not affect the welfare of an animal that has been made unconscious before being killed, since the suspension does not take place until the animal is unconscious; but it has horrible results if the animal must be conscious when killed. Instead of being quickly knocked to the floor and killed almost as they hit the ground, animals being ritually slaughtered in the United States are shackled around a rear leg, hoisted into the air, and then hang, fully conscious, upside down on the conveyor belt for between two and five minutes—and occasionally much longer if something goes wrong on the "killing line"—before the slaughterer makes his cut. The process has been described as follows:

> When a heavy iron chain is clamped around the leg of a heavy beef animal weighing between 1,000 and 2,000 pounds, and then the steer is jerked off its feet, the skin will open and slip away from the bone. The canon bone will often be snapped or fractured.[89]

The animal, upside down, with ruptured joints and often a broken leg, twists frantically in pain and terror, so that it must be gripped by the neck or have a clamp inserted in its nostrils to enable the slaughterer to kill the animal with a single stroke, as the religious law prescribes. It is difficult to imagine a clearer example of how sticking strictly to the letter of a law can pervert its spirit.*

Those who do not follow Jewish or Moslem dietary laws may believe that the meat they buy has not been killed in this barbaric fashion; but if they live in an area with a large Jewish population this confidence may not be founded on fact. For meat to be passed as "kosher" by the Orthodox rabbis, it must, in addition to being from an animal killed while conscious, have had the blood vessels cut out. Cutting these vessels out of the hindquarters of an animal is a laborious business and so in the United States, where labor costs are high, only the forequarters—which have

---

* It should be noted, however, that even among Orthodox rabbis there is not unanimity on the prohibition of stunning prior to killing; in Sweden and one or two other countries the rabbis have accepted legislation requiring stunning with no exemptions for ritual slaughter.

It is also worth noting that the ASPCA has developed a "casting pen" which permits a conscious animal to be killed in compliance with US hygiene regulations without being hoisted by the leg. Though this characteristic ASPCA compromise is acceptable to the rabbis, its $10,000–$15,000 initial cost has been sufficient to prevent it being used widely.

larger blood vessels, more easily removed—are sold as kosher meat, and the remainder usually ends up on supermarket shelves without any indication of its origin. This means that far more animals are slaughtered without prior stunning than would be necessary to supply the demand for this type of meat. It has been estimated that over 90 percent of the animals slaughtered in New Jersey—whose slaughterhouses supply New York City as well as their own state—are slaughtered by the ritual method. Only some of this meat is labeled kosher, so much of the nonkosher meat on sale in New York City and New Jersey comes from animals that were shackled by the leg and hoisted, fully conscious, into the air before they had their throats cut.

The slogan "religious freedom" and the charge that those who attack ritual slaughter are motivated by anti-Semitism have sufficed to prevent legislative interference with this practice in the United States, Britain, and many other countries. Actually it should be obvious to any compassionate person that one does not have to be anti-Semitic to oppose what is done to animals in the name of Orthodox Judaism today; and, fortunately, there have been many Jewish voices raised against the practice. Nor should the legitimate claim to religious freedom be extended so far as to allow the infliction of pain on animals in the name of religion. A ban on ritual slaughter would force Orthodox members of the Jewish and Moslem faith to choose between adherence to their religious laws, as currently interpreted, and their desire to eat meat; but it would not in any way compel them to violate a religious duty, since there is no duty, in these religions, to eat meat at all. There are many Orthodox Jews who follow a vegetarian diet, sometimes eating fish as well, but not meat.

If, to preserve religious laws intact, a choice must be made between the taste for meat and the agony of millions of animals, surely it is justifiable to ask those who follow the religious laws to do without meat. "Freedom of religion" means that people should be free to worship according to their own religion, and should not be forced to violate the laws of their religion; it does not mean that they must be able to do everything they would *like* to do, although their religion does not compel them to do it, and it can only be done by inflicting suffering on other beings. (As the next chapter will make clear I am not, in any case, asking Orthodox Jews and Moslems to do anything more than I ask everyone to do, although the case for asking them to do it is especially strong.)

As a conclusion to this chapter let us turn away from the older methods of slaughter, back to slaughter at its best. If we could do away with inhumane slaughter this would be the final outcome of the lives of all the animals we raise for meat. Shorn of all brutality and cruelty, quick, clean, and technically efficient, slaughter at its best still is based on the attitude that animals are means to our ends —and this is the attitude that lies behind all the abuses described in this chapter. The following account of a modern slaughterhouse is by Richard Rhodes, a writer who grew up on a farm, was familiar with the killing of animals from childhood, and still regards this killing as "necessary." The account is of the operation of a fair-sized slaughterhouse in Des Moines, Iowa, which specializes in killing pigs and kills them at a rate of 450 an hour. It is a slaughterhouse which, Rhodes says, is doing its job "as humanely as possible," and, unlike other slaughterhouses, it is one which was prepared to let Rhodes watch the killing:

Before they reach their end, the pigs get a shower, a real one. Water sprays from every angle to wash the farm off them. Then they begin to feel crowded. The pen narrows like a funnel; the drivers behind urge the pigs forward, until one at a time they climb onto the moving ramp. . . . Now they scream, never having been on such a ramp, smelling the smells they smell ahead. I do not want to overdramatize because you have read all this before. But it was a frightening experience, seeing their fear, seeing so many of them go by it had to remind me of things no one wants to be reminded of anymore, all mobs, all death marches, all mass murders and extinctions. . . .[90]

At the top of the moving ramp an operator positions electrodes on either side of the pig's head and causes an electric current to pass through them. The pig drops instantly, and the process of turning the animal into bacon, ham, and pork chops begins.

NOTES

1. *Washington Post,* 3 October 1971; see also the testimony before the Subcommittee on Monopoly of the Select Committee on Small Business of the US Senate, in the *Hearings on the Role of Giant Corporations,* especially the testimony by Jim Hightower of the Agribusiness Accountability Project.

2. Ruth Harrison, *Animal Machines* (London: Vincent Stuart, 1964), p. 3.

3. Harrison Wellford, *Sowing the Wind: The Report on the Politics of Food Safety* (New York: Grossman Press, 1972), p. 104.

4. *Wall Street Journal,* 9 August 1967.

5. Konrad Lorenz, *King Solomon's Ring* (London: Methuen and Co., 1964), p. 147.

6. Ian Duncan, "Can the Psychologist Measure Stress?" *New Scientist,* 18 October 1973.

7. *Farming Express,* 1 February 1962; quoted by Ruth Harrison, *Animal Machines,* p. 18.

8. *The Smallholder,* 6 January 1962; quoted by Ruth Harrison, *Animal Machines,* p. 18.

9. *Report of the Technical Committee to Enquire into the Welfare of Animals Kept under Intensive Livestock Husbandry Systems* (hereafter referred to as the Brambell Report), Command Paper 2836 (London: Her Majesty's Stationery Office, 1965), paragraph 97.

10. *Contours of Change:* Yearbook for 1970, US Department of Agriculture, p. xxxiii.

11. *American Agriculturist,* March 1967.

12. *Farm Journal,* June/July 1973; see also G. W. Chaloupka and others, "Growing Broilers in a Cage-Coop System," *Progress Report of the University of Delaware Agricultural Experiment Station,* Newark, Delaware, April-September 1970.

13. *Poultry World* (England), 23 December 1971.

14. *Farmer's Weekly* (England), 29 September 1972.

15. Transcript of advertisement and confirmation that Perdue chickens are de-beaked supplied by Mr. F. Perdue, in a private communication to the author.

16. *Poultry Tribune,* January 1974.

17. *Farmer and Stockbreeder,* 30 January 1962; quoted by Ruth Harrison, *Animal Machines,* p. 50.

18. *American Agriculturist,* July 1966.

19. *Upstate,* 5 August 1973, report by Mary Rita Kiereck.

20. *National Geographic Magazine,* February 1970.

21. *American Agriculturist,* March 1967.

22. *Poultry Tribune*, February 1974.

23. *Federal Register*, 24 December 1971, p. 24926.

24. W. H. Thorpe, "Welfare of Domestic Animals," *Nature*, 4 October 1969.

25. *National Geographic Magazine*, February 1970.

26. *Daily News*, 1 September 1971.

27. *American Agriculturist*, August 1968, April 1974.

28. *Upstate*, 5 August 1973.

29. Roy Bedichek, *Adventures with a Naturalist*, quoted by Ruth Harrison, *Animal Machines*, p. 154.

30. *Upstate*, 5 August 1973.

31. *Plain Truth* (Pasadena, California), March 1973.

32. C. E. Ostrander and R. J. Young, "Effects of Density on Caged Layers," *New York Food and Life Sciences*, vol. 3, no. 3 (1970).

33. *American Agriculturist*, January 1966, July 1966.

34. *Poultry Tribune*, March 1974.

35. Ian Duncan, "Can the Psychologist Measure Stress?" *New Scientist*, 18 October 1973.

36. *Farmer's Weekly*, 7 November 1961, quoted by Ruth Harrison, *Animal Machines*, p. 97.

37. *American Agriculturist*, November 1965; see also *Farm Journal*, October 1969.

38. *Farm Journal*, May 1974, and *Swine Stress*, published by the National Livestock Safety Committee and Livestock Conservation, Inc., no date.

39. *Farmer and Stockbreeder* (England), 22 January 1963; quoted by Ruth Harrison, *Animal Machines*, p. 95.

40. *Farm Journal*, August 1966, and elsewhere.

41. *Farm Journal*, November 1968.

42. *People and Land*, Summer 1974; the report is by the Center for Rural Affairs, Walthill, Nebraska.

43. *Poultry World*, 28 June 1973.

44. *Farm Journal*, May 1973.

45. *Farmer and Stockbreeder*, 11 July 1961; quoted by Ruth Harrison, *Animal Machines*, p. 148.

46. *Farm Journal*, November 1968.

47. *Sunday Times* (London), 12 December 1971; *Farm Journal*, March 1973.

48. *Farm Journal*, April 1970.

49. *Hog Farm Management*, July 1974; *Farm Journal*, August 1968.

50. Roger Ewband, "The Trouble With Being a Farm Animal," *New Scientist*, 18 October 1973.

51. *Farm Journal*, April 1970.

52. *Times* (London), 11 November 1968.

53. Quoted in *An Enquiry into the Effects of Modern Livestock Production on the Total Environment* (The Farm and Food Society, London, 1972), p. 12.

54. *The Stall Street Journal*, July 1972.

55. *Times* (London), 23 August 1972.

56. Ruth Harrison, *Animal Machines*, p. 72.

57. *The Stall Street Journal*, November 1973.

58. *The Stall Street Journal*, April 1973.

59. *The Stall Street Journal*, November 1973.

60. *Farmer and Stockbreeder,* 13 September 1960, quoted by Ruth Harrison, *Animal Machines,* p. 70.

61. *The Stall Street Journal,* April 1973.

62. "Some General Remarks Concerning Farm Animal Welfare in Intensive Farming Systems," by G. van Putten, Research Institute for Animal Husbandry "Schoonoord," Driebergseweg, Zeist, The Netherlands (unpublished), p. 2.

63. Ibid., p. 3.

64. Vance Bourjaily, "Eight Months on Full Feed," *Harper's,* March 1972.

65. *Los Angeles Times Outlook,* 20 August 1961; quoted by Beatrice Trum Hunter, *Consumer Beware* (New York: Simon & Schuster, 1971), p. 113.

66. *New Scientist,* 18 October 1973.

67. *Farmland News* (Kansas City), 31 January 1973.

68. R. E. Smith, superintendent, West Central Experimental Station, Morris, Minnesota, quoted in *Farm Journal,* December 1973.

69. *Farm Journal,* August 1967, March 1968.

70. *Farm Journal,* December 1970; *Compassion in World Farming Newsletter* (Greatham, Hampshire, England), April 1971.

71. Brambell Report, pars. 65-67.

72. Brambell Report, par. 92.

73. Brambell Report, pars. 160, 164-169.

74. *Times* (London), 23 June 1969.

75. *Times* (London), 25 June 1969.

76. *Dehorning, Castrating, Branding, Vaccinating Cattle,* Publication No. 384 of the Mississippi State University Extension Service, cooperating with the US Department of Agriculture; see also *Beef Cattle: Dehorning, Castrating, Branding and Marking,* US Department of Agriculture, Farmers' Bulletin No. 2141, September 1972.

77. *Progressive Farmer,* February 1969.

78. *Pig Farming* (England), September 1973.

79. *Hot-Iron Branding,* University of Georgia College of Agriculture, Circular 551.

80. *Beef Cattle: Dehorning, Castrating, Branding and Marking.*

81. R. A. Ivie, "Why Do Feeder Calves Fail to Perform When They Reach the Feedlot?" published in the Report of a Preconditioning Seminar held at Oklahoma State University, September 1967, p. 12.

82. R. F. Bristol, "Preconditioning of Feeder Cattle Prior to Interstate Shipment," Preconditioning Seminar Report, p. 65.

83. H. L. Self, "Factors Affecting Shrink in Feeder Cattle," Preconditioning Seminar Report, pp. 75-81.

84. *Official Proceedings,* 58th Annual Meeting, Livestock Conservation, Inc., Omaha, Nebraska, May 1974, pp. 44, 93.

85. *Guide to the Safe Handling of Livestock,* Livestock Conservation, Inc., Service Series I-61, no date.

86. *Official Proceedings,* 58th Annual Meeting, Livestock Conservation, Inc., pp. 49-50.

87. "Animals into Meat: A Report on the Pre-Slaughter Handling of Livestock," *Argus Archives* (New York), vol. 2, no. 1 (March 1971). These are 1970 figures, as are those in the remainder of this section. Other unattributed information in this section comes from the same report.

88. See H. E. Bywater, "Humane Slaughtering of Food Animals," *Veterinary Annual 1968*, John Wright and Sons, Bristol; and L. L. Nangeroni and P. D. Kennett, "Electroencephalographic Studies on the Effect of Shechitah Slaughter on Cortical Function in Ruminants," New York (State) University College Report, 1963-4. Both items cited in "Animals into Meat."

89. "Animals into Meat," pp. 16-17; the description is by John MacFarlane, a vice president of Livestock Conservation, Inc.

90. Richard Rhodes, "Watching the Animals," *Harper's*, March 1970.

4

Becoming a Vegetarian . . .

or how to reduce animal
suffering and human starvation
at the same time.

Now that we have understood the nature of speciesism and seen the consequences it has for nonhuman animals it is time to ask: what can we do about it?

There are many things that we can and should do about speciesism. We should, for instance, write to our political representatives about the issues discussed in this book; we should make our friends aware of these issues; we should educate our children to be concerned about the welfare of all sentient beings; and we should protest publicly on behalf of nonhuman animals whenever we have an effective opportunity to do so.

While we should do all these things, there is one other thing we can do that is of supreme importance; it underpins, makes consistent, and gives meaning to all our other activities on behalf of animals. This one thing is that we cease to eat animals.

Many people who are opposed to cruelty to animals draw the line at becoming a vegetarian. It was of such people that Oliver Goldsmith, the eighteenth-century humanitarian essayist, wrote: "They pity, and they eat the objects of their compassion."[1]

As a matter of strict logic, perhaps, there is no contradiction in taking an interest in animals on both compassionate and gastronomic grounds. If a person is opposed to the infliction of suffering on animals, but not to the painless killing of animals, he could consistently eat animals that had lived free of all suffering and been instantly, painlessly slaughtered. Yet practically and psychologically it is impossible to be consistent in one's concern for nonhuman animals while continuing to dine on them. If we are prepared to take the life of another being merely in order to satisfy our taste for a particular type of food, then that being is no more than a means to our end. In time we will come to regard pigs, cattle, and chickens as things for us to use, no matter how strong our compassion may be; and when we find that to continue to obtain supplies of the bodies of these animals at a price we are able to pay it is necessary to change their living conditions a little, we will be unlikely to regard these changes too critically. The factory farm is nothing more than the application of technology to the idea that animals are means to our ends. Our eating habits are dear to us and not easily altered. We have a strong interest in convincing ourselves that our concern for other animals does not require us to stop eating them. No one in the habit of eating an animal can be completely without bias in judging whether the conditions in which that animal is reared cause suffering.

In practical terms it is not possible to rear animals for food on a large scale without inflicting suffering. Even if intensive methods are not used, traditional farming involves castration, the separation of mother and young, the breaking up of herds, branding, transportation to the slaughterhouse, and finally slaughter itself. It is difficult to imagine how animals could be reared for food without suffering in any of these ways. Possibly it could be done on a small scale, but we could never feed today's huge urban populations with meat raised in this manner. If it could be done at all, the animal flesh thus produced would be vastly more expensive than animal flesh is today—and rearing animals is, already, an expensive and inefficient way of producing protein. The flesh of animals reared and killed without suffering would be a delicacy available only to the rich.

All this is, in any case, quite irrelevant to the immediate question of the ethics of our daily diet. Whatever the theoretical possibilities of rearing animals without suffering may be, the fact is that the meat available from butchers and supermarkets comes from animals who did suffer while being reared. So we must ask ourselves, not: is it *ever* right to eat meat? but: is it right to eat *this* meat? Here I think that those who are opposed to the needless killing of animals and those who oppose only the infliction of suffering must join together and give the same, negative answer.

Becoming a vegetarian is not merely a symbolic gesture. Nor is it an attempt to isolate oneself from the ugly realities of the world, to keep oneself pure and so without responsibility for the cruelty and carnage all around. Becoming a vegetarian is the most practical and effective step one can take toward ending both the killing of nonhuman animals and the infliction of suffering upon them. Assume, for the moment, that it is only the suffering that we disapprove of, not the killing. How can we stop the use of the intensive methods of animal rearing described in the previous chapter?

So long as people are prepared to buy the products of intensive farming, the usual forms of protest and political action will never bring about a major reform. Even in supposedly animal-loving Britain, although the wide controversy stirred by the publication of Ruth Harrison's *Animal Machines* forced the government to appoint a group of impartial experts (the Brambell committee) to investigate the issue and make recommendations, when the committee reported the government refused to implement its recommendations. These recommendations were already a compromise between the standards the committee considered necessary to safeguard the welfare of farm animals and the standards the committee thought Parliament and the farmers might be persuaded to accept. If this was the fate of the movement for reform in Britain, nothing better can be expected in the United States, where the agribusiness lobby is still more overwhelming.

The links between agribusiness and the US Department of Agriculture are formidable. To give just two out of many possible examples: when Clifford Hardin resigned as secretary of agriculture in 1970 he went straight to a top position at Ralston Purina, one of the largest agribusiness corporations; his successor, Earl Butz, was a director of Ralston Purina prior to becoming secretary. On issues much less threatening to its interests than the abolition of intensive farming—issues like the inspection of meat for wholesomeness—the agribusiness lobby has been able to block and delay effective legislation, and when legislation has finally been passed it cannot be effectively enforced.[2]

This is not to say that the normal channels of protest and political action are useless and should be abandoned. On the contrary, they are a necessary part of the over-all struggle for effective change, and in Britain especially the small protest organizations have done invaluable work in keeping the issue alive; but in themselves, these methods are not enough.

The people who profit by exploiting large numbers of animals do not need our approval. They need our money. The purchase of the corpses of the animals they rear is the only support the factory farmers ask from the public. They will use intensive methods as long as they continue to receive this support; they will have the resources needed to fight reform politically; and they will be able to defend themselves against criticism with the reply that they are only providing the public with what it wants.

Hence the need for each one of us to stop buying the produce of modern animal farming—even if we are not convinced that it would be wrong to eat animals that have lived pleasantly and died painlessly. Vegetarianism is a form of boycott. For most vegetarians the boycott is a permanent one, since once they have broken away from flesh-eating habits they can no longer approve of slaughtering animals in order to satisfy the trivial desires of their palates. But the moral obligation to boycott the meat available in butcher shops and supermarkets today is just as inescapable for those who disapprove only of inflicting suffering, and not of killing. In recent years Americans have boycotted lettuce and grapes because the system under which those particular lettuces and grapes had been produced exploited farm laborers, not because lettuce and grapes can never be produced without exploitation. The same line of reasoning leads to boycotting meat. Until we boycott meat we are, each one of us, contributing to the continued existence, prosperity, and growth of factory farming and all the other cruel practices used in rearing animals for food.

It is at this point that the consequences of speciesism intrude directly into our lives, and we are forced to attest personally to the sincerity of our concern for nonhuman animals. Here we have an opportunity to *do* something, instead of merely talking and wishing the politicians would do something. It is easy to take a stand about a remote issue, but the speciesist, like the racist, reveals his true nature when the issue comes nearer home. To protest about bull-fighting in Spain or the slaughter of baby seals in Canada while continuing to eat chickens that have spent their lives crammed into cages, or veal from calves that have been deprived of their mothers, their proper diet, and the freedom to lie down with their legs extended, is like denouncing apartheid in South Africa while asking your neighbors not to sell their houses to blacks.

To make the boycott aspect of vegetarianism more effective, we must not be shy about our refusal to eat flesh. A vegetarian in an omnivorous society is always being asked about the reasons for his strange diet. This can be irritating, or even embarrassing, but it also provides opportunities to tell people about cruelties they may be unaware of. (I first learned of the existence of factory farming from a vegetarian who took the time to explain to me why he wasn't eating the same food I was.) If a boycott is the only way to stop cruelty, then we must encourage as many as possible to join the boycott. We can only be effective in this if we ourselves set the example.

People sometimes attempt to justify eating flesh by saying that the animal was already dead when they bought it. The weakness of this rationalization—which I have heard used, quite seriously, many times—should be obvious as soon as we consider vegetarianism as a form of boycott. The nonunion grapes available in stores during the grape boycott inspired by Cesar Chavez's efforts to improve the wages and conditions of the grape-pickers had already been produced by underpaid laborers, and we could no more raise the pay those laborers had received for picking those grapes than we could bring our steak back to life. In both cases the aim of the boycott is not to alter the past but to prevent the continuation of the conditions to which we object.

I have emphasized the boycott element of vegetarianism so much that the reader may ask whether, if the boycott does not spread and prove effective, anything has been achieved by becoming a vegetarian. Now we must often venture when we cannot be certain of success, and it would be no argument against becoming a vegetarian if this were all that could be said against it, since none of the great movements against oppression and injustice would have existed if their leaders had made no efforts until they were assured of success. In the case of vegetarianism, however, I believe we do achieve something by our individual acts, even if the boycott as a whole should not succeed. George Bernard Shaw once said that he would be followed to his grave by numerous sheep, cattle, pigs, chickens, and a whole shoal of fish, all grateful at having been spared from slaughter because of his vegetarian diet. Although we cannot identify any individual animals whom we have benefited by becoming a vegetarian, we can assume that our diet has some impact on the number of animals raised in factory farms and slaughtered for food. This assumption is reasonable because the number of animals raised and slaughtered depends on the profitability of this process, and this profit depends in part on the demand for the product. The smaller the demand, the lower the price and the lower the profit. The lower the profit, the fewer the animals that will be raised and slaughtered. This is elementary economics, and it can easily be observed in tables published by the poultry trade journals, for instance, that there is a direct correlation between the price of poultry and the number of chickens placed in broiler sheds to begin their joyless existence.

So vegetarianism is really on even stronger ground than most other boycotts or protests. The person who boycotts South African produce in order to bring down apartheid achieves nothing unless the boycott succeeds in forcing white South Africans to modify their policies (though the effort may have been well worth making, whatever the outcome); but the vegetarian knows that he does, by his actions, contribute to a reduction in the suffering and slaughter of animals, whether or not he lives to see his efforts spark off a mass boycott of meat and an end to cruelty in farming.

In addition to all this, becoming a vegetarian has a special significance because the vegetarian is a practical, living refutation of a common, yet utterly false, defense of factory farming methods. It is sometimes said that these methods are needed to feed the world's soaring population. Because the true facts here are so important—important enough, in fact, to amount to a compelling case for vegetarianism that is quite independent of the question of animal welfare that I have emphasized in this book—I shall digress briefly to discuss the fundamentals of food production.

At this moment, millions of people in many parts of the world do not get enough to eat. Millions more get a sufficient quantity, but they do not get the right kind of food; mostly, they do not get enough protein. The question is, does the raising of food by the methods practiced in the affluent nations make a contribution to the solution of the hunger problem?

Every animal has to eat in order to grow to the size and weight at which it is considered ready for humans to eat. If a calf, say, grazes on rough pasture land that grows only grass and could not be planted with corn or any other crop that provides food edible by humans, the result will be a net gain of protein for humans, since the grown calf provides us with protein that we cannot—yet—extract economically from grass. But if we take that same calf and place him in a feedlot, or any other confinement system, the picture changes. The calf must now be fed. No matter how little space he and his companions are crowded into, land must be used to grow the corn, sorghum, soybeans, or whatever it is that the calf eats. Now we are feeding the calf food that we ourselves could eat. The calf needs most of this food for the ordinary physiological processes of day-to-day living. No matter how severely the calf is prevented from exercising, his body must still burn food merely to keep him alive. The food is also utilized to build inedible parts of the calf's body, like bones. Only the food left over after these needs are satisfied can be turned into flesh, and eventually be eaten by humans.

How much of the protein in his food does the calf use up, and how much is available for humans? The answer is surprising. It takes twenty-one pounds of protein fed to a calf to produce a single pound of animal protein for humans. We get back less than 5 percent of what we put in. No wonder that Frances Moore Lappé has called this kind of farming "A protein factory in reverse"![3]

We can put the matter another way. Assume we have one acre of fertile land. We can use this acre to grow a high-protein plant food, like peas or beans. If we do this, we will get between 300 and 500 pounds of protein from our acre. Alternatively we can use our acre to grow a crop that we feed to animals, and then kill and eat the animals. Then we will end up with between forty and fifty-five pounds of protein from our acre. Interestingly enough, although most animals convert plant protein into animal protein more efficiently than cattle—a pig, for instance, need be fed "only" eight pounds of protein to produce one pound for humans—this advantage is almost eliminated when we consider how much protein we can produce per acre, because cattle can make use of sources of protein that are indigestible for pigs. So most estimates conclude that plant foods yield about ten times as much protein per acre as meat does, although estimates vary, and the ratio sometimes goes as high as twenty to one.[4]

If instead of killing the animals and eating their flesh we use them to provide us with milk or eggs we improve our return considerably. Nevertheless the animal must still use protein for its own purposes and the most efficient forms of egg and milk production do not yield more than a quarter of the protein per acre that can be provided by plant foods.

The implications of all this for the world food situation are staggering. In late 1974, as a famine situation began to develop in India and Bangladesh, Lester Brown of the Overseas Development Council estimated that if Americans were to reduce their meat consumption by only 10 percent for one year, it would free at least 12 million tons of grain for human consumption—or enough to feed 60 million people, which would be more than enough to save those threatened in India and Bangladesh. Indeed, if Americans were to stop eating grain-fed beef altogether the grain thus released would be enough to feed *all* the 600 million people in India.[5] According to another estimate, 20 million tons of protein obtained primarily from sources that could have been consumed by humans were fed to livestock (excluding dairy cows) in the United States in the year 1968. The livestock thus fed provided only 2 million tons of protein. The 18 million tons of protein wasted by this process were equivalent to 90 percent of the yearly world protein deficit. If we add to this figure similar wastage in other affluent nations we get a figure in excess of the *total shortfall of protein throughout the world*. Considering food of all kinds, and not merely protein, Don Paarlberg, a former US assistant secretary of agriculture, has said that merely reducing the US livestock population by half would make available enough food to make up the calorie deficit of the nonsocialist underdeveloped nations *nearly four times over*. Taking these two facts together we find that the food wasted by animal production in the affluent nations would be sufficient, it properly distributed, to end both hunger and malnutrition throughout the world.

The simple answer to our question, then, is that the raising of animals for food by the methods used in the industrial nations does not contribute to the solution of the hunger problem. On the contrary, it aggravates it enormously. Livestock feeding wastes a gigantic amount of food that could be used to fight hunger throughout the world. When, as in 1973 and 1974, grains and soybeans are in relatively short supply and fetch prices so high that India, Bangladesh, the nations of sub-Saharan Africa, and other famine-prone areas can no longer afford to buy them, it is

only because we are feeding these valuable foods to livestock that the supply is short.

This does not mean that all we have to do to end famine
throughout the world is to stop eating meat. We would
still have to see that the grain thus saved actually got to
the people who needed it. Costs of shipment, inadequate
systems of transportation, and inequitable social structures
in some of the nations that need assistance would all present serious problems. But these problems may not be insuperable. While significant amounts of government aid do
not reach those for whom they are intended, some of the
smaller nongovernmental charitable organizations, with relief workers on the spot where the food is needed, have a
much better record in this respect.

At present, after feeding our livestock, we do not have
enough surplus grain to feed the hungry even if we did
have an adequate system of distributing it. Attempts to
raise the total world harvest by such means as the "Green
Revolution" appear to be blocked by the high costs of oil
and fertilizer. Therefore making more efficient use of the
grain we now produce is an indispensable first step to a
solution of the global food problem.

Another point to note is that in many cases the proteins
that we are wasting have actually been imported into the
affluent nations from the countries that need them most.
As N. W. Pirie, an authority on the world protein situation,
has said:

A distressing feature of the way the world is now
handling its protein supplies is that oil-seeds from pro-
tein-deficient countries such as India and Nigeria supply much of the feed protein used to produce pigs,
eggs and broiler chickens in countries such as Britain.[6]

All the indications are that the world is going to go
through a crisis period in food supplies. It is entirely possible that deaths from starvation will be numbered in the
hundreds of millions in the next few years. Yet if India,
Bangladesh, and the poorer nations of Latin America and
Africa can increase production to anything near the productivity that has been achieved in Japan, Taiwan, and

mainland China, there will be food enough even for the growing populations of these areas—and the indications are that when poverty is alleviated, population growth can also be reduced.

An urgent moral question now faces all who live in affluent nations. The average American now consumes nearly a ton of grain a year—93 percent of it having been first converted into meat, milk, and eggs. The average Indian consumes about 400 lbs. of grain annually, 85 percent directly in the plant form. Between 1950 and 1972 American per capita meat consumption nearly doubled; yet in 1950 most Americans were already eating as much meat as their bodies could use. If Americans were to reduce their level of meat consumption to the 1950 level, there would be, for every American who did so, enough grain saved to keep alive at least one, and probably two, people who would otherwise starve.[7] The question is, then, are we going to do this? Or are we going to continue to eat our steak, hamburger, and pork chops, and then settle back to watch millions of people starve to death on our television screens. This would, as C. P. Snow once prophesied, mark the end of any human moral community. Whether this will happen is not going to be decided by governments. It is going to be decided by each and every one of us.

So the case for becoming a vegetarian based on Animal Liberation is powerfully buttressed by the facts of the world food situation. Concern for human beings points urgently in the same direction as concern for other animals.

It is therefore a double tragedy that political interests in the United States have forced the government to give huge financial aid to meat producers, thus making economically possible the American reliance on meat, particularly beef, which has been called "the single largest inefficiency in world dietary patterns."[8] In 1974, for instance, as famine loomed in many parts of the world, Congress authorized a $2 billion loan guarantee program for beef producers. In addition US trade policies have been explicitly designed to encourage meat consumption in Japan and Western Europe, to provide an export market for US grains. Countries like India, which need grain to feed people instead of cattle, cannot pay as high a price for it as these more affluent nations.[9]

Given the combination of human and nonhuman welfare that dictates a drastic reduction in the consumption of animal flesh, it should hardly be necessary to add that in purely economic terms countries like the United States and Britain have strong incentives to phase out animal production. For Britain the need to import vast quantities of vegetable protein to feed pigs, cattle, and chickens is a major burden on the balance of payments, increasing the country's dependence on overseas suppliers. In the United States, the consumption of meat diminishes stocks of soybeans, now the nation's most valuable export and the best hope of paying for imports of costly items like oil. The US now produces three-quarters of the world's soybeans. But about 95 percent of the American soybean crop is fed to animals. According to a recent article in *Scientific American:*

> To put the matter rather crudely, the American public may have to choose between steak and pleasure trips . . . a shift towards meat analogues ["meat" made from vegetable protein] and other high-protein foods based on vegetable sources—soybeans foremost among them—could reduce the requirement for feed crops within the country and allow for higher exports of agricultural products to pay for petroleum and other essential imports while keeping the foreign trade account in balance.[10]

How far should we go? The case for a radical break in our eating habits is clear; but should we eat nothing but vegetables? Where exactly do we draw the line?

Drawing precise lines is always difficult. I shall make some suggestions, but the reader might well find what I say here less convincing than what I have said before about the more clear-cut cases. You must decide for yourself where you are going to draw the line, and your decision may not coincide exactly with mine. This does not matter all that much. We can distinguish bald men from men who are not bald without deciding every borderline case. It is agreement on the fundamentals that is important.

I hope that anyone who has read this far will recognize the moral necessity of refusing to buy or eat the flesh of animals that have been reared in modern factory farm conditions. This is the clearest case of all, the absolute minimum that anyone with the capacity to look beyond considerations of narrow self-interest should be able to accept.

Let us see what this minimum involves. It means that, unless we can be sure of the origin of the particular item we are buying, we must avoid chicken, turkey, rabbit, pork, veal, and beef. At the present time relatively little lamb is intensively produced; but some is, and more may be in future. It is possible to obtain supplies of all these meats that do not come from factory farms, but unless you live in a rural area this takes a lot of effort. Most butchers have no idea how the animals whose bodies they are selling were raised. In some cases, such as that of chickens, traditional methods of rearing have disappeared so completely that it is almost impossible to buy a chicken that was free to roam outdoors; and veal is a meat that simply cannot be produced humanely. Even when meat is described as "organic" this may mean no more than that the animals were not fed the usual doses of antibiotics, hormones, or other drugs; small solace for an animal that was not free to walk around outdoors.

My guess is that most people who are sincere in their efforts to boycott intensive farming will soon find it simpler to stop buying poultry, pork, veal, and beef altogether than to search for humanely raised produce. People who have had no experience of how satisfying an imaginative vegetarian diet can be may doubt this, but if they follow the suggestions in Appendix 1 of this book I think they will come to realize that the flesh of dead animals is not an essential part of a pleasing and satisfying meal.

Once you have stopped eating poultry, pork, veal, and beef the next step is to refuse to eat any slaughtered bird or mammal. This is only a very small additional step, since so few of the birds or mammals commonly eaten are not intensively reared. The reason for taking this extra step may be the belief that it is wrong to kill these creatures for the trivial purpose of pleasing our palates; or because even when these animals are not intensively raised they suffer in the various other ways that were described in the previous chapter.

Now more difficult questions arise. How far down the evolutionary scale shall we go? Shall we eat fish? What about shrimps? Oysters? To answer these questions we must bear in mind the central principle on which our concern for other beings is based. As I said in the first chapter, the only legitimate boundary to our concern for the interests of other beings is the point at which it is no longer accurate to say that the other being has interests. To have interests, in a strict nonmetaphorical sense, a being must be capable of suffering or experiencing pleasure. If a being suffers, there can be no moral justification for disregarding that suffering, or for refusing to count it equally with the like suffering of any other being. But the converse of this is also true. If a being is not capable of suffering, or of enjoyment, there is nothing to take into account.

So the problem of drawing the line is the problem of deciding when we are justified in assuming that a being is incapable of suffering. In my earlier discussion of the evidence we have that nonhuman animals are capable of suffering, I suggested two indicators of this capacity: the behavior of the being, whether it writhes, utters cries, attempts to escape from the source of pain, and so on; and the similarity of the nervous system of the being to our own. As we proceed down the evolutionary scale we find that on both these grounds the strength of the evidence for a capacity to feel pain diminishes. With birds and mammals the evidence is overwhelming. Reptiles and fish have nervous systems that differ from those of mammals in some important respects but share the basic structure of centrally organized nerve pathways. Fish and reptiles show most of the pain behavior that mammals do. In most species there is even vocalization, although it is not audible to our ears. Fish, for instance, make vibratory sounds and different "calls" have been distinguished by researchers, including sounds indicating "alarm" and "aggravation."[11] Fish also show signs of distress when they are taken out of

the water and allowed to flap around in a net or on dry
land until they die. Surely it is only because fish do not
yelp or whimper in a way that we can hear that otherwise
decent people can think it a pleasant way of spending an
afternoon to sit by the water dangling a hook while previously caught fish die slowly beside them. The evidence that
fish and other reptiles can suffer seems strong, if not quite
as conclusive as it is with mammals.

People more concerned about causing pain than about
killing may ask: assuming fish *can* suffer, how much *do*
they actually suffer in the normal process of commercial
fishing? Fish, unlike birds and mammals, are not made to
suffer in the process of rearing them for our tables, since
they are usually not reared at all; man interferes with
them only to catch and kill them. (Some "fish farms" are
now being established, but even here the conditions of the
fish are closer to their natural environment than is the case
with other intensively reared animals.) On the other hand,
the death of a commercially caught fish is much more
drawn out than the death of, say, a chicken, since fish are
simply hauled up into the air and left to die. Since their
gills can extract oxygen from water but not from air, fish
out of the water cannot breathe. The fish on sale in your
fish shop died slowly, from suffocation.

Since fish are not reared, the ecological argument against
eating intensively reared animals does not apply to fish. We
do not waste grain or soybeans by feeding them to fish in
the ocean. Yet there is a different ecological argument that
counts against the extensive commercial fishing of the
oceans now practiced, and this is that we are rapidly fishing
out the oceans. In recent years fish catches have declined
dramatically. Several once-abundant species of fish, such as
the herrings of Northern Europe, the California sardines,
and the New England haddock, are now so scarce as to
be, for commercial purposes, extinct. Countries like Ice-
land and Peru are desperately trying to extend their fishing
limits so that they can save their traditional fishing areas
from disappearing altogether. Modern fishing fleets trawl
the fishing grounds systematically with fine-gauge nets that
catch everything in their way. The nets used by the tuna
fishing industry also catch thousands of dolphins every

year, trapping them underwater and drowning them. In addition to the disruption of ocean ecology caused by all this overfishing there are bad consequences for humans too. All over the world small coastal villages that live by fishing are finding their traditional source of food and income drying up. From the communities on Ireland's west coast to the Burmese and Malayan fishing villages the story is the same. The fishing industry of the developed nations has become one more form of redistribution from the poor to the rich.

So out of concern for both fish and humans we should avoid eating fish. Certainly those who continue to eat fish while refusing to eat other animals have taken a major step away from speciesism; but those who eat neither have gone one step further.

When we go beyond fish to the other forms of marine life commonly eaten by humans the existence of a capacity for pain becomes more questionable. Crustaceans—crabs, shrimps, prawns, lobsters—have nervous systems that are more like those of insects than like those of vertebrate animals. They are complex enough but so differently organized from our own that it is difficult to be confident one way or the other about whether they feel pain. We cannot exclude the hypothesis that the reaction of crustaceans to what would for us be a source of pain is, for them, an automatic response that does not operate at the level of consciousness; but we cannot assume that this hypothesis is true either. Crustaceans do act as if they feel pain, in the appropriate circumstances. There may be room for doubt, but it does seem that crustaceans deserve the benefit of the doubt.

Some other edible sea creatures, however, belong to a very different order. Oysters, clams, mussels, scallops, and the like are mollusks, and mollusks are in general very primitive organisms. (There is an exception: the octopus is a mollusk, but incomparably more developed, and presumably more sentient, than his distant mollusk relatives.) Most mollusks are such rudimentary beings that it is difficult to imagine them feeling pain, or having other mental states. Those who want to be absolutely certain that they are not causing suffering will not eat mollusks either; but

somewhere between a shrimp and an oyster seems as good
a place to draw the line as any, and better than most.

Granted, no single line of demarcation will please everyone. What I have just written may surprise some vegetarians, since, after all, mollusks are animals. But even the
line between the animal and vegetable realms is not precise,
as disagreements among biologists about newly discovered
micro-organisms regularly show. So long as we keep in
mind the reasons for being a vegetarian we will be less
concerned with a rigid adherence to the animal/vegetable
distinction, and more concerned with the nature and capacities of the being we are thinking of eating.

If my toleration of mollusk-eating will seem anomalous
to some vegetarians, there is an aspect of the normal vegetarian diet that has drawn the same charge from critics;
the use of animal products, especially eggs and milk. Some
have tried to accuse vegetarians of inconsistency here.
"Vegetarian," they say, is a word that has the same root as
"vegetable" and a vegetarian should eat only food of
vegetable origin. Taken as a verbal quibble, this criticism
is historically inaccurate. The term "vegetarian" came into
general use as a result of the formation of the Vegetarian
Society in England in 1847. Since the rules of the society
permit the use of eggs and milk, the term "vegetarian" is
properly applied to those who use these animal products.
Recognizing this linguistic *fait accompli,* those who eat
neither animal flesh nor eggs nor milk nor foods made from
milk have begun to call themselves "vegans." The verbal
point, however, is not the important one. What we should
ask is whether the use of these other animal products is
morally justifiable. This question is a real one because it is
possible to be adequately nourished without consuming any
animal products at all—a fact that is not widely known,
although most people now know that vegetarians can live
long and healthy lives. I shall say more on the topic of
nutrition later in this chapter; for the present it is enough
that the reader know that we can do without eggs and
milk. But is there any reason why we should?

We have seen that the egg industry is one of the most
ruthlessly intensive forms of modern factory farming, exploiting hens relentlessly to produce the most eggs at the

least cost. Our obligation to boycott this type of farming is as strong as our obligation to boycott intensively produced pork or chicken. All but a tiny fraction of the eggs produced in industrialized nations now come from hens kept in cages. If we are to continue to use eggs, we should find a source of eggs that come from hens able to walk around outside. In Britain these eggs are referred to as "free range"; in the United States they are sometimes called "organic eggs," but this term is inexact, and may only mean that the birds received no hormones or other drugs in their food. In both countries health food shops are the usual suppliers of these eggs, unless you are fortunate enough to know someone who keeps free-ranging hens. Free-range eggs fetch a higher price than others; many people say they taste better, and they have been found to have a higher vitamin B_{12} content. Unfortunately the higher price has led to swindling, and the labels on egg boxes are not always reliable. If you can, ask your health food shop for the name and address of their supplier and check it out.

Assuming you can get free-range eggs, the ethical objections to eating them are relatively minor. Hens provided with both shelter and an outdoor run to walk and scratch around in live comfortably. They do not appear to mind the removal of their eggs. They will be killed when they cease to lay productively, but they will have a pleasant existence until that time.

Milk and milk products like cheese and yoghurt raise different issues. Dairy production is coming under pressures similar to those that have intensified other areas of animal husbandry. So far the dairy cow remains considerably better off than most other domestic animals, but this could change if anything like the "Unicar" system, described in the previous chapter, were to be widely adopted. Fortunately such systems have yet to prove themselves economical—it may be that cows need to be reasonably content to produce large quantities of milk.

Intensification, however, is not the only ethical issue raised by dairying. In both traditional and modern dairying it is necessary to make the cows pregnant at regular intervals—maybe once a year—in order to prevent the cow's milk from drying up. The calf will be taken away from its

mother, to be slaughtered immediately or raised for veal.
The milk that the calf would have drunk thus becomes
available for human consumption. Of this practice the
British expert committee under Professor Brambell said:

> Separating the calf from its mother shortly after birth
> undoubtedly inflicts anguish on both. Maternal care for
> the young is highly developed in cattle, and it is only
> necessary to observe the behavior of the cow and of the
> calf when they are separated to appreciate this. It is a
> consequence of keeping cows to produce milk for
> human consumption and we regret that we know of no
> way by which it can be avoided.[12]

So it seems that to produce milk economically we must
cause some suffering to the dairy cow and its calf. In an
ideal world, free of all speciesist practices, we would not
use animal milks, except for the use of human milk for
feeding human infants. Instead of cow's milk we would use
substitutes made directly from plants. Some of these are
already on the market (see Appendix 1) and although the
limited demand for them means that they are at present
more expensive than cow's milk they should eventually
become considerably cheaper, since the production of cow's
milk is, like meat production but to a lesser degree, a wasteful method of obtaining protein. Cheeses, yoghurts, and ice
cream made from vegetable protein sources are now also
at the research stage, while drinks based on soybeans compete successfully with other soft drinks in Hong Kong and
several other countries.

"Vegans," then, are right to say that we ought not to use
dairy products. They are living demonstrations of the prac-
ticality and nutritional soundness of a diet that is totally
free from the exploitation of other animals. At the same
time, it should be said that, in our present speciesist world,
it is not easy to keep so strictly to what is morally right.
Most people have difficulty enough in taking the step to
vegetarianism; if asked to give up milk and cheese at the
same time they could be so alarmed that they end up doing
nothing at all. A reasonable and defensible plan of action is
to tackle the worst abuses first and move on to lesser issues

when substantial progress has been made. It is more important to encourage people to stop eating animal flesh and factory farm eggs than it is to condemn them for continuing to eat milk products. While someone who gave up animal flesh and simply replaced it with an increased amount of cheese would not really be doing very much for animals, anyone who replaces animal flesh with vegetable protein, while continuing to eat milk products occasionally, has made a major step toward the liberation of animals.

Eliminating speciesism from one's dietary habits is very difficult to do all at once. People who become vegetarians have made a clear public commitment to the movement against animal exploitation. The most urgent task of the animal liberation movement is to persuade as many people as possible to make this commitment, so that the boycott will spread and gain attention. If, because of an admirable desire to stop *all* forms of exploitation of animals immediately, we convey the impression that unless one gives up milk products one is no better than those who still eat animal flesh, the result may be that many people are deterred from doing anything at all, and the exploitation of animals will continue as before.

And that, I think, takes care of most of the problems that are likely to face a nonspeciesist who asks what he should and should not eat. As I said at the beginning of this section, my remarks are intended to be no more than suggestions. Sincere nonspeciesists may well disagree among themselves about the details. So long as there is agreement on the fundamentals this should not disrupt efforts toward a common goal.

On an intellectual level many people are willing to admit that the case for vegetarianism is strong. Too often, though, there is a gap between intellectual conviction and the action needed to break a lifetime habit. There is no way in which a book can bridge this gap; ultimately it is up to the reader to put his convictions into practice. But a book can narrow the gap. It can make the transition from an omnivorous diet to a vegetarian one much easier and more attractive, so that instead of seeing the change of diet as an unpleasant duty the reader looks forward to a new and interesting cuisine,

full of fresh foods as well as unusual meatless dishes from
Europe, India, China, and the Middle East, dishes so varied
as to make the habitual meat, meat, and more meat of
most Western diets stale and repetitive by comparison; a
cuisine, moreover, the enjoyment of which is enhanced by
the knowledge that its good taste and nourishing qualities
were provided directly by the earth, neither wasting what
the earth produces, nor requiring the suffering and death of
any sentient being.

Vegetarianism brings with it a new relationship to food,
plants, and nature. Flesh taints our meals. Disguise it as we
may, the fact remains that the centerpiece of our dinner
has come to us from the slaughterhouse, dripping blood.
Untreated and unrefrigerated, it soon begins to putrefy and
stink. When we eat it, it sits heavily in our stomachs, block-
ing our digestive processes until, days later, we struggle to
excrete it.* When we eat plants, food takes on a different
quality. We take from the earth food that is ready for us
and does not fight against us as we take it. Without meat to
deaden the palate there is an extra delight in fresh vegetables
taken straight from the ground. Personally, I found the idea
of picking my own dinner so satisfying that shortly after
becoming a vegetarian I began digging up part of our back-
yard and growing some of my own vegetables—something
that I had never thought of doing previously, but which
several of my vegetarian friends were also doing. In this
way dropping flesh-meat from my diet brought me into
closer contact with plants, the soil, and the seasons.

Cooking, too, was something that I became interested
in only after I became a vegetarian. For those brought up
on the usual Anglo-Saxon menus in which the main dish
consists of meat supplemented by two overcooked vege-

---

* "Struggle" is not altogether a joke. According to a comparative
study published in The Lancet (30 December 1972), the "mean
transit time" of food through the digestive system of a sample
group of nonvegetarians on a Western type of diet was 76–83
hours; for vegetarians, 42 hours. The authors suggest a possible
connection between the length of time the stool remains in the
colon and the incidence of cancer of the colon and related diseases which have increased rapidly in nations whose consumption
of meat has increased but are almost unknown among rural Africans who, like vegetarians, have a diet low in meat and high in
roughage.

tables, the elimination of meat poses an interesting challenge to the imagination. When I speak in public about the issues discussed in this book, I am often asked about what one can eat instead of meat, and it is clear from the way the question is phrased that the questioner has mentally subtracted his chop or hamburger from his plate, leaving the mashed potatoes and boiled cabbage, and is wondering what to put in place of the meat. A heap of soybeans perhaps?

There may be those who would enjoy such a meal, but for most tastes the answer is to rethink the whole idea of the main course, so that it consists of a combination of ingredients, perhaps with a salad on the side, instead of detached items. Good Chinese dishes, for instance, are superb combinations of a high-protein ingredient—in vegetarian Chinese cooking this may be one or more of bean curd, nuts, bean sprouts, eggs, mushrooms, or wheat gluten—with fresh, lightly cooked vegetables and rice. An Indian curry using lentils for protein served over brown rice with some fresh sliced cucumber for light relief makes an equally satisfying meal, as does an Italian pizza or meatless lasagna with salad. A more simple meal might consist of whole grains and vegetables. Most Westerners eat very little millet, whole wheat, or buckwheat, but these grains can form the basis of a dish that is a refreshing change. The recipes and hints in Appendix 1 will give you details on how to cook these meals and many others, and should help you make the transition to vegetarianism. Some people find it hard, at first, to change their attitude to a meal. Getting used to meals without a central piece of animal flesh may take time, but once it has happened you will have so many interesting new dishes to choose from that you will wonder why you ever thought it would be difficult to do without flesh foods.

Apart from the tastiness of their meals, people contemplating vegetarianism are most likely to worry about whether they will be adequately nourished. These worries are entirely groundless. In numerous parts of the world there have been vegetarian cultures whose members have been as healthy, and often healthier, than nonvegetarians living in similar areas. Strict Hindus have been vegetarians for more than 2,000 years. Gandhi, a lifelong vegetarian, was near eighty when an assassin's bullet ended his active life. In Britain, where there has now been an official vegetarian movement for more than 125 years, there are third and fourth generation vegetarians. Many prominent vegetarians, like Leonardo da Vinci, Leo Tolstoy, and George Bernard Shaw, have lived long, immensely creative lives. Indeed, most people who have reached exceptional old age have eaten little or no meat. The inhabitants of the Vilcabamba valley in Ecuador frequently live to be more than 100 years old, and men as old as 123 and 142 years were recently found by scientists; these people eat less than one ounce of meat a week. A study of all living centenarians in Hungary found that they were largely vegetarian.[13] That meat is unnecessary for physical endurance is shown by a long list of successful athletes who do not eat it, a list that includes Olympic long-distance swimming champion Murray Rose and the famous distance runner Paavo Nurmi, known as "The Flying Finn."

Many vegetarians claim that they feel fitter, healthier, and more zestful than when they ate meat. Certainly your digestive system will find the new diet easier to cope with, and you will feel better after a big meal. Those with a high cholesterol level will benefit too; in fact the American Heart Association has recommended that Americans reduce their meat intake.[14] You also have the advantage of "getting off the top of the food chain," which means that you consume far fewer pesticide residues.[15]

Nutritional experts no longer dispute about whether animal flesh is essential; they now agree that it is not. If ordinary people still have misgivings about doing without it, these misgivings are based on ignorance. Most often this ignorance is about the nature of protein. We are frequently told that protein is an important element in a sound diet, and that meat is high in protein. Both these statements are true, but there are two other things that we are told less often. The first is that the average American eats too much protein. The protein intake of the average American exceeds the generous level recommended by the National Academy of Sciences by 45 percent. Other estimates say that most Americans consume between two and four times as much meat as the body can use. Excess protein cannot be stored. Some of it is excreted, and some may be converted by the body to carbohydrate, which is an expensive way to increase your carbohydrate intake.[16]

The second thing to know about protein is that meat is only one among a great variety of foods containing protein, its chief distinction being that it is the most expensive. It was once thought that meat protein is of superior quality, but as long ago as 1950 the British Medical Association's Committee on Nutrition stated:

> It is generally accepted that it is immaterial whether the essential protein units are derived from plant or animal foods, provided that they supply an appropriate mixture of the units in assimilable form.[17]

More recent research has provided further confirmation of this conclusion. We now know that the nutritional value of protein consists in the essential amino acids it contains, since these determine how much of the protein the body can use. While it is true that animal foods, especially eggs and milk, have a very well-balanced amino acid composition, plant foods like soybeans and nuts also contain a broad range of these nutrients. Moreover by eating different kinds of plant proteins at the same time it is easy to put together a meal that provides protein entirely equivalent to that of animal protein. This principle is called "protein complementarity," but you do not need to know a lot about nutrition to do it. The peasant who eats his beans or lentils with rice or corn is practicing protein complementarity. So is the mother who gives her child a peanut butter sandwich on whole wheat bread—a combination of peanuts and wheat, both of which contain protein. The different forms of protein in the different foods combine with each other in such a way that the body absorbs more protein if they are eaten together than if they were eaten separately.[18]

We have already seen how much more land and labor is required to produce a pound of protein via animals rather than directly from the earth. It should be no surprise to find that this difference is reflected in the retail prices of the different forms of protein. In order to compare prices you have to remember that one pound of beef gives you no more than three ounces of protein—the rest is water and fat. One pound of dried soybeans contains as much protein as two pounds of meat or fish. One pound of defatted soy flour, which is an even cheaper form of protein, costs at the present time around sixty cents. You need 2.5 pounds of boneless meat to get an equivalent amount of protein, and that will cost three dollars or more.[19]

Soybeans have risen sharply in price in the last year or two, but they retain their advantage over meat because they themselves are an ingredient in meat production and hence a factor in determining the cost of meat. According to the Agriculture Department's Research Service, peanut butter is the cheapest source of protein readily available at any American grocery store. The quantity necessary to yield 20 grams of protein—the recommended intake for an adult at each meal—cost 15 cents in August 1974; by comparison the amount of steak necessary to yield the same quantity of protein cost seventy-four cents.[20] Other economical plant proteins are dried peas, chick peas (or garbanzos), wheat germ, sesame seeds, lentils, and other varieties of dried beans. Eggs, milk, and cheese fall between the cheapest vegetable proteins and meat in cost, except for skim milk powder and cottage cheese made from skimmed milk, both among the most economical forms of protein.

Protein is not the only nutrient in meat, but the others can all easily be obtained from a vegetarian diet without special care. Only "vegans," who take no animal products at all, need to be especially careful about their diet. There appears to be one, and only one, necessary nutrient that is not normally available from plant sources, and this is vitamin B_{12}, which is present in eggs and milk, but not in a readily assimilable form in plant foods. For this reason the British Vegan Society recommends its members to take yeast tablets fortified with vitamin B_{12}. This vitamin is obtained from bacteria grown on vegetable products. Artificial "plant milks" fortified with B_{12} are also available in health food stores for those who do not drink milk. Studies of children in British "vegan" families have found that they develop normally on diets that contain a B_{12} supplement but no animal protein after weaning.[21]

Sometimes people are concerned that they will gain

weight if they become vegetarians. If the arguments of this
book have any substance at all this is more of an excuse
than a reason, since the disadvantage of being a little over-
weight hardly compares with the disadvantages the animals
suffer. Still, if this thought had crossed your mind you can
be reassured. Many of the foods vegetarians eat are high in
roughage. The roughage may contain carbohydrate, but this
carbohydrate is in a form that cannot be absorbed by the
human body, and so it passes through. Dry soybeans, for
instance, contain only 12 percent available carbohydrate—
so little that they can be used by diabetics. A calculation of
the number of calories contained in a food per gram of
usable protein shows that many vegetarian foods, including
soybean sprouts, soybean curd (Chinese bean cake or tofu),
mushrooms, eggs, cottage cheese, and wheat germ compare
well with steak, and all will give you more protein for
fewer calories than a lamb chop.[22] Two studies of "vegans"
have found them to weigh less than comparable omnivores,
which is a healthy sign as most people in affluent nations
tend to weigh too much rather than too little.[23] In my own
case—to add a personal note—I have lost about seven
pounds since becoming a vegetarian. So you needn't
expect to gain weight on becoming a vegetarian, although
you shouldn't expect automatically to lose it either; your
weight usually has more to do with the amount of sweet,
nutritionally worthless junk food you eat than with whether
you eat meat.

This chapter should have answered those doubts about
becoming a vegetarian that can easily be articulated and
expressed. But there is a deeper resistance among some
people which makes them hesitate. Perhaps the reason for
hesitation is a fear of being thought a crank by one's
friends. When my wife and I began to think about becoming vegetarians we talked about this. We worried that we
would be cutting ourselves off from our nonvegetarian
friends—and at that time none of our long-established
friends was vegetarian. The fact that we became vegetarians
together certainly made the decision easier for both of us,
but as things turned out we need not have worried. We explained our decision to our friends and they saw that we
had good reasons for it. They did not all become vege-

tarians, but they did not cease to be our friends either; in fact I think they rather enjoyed inviting us to dinner and showing us how well they could cook without meat. Of course, it is possible that you will encounter people who consider you a crank. If this happens, remember that you are in good company. All the best reformers—those who first opposed the slave trade, nationalistic wars, and the exploitation of children working a fourteen-hour day in the factories of the Industrial Revolution—were at first derided as cranks by those who had an interest in the abuses they were opposing.

NOTES

1. Oliver Goldsmith, *The Citizen of the World,* in *Collected Works,* ed. A. Friedman (Oxford: Clarendon Press, 1966), vol. 2, p. 60. Apparently Goldsmith himself fell into this category, however, since according to Howard Williams in *The Ethics of Diet* (abridged edition, Manchester and London, 1907, p. 149), Goldsmith's sensibility was stronger than his self-control.

2. For a detailed account see the study sponsored by Ralph Nader's consumer organization: Harrison Wellford, *Sowing the Wind: The Report on the Politics of Food Safety* (New York: Grossman, 1972; Bantam Books, 1973).

3. Frances Moore Lappé, *Diet for a Small Planet* (New York: Friends of the Earth/Ballantine, 1971), pp. 4-11. This book is the best brief introduction to the topic, and figures not otherwise attributed in this section have been taken from this book. (A revised edition was published in April 1975.) The main original sources are *The World Food Problem,* a Report of the President's Science Advisory Committee (1967), *Feed Situation,* February 1970, US Department of Agriculture, and *National and State Livestock-Feed Relationships,* US Department of Agriculture, Economic Research Service, Statistical Bulletin No. 446, February 1970.

4. The higher ratio is from Folke Dovring, "Soybeans," *Scientific American,* February 1974.

5. Boyce Rensberger, "Curb on U.S. Waste Urged to Help World's Hungry," *New York Times,* 25 October 1974.

6. N. W. Pirie, *Food Resources Conventional and Novel* (Middlesex, England, and Baltimore, Maryland: Penguin Books, 1969), p. 124.

7. *New York Times,* 25 October 1974 and Barbara Ward, "The Fat and the Lean," *The Economist,* 2 November 1974. According to Dr. Ward, even a return to 1965 levels of meat production would spare enough grain, per person, to keep another person alive.

8. *New York Times,* 25 October 1974.

9. See Emma Rothschild, "Running Out of Food," *New York Review of Books,* September 19, 1974; and also the "Flanigan Report" of the President's Council on International Economic Policy, published by the Senate Committee on Agriculture, April 1973.

10. Folke Dovring, "Soybeans."

11. L. and M. Milne, *The Senses of Men and Animals* (Middlesex, England, and Baltimore, Maryland: Penguin Books, 1965), ch. 5.

12. The Brambell Report, p. 36.

13. David Davies, "A Shangri-La in Ecuador," *New Scientist,* 1

February 1973. On the basis of other studies, Ralph Nelson of the Mayo Medical School has suggested that a high protein intake causes us to "idle our metabolic engine at a faster rate" (*Medical World News*, 8 November 1974, p. 106). This could explain the correlation between longevity and little or no meat consumption.

14. *New York Times*, 25 October 1974.

15. See Frances Moore Lappé, *Diet for a Small Planet*, pp. 19-28.

16. *Diet for a Small Planet*, pp. 28-29; see also *New York Times*, 25 October 1974; *Medical World News*, 8 November 1974, p. 106.

17. Quoted in F. Wokes, "Proteins," *Plant Foods for Human Nutrition*, vol. 1, p. 38 (1968).

18. *Diet for a Small Planet*, pp. 51-4; Ellen B. Ewald, *Recipes for a Small Planet* (New York: Ballantine, 1973). In addition to explaining the theory of protein complementarity, both of these books contain recipes utilizing the principle.

19. The protein comparisons come from Mildred Lager and Dorothea van Gundy Jones, *The Soybean Cookbook* (New York: Arc Books, Inc., 1971), p. 9. The prices are November 1974 in New York City.

20. *New York Times*, 25 October 1974.

21. F. R. Ellis and W. M. E. Montegriffo, "The Health of Vegans," *Plant Foods for Human Nutrition*, vol. 2, pp. 93-101 (1971). Some vegans claim that B_{12} supplements are not necessary, on the grounds that the human intestine can synthesize this vitamin from other B group vitamins. The question is, however, whether this synthesis takes place sufficiently early in the digestive process for the B_{12} to be absorbed rather than excreted. At present the nutritional adequacy of an all-plant diet without supplementation is an open scientific question; accordingly it seems safer to take supplementary B_{12}. See also F. Wokes, "Proteins," *Plant Foods for Human Nutrition*, p. 37.

22. *Diet for a Small Planet*, pp. 269-270.

23. Ellis and Montegriffo, "The Health of Vegans."

5

Man's Dominion . . .

a short history of speciesism.

To end tyranny we must first understand it. As a practical matter, the rule of the human animal over other animals expresses itself in the manner we have seen in Chapters 2 and 3, and in related practices like the slaughter of wild animals for sport or for their furs. These practices should not be seen as isolated aberrations. They can be properly understood only as the manifestations of the ideology of our species—that is, the attitudes which we, as the dominant animal, have toward the other animals.

In this chapter we shall see how, at different periods, outstanding figures in Western thought formulated and defended the attitudes to animals which we have inherited. I focus on the "West" not because other cultures are inferior —the reverse is true, so far as attitudes to animals are concerned—but because Western ideas have, over the past two or three centuries, spread out from Europe until today they set the mode of thought for most human societies, whether capitalist or communist.

Though the material which follows is historical, my aim in presenting it is not. When an attitude is so deeply ingrained in our thought that we take it as an unquestioned truth, a serious and consistent challenge to that attitude runs the risk of ridicule. It *may* be possible to shatter the

complacency with which the attitude is held by a frontal
attack. This is what I have tried to do in the preceding
chapters. An alternative strategy is to attempt to undermine
the plausibility of the prevailing attitude by revealing its
historical origins.

The attitudes toward animals of previous generations are
no longer convincing because they draw on presuppositions
—religious, moral, metaphysical—that are now obsolete.
Because we do not defend our attitudes to animals in the
way that St. Thomas Aquinas, for example, defended his
attitudes to animals, we may be ready to accept that
Aquinas used the religious, moral, and metaphysical ideas
of his time to mask the naked self-interest of human deal-
ings with other animals. If, then, we can see that past generations accepted as right and natural attitudes that we
recognize as ideological camouflages for self-serving practices; and if, at the same time, it cannot be denied that we
continue to use animals to further our own minor interests
in violation of their major interests, we may be persuaded to
take a more skeptical view of those justifications of our own
practices that we ourselves have taken to be right and
natural.

Western attitudes to animals have two roots: Judaism
and Ancient Greece. These roots unite in Christianity, and it
is through Christianity that they came to prevail in Europe.
A more enlightened view of our relations with animals
emerges only gradually, as thinkers begin to take positions
that are relatively independent of the Church; and in the
most fundamental respects we still have not broken free of
the attitudes that were unquestioningly accepted in Europe
until the eighteenth century. We may divide our historical
discussion, therefore, into three parts: pre-Christian, Christian, and the Enlightenment and after.

Pre-Christian Thought

The creation of the universe seems a fit starting point.
The biblical story of the creation sets out very clearly the
nature of the relationship between man and animal as the

Hebrew people conceived it to be. It is a superb example of myth echoing reality:

> And God said, Let the earth bring forth the living creature after his kind, cattle and creeping thing, and beast of the earth after his kind: and it was so.
>
> And God made the beast of the earth after his kind, and cattle after their kind, and every thing that creepeth upon the earth after his kind: and God saw that it was good.
>
> And God said, Let us make man in our image, after our likeness: and let them have dominion over the fish of the sea, and over the fowl of the air, and over the earth, and over every creeping thing that creepeth upon the earth.
>
> So God created man in his own image, in the image of God created he him; male and female created he them.
>
> And God blessed them, and God said upon them, Be fruitful, and multiply, and replenish the earth, and subdue it; and have dominion over the fish of the sea, and over the fowl of the air, and over every living thing that moveth upon the earth.[1]

The Bible tells us that God made man in His own image. We may regard this as man making God in his own image. Either way, it allots man a special position in the universe, as a being that, alone of all living things, is God-like. Moreover God is explicitly said to have given man dominion over every living thing. It is true that, in the Garden of Eden, this dominion may not have involved killing other animals for food. Verse 29 of the first chapter of Genesis suggests that at first man lived off the herbs and fruits of the trees, and Eden has often been pictured as a scene of perfect peace, in which killing of any kind would have been out of place. Man ruled, but in this earthly paradise his was a benevolent despotism.

After the Fall of man (for which the Bible holds a woman and an animal responsible), killing animals clearly was permissible. God himself clothed Adam and Eve in animal skins before driving them out of the Garden of

Eden. Their son Abel was a keeper of sheep and made offerings of his flock to the Lord. Then came the flood, when the rest of creation was nearly wiped out to punish man for his wickedness. When the waters subsided Noah thanked God by making burnt offerings "of every clean beast, and of every clean fowl." In return, God blessed Noah and gave the final seal to man's dominion:

> And God blessed Noah and his sons, and said unto them, Be fruitful, and multiply, and replenish the earth.
>
> And the fear of you and the dread of you shall be upon every beast of the earth, and upon every fowl of the air, upon all that moveth upon the earth, and upon all the fishes of the sea; into your hands are they delivered.
>
> Every moving thing that liveth shall be meat for you; even as the green herb have I given you all things.[2]

This is the basic position of the ancient Hebrew writings toward nonhumans. It is true that the prophet Isaiah condemned animal sacrifices, and the book of Isaiah does contain a lovely vision of the time when the wolf will dwell with the lamb, the lion will eat straw like the ox, and "they shall not hurt nor destroy in all my holy mountain." This, however, is a utopian vision, not a command for immediate adoption. There are other scattered passages in the Old Testament encouraging some degree of kindliness toward animals, so that it is possible to argue that wanton cruelty was prohibited; but there is nothing to challenge the over-all view, set down in Genesis, that man is the pinnacle of creation, that all the other creatures have been delivered into his hands, and that he has divine permission to kill and eat them.

The second ancient tradition of Western thought is that of Greece. Here we find, at first, conflicting tendencies. Greek thought was not uniform, but divided into rival schools, each taking their basic doctrines from some great founder. One of these, Pythagoras, was a vegetarian and encouraged his followers to treat animals with respect, apparently because he believed that the souls of dead men migrated to animals. But the most important school was that of Plato and his pupil, Aristotle.

Aristotle's support for slavery is well known; he thought that some men are slaves by nature and that slavery is both right and expedient for them. I mention this not in order to discredit Aristotle, but because it is essential for understanding his attitude to animals. Aristotle holds that animals exist to serve the purposes of humans, although, unlike the author of Genesis, he does not drive any deep gulf between humans and the rest of the animal world.

Aristotle does not deny that man is an animal; in fact he defines man as a rational animal. Sharing a common animal nature, however, is not enough to justify equal consideration. For Aristotle the man who is by nature a slave is undoubtedly a human being, and is as capable of feeling pleasure and pain as any other human being; yet because he is supposed to be inferior to the free man in his reasoning powers, Aristotle regards him as a "living instrument." Quite openly, Aristotle juxtaposes the two elements in a single sentence: the slave is one who "though remaining a human being, is also an article of property."[3]

If the difference in reasoning powers between human beings is enough to make some masters and others their property, Aristotle must have thought the rights of humans to rule over other animals too obvious to require much argument. Nature, he held, is essentially a hierarchy in which those with less reasoning ability exist for the sake of those with more:

. . . Plants exist for the sake of animals, and brute beasts for the sake of man—domestic animals for his use and food, wild ones (or at any rate most of them) for food and other accessories of life, such as clothing and various tools.

Since nature makes nothing purposeless or in vain, it is undeniably true that she has made all animals for the sake of man.[4]

It was the views of Aristotle, rather than those of Pythagoras, that were to become part of the later Western tradition.

Christian Thought

Christianity was in time to unite Jewish and Greek ideas about animals. But Christianity was founded and became powerful under the Roman Empire, and we can see its initial effect best if we compare Christian attitudes with those they replaced.

The Roman Empire was built by wars of conquest, and needed to devote much of its energy and revenue to the military forces that defended and extended its vast territory. These conditions did not foster sentiments of sympathy for the weak. The martial virtues set the tone of the society. Within Rome itself, far from the fighting on the frontiers, the character of Roman citizens was supposedly toughened by the so-called "games."

Although every schoolboy knows how Christians were thrown to the lions in the Colosseum, the significance of the games as an indication of the possible limits of sympathy and compassion of apparently—and in other respects genuinely—civilized people is rarely appreciated. Men and women looked upon the slaughter of both human beings and other animals as a normal source of entertainment; and this continued for centuries with scarcely a protest.

The nineteenth-century historian W. E. H. Lecky gives the following account of the development of the Roman games from their beginning as a combat between two gladiators:

The simple combat became at last insipid, and every variety of atrocity was devised to stimulate the flagging interest. At one time a bear and a bull, chained together, rolled in fierce combat across the sand; at another, criminals dressed in the skins of wild beasts were thrown to bulls, which were maddened by red-hot irons, or by darts tipped with burning pitch. Four hundred bears were killed on a single day under Caligula. . . . Under Nero, four hundred tigers fought with bulls and elephants. . . . In a single day, at the dedication of the Colosseum by Titus, five thousand animals perished. Under Trajan, the games continued for one hundred and twenty-three successive days. Lions, tigers, elephants, rhinoceroses, hippopotami, giraffes, bulls, stags, even crocodiles and serpents were employed to give novelty to the spectacle. Nor was any form of human suffering wanting. . . . Ten thousand men fought during the games of Trajan. Nero illumined his gardens during the night by Christians burning in their pitchy shirts. Under Domitian, an army of feeble dwarfs was compelled to fight. . . . So intense was the craving for blood, that a prince was less unpopular if he neglected the distribution of corn than if he neglected the games.[5]

The Romans were not without any moral feelings. They showed a high regard for justice, public duty, and even kindness to others. What the games show, with hideous clarity, is that there was a sharp limit to these moral feelings. If a being came within this limit, activities comparable to what occurred at the games would have been an intolerable outrage; when a being was outside the sphere of moral concern, however, the infliction of suffering was merely entertaining. Some human beings—criminals and military captives especially—and all animals fell outside this sphere.

It is against this background that the impact of Christianity must be assessed. Christianity brought into the Roman world the idea of the uniqueness of man, which it inherited from the Jewish tradition but insisted upon with still greater emphasis because of the importance it placed on man's immortal soul. Man, and man alone of all beings living on earth, was destined for a life after his bodily death. With this came the distinctively Christian idea of the sanctity of all human life.

There have been religions, especially in the East, which have taught that all life is sacred; and there have been many others that have held it gravely wrong to kill members of one's own social, religious, or ethnic group; but

Christianity spread the idea that every human life—and only human life—is sacred. Even the new-born infant and the fetus in the womb have immortal souls, and so their lives are as sacred as those of adults.

In its application to human beings, the new doctrine was in many ways very progressive, and involved a tremendous expansion of the limited moral sphere of the Romans; so far as other species are concerned, however, this same doctrine served to confirm and further depress the lowly position nonhumans had in the Old Testament. While it asserted man's complete dominance over other species, the Old Testament did at least show flickers of concern for their sufferings. The New Testament is completely lacking in any injunction against cruelty to animals, or any recommendation to consider their interests. Jesus himself showed indifference to the fate of nonhumans when he induced two thousand swine to hurl themselves into the sea—an act which was, apparently, quite unnecessary, since Jesus was able to cast out devils without inflicting them upon any other creature.[6] St. Paul insisted on reinterpreting the old Mosaic law which forbade muzzling the ox that trod out the corn: "Doth God care for oxen?" Paul asks scornfully. No, he answered, the law was somehow intended "altogether for our sakes."[7]

The example given by Jesus was not lost on later Christians. Referring to the incident of the swine and the episode in which Jesus cursed a fig tree, St. Augustine wrote:

Christ himself shows that to refrain from the killing of animals and the destroying of plants is the height of superstition, for judging that there are no common rights between us and the beasts and trees, he sent the devils into a herd of swine and with a curse withered the tree on which he found no fruit. . . . Surely the swine had not sinned, nor had the tree.

Jesus was, according to Augustine, trying to show us that we need not govern our behavior toward animals by the moral rules which govern our behavior toward men. That is why he transferred the devils to swine instead of destroying them as he could easily have done.[8]

On this basis the outcome of the interaction of Christian and Roman attitudes is not difficult to guess. It can be seen most clearly by looking at what happened to the Roman games after the conversion of the Empire to Christianity. Christian teaching was implacably opposed to gladiatorial combats. The gladiator who survived by killing his opponent was regarded as a murderer. Mere attendance at these combats made the Christian liable to excommunication, and by the end of the fourth century combats between human beings had been suppressed altogether. On the other hand, the moral status of killing or torturing any nonhuman remained unchanged. Combats with wild animals continued into the Christian era, and apparently declined only because the declining wealth and extent of the Empire made wild animals more difficult to obtain. Indeed they may still be seen, in the modern form of the bullfight, in Spain and Latin America.

What is true of the Roman games is also true more generally. Christianity left nonhumans as decidedly outside the pale of sympathy as they ever were in Roman times. Consequently, while attitudes to human beings were softened and improved beyond recognition, attitudes to other animals remained as callous and brutal as they were in Roman times. Indeed, not only did Christianity fail to temper the worst of Roman attitudes toward other animals; it unfortunately succeeded in extinguishing for a long, long time the spark of a wider compassion that had been kept alight by a tiny number of more gentle people.

There had been just a few Romans who had shown compassion for suffering, whatever the being that suffered, and repulsion at the use of sentient creatures for human pleasure, whether at the gourmet's table or in the arena. Ovid, Seneca, Porphyry, and Plutarch all wrote along these lines, Plutarch having the honor, according to Lecky, of being the first to advocate strongly the kind treatment of animals on the grounds of universal benevolence, independently of any belief in the transmigration of souls.[9] We have to wait nearly sixteen hundred years, however, before any Christian writer attacks cruelty to animals on any ground other than that it may encourage a tendency toward cruelty to humans.

Instead of tracing the development of Christian views on animals through the early Church Fathers to the medieval scholastics—a tedious process, since there is more repetition than development—it will be better to consider in more detail than would otherwise be possible the position of St. Thomas Aquinas.

Aquinas's enormous *Summa Theologica* was an attempt to grasp the sum of theological knowledge and reconcile it with the worldly wisdom of the philosophers—though for Aquinas, Aristotle was so preeminent in his field that he is referred to simply as "the philosopher." If any single writer may be taken as representative of Christian philosophy prior to the Reformation, and of Roman Catholic philosophy to this day, it is Aquinas.

We may begin by asking whether, according to Aquinas, the Christian prohibition on killing applies to creatures other than humans, and if not, why not. Aquinas answers:

There is no sin in using a thing for the purpose for which it is. Now the order of things is such that the imperfect are for the perfect . . . things, like plants which merely have life, are all alike for animals, and all animals are for man. Wherefore it is not unlawful if men use plants for the good of animals, and animals for the good of man, as the Philosopher states (*Politics*, I, 3).

Now the most necessary use would seem to consist in the fact that animals use plants, and men use animals, for food, and this cannot be done unless these be deprived of life, wherefore it is lawful both to take life from plants for the use of animals, and from animals for the use of men. In fact this is in keeping with the commandment of God himself (*Genesis* i, 29, 30 and *Genesis* ix, 3).[10]

For Aquinas the point is not that killing for food is in itself necessary and therefore justifiable (since Aquinas knew of sects like the Manichees in which the killing of animals was forbidden, he could not have been entirely ignorant of the fact that human beings can live without killing animals, but we shall overlook this for the mo-

ment); it is only the "more perfect" who are entitled to
kill for this reason. Animals that kill human beings for
food are in a quite different category:

> Savagery and brutality take their names from a like-
> ness to wild beasts. . . . For animals of this kind attack
> man that they may feed on his body, and not for some
> motive of justice, the consideration of which belongs
> to reason alone.[11]

Man, of course, would not kill for food unless he had first
considered the justice of so doing!

So man may kill other animals and use them for food;
but are there perhaps other things that he may not do to
them? Is the suffering of other creatures in itself an evil?
If so, would it not for that reason be wrong to make them
suffer, or at least to make them suffer unnecessarily?

Aquinas does not say that cruelty to "irrational animals"
is wrong. He has no room for wrongs of this kind in his
moral schema, for he divides sins into those against God,
those against oneself, and those against one's neighbor. So
the limits of morality once again exclude nonhumans.
There is no category for sins against them.[12]

Perhaps although it is not a sin to be cruel to nonhumans, it is charitable to be kind to them? No, Aquinas
explicitly excludes this possibility as well. Charity, he says,
does not extend to irrational creatures for three reasons:
they are "not competent, properly speaking, to possess
good, this being proper to rational creatures"; we have no
fellow-feeling with them; and because, finally, "charity is
based on the fellowship of everlasting happiness, to which
the irrational creatures cannot attain." It is only possible
to love these creatures, we are told, "if we regard them as
the good things that we desire for others," that is, "to
God's honor and man's use." In other words, we cannot
lovingly give food to a turkey because it is hungry, but
only if we think of it as someone's Christmas dinner.[13]

All this might lead us to suspect that Aquinas simply
doesn't believe that animals other than humans are capable
of suffering at all. This view has been held by other philosophers and, for all its apparent absurdity, to attribute it to

Aquinas would at least excuse him of the charge of indifference to suffering. This interpretation, however, is ruled out by our author's own words. In the course of a discussion of some of the mild injunctions against cruelty to animals in the Old Testament, Aquinas proposes that we distinguish reason and passion. So far as reason is concerned, he tells us:

> . . . . it matters not how man behaves to animals, because God has subjected all things to man's power . . . and it is in this sense that the Apostle says that God has no care for oxen, because God does not ask of man what he does with oxen or other animals.

On the other hand, where passion is concerned, our pity is aroused by animals, because "even irrational animals are sensible to pain"; nevertheless, the Old Testament injunctions are not intended to spare irrational animals pain:

> Now it is evident that if a man practice a pitiable affection for animals, he is all the more disposed to take pity on his fellow-men, wherefore it is written (*Proverbs* xii, 10) "The just regardeth the life of his beast. . . ."[14]

So Aquinas comes out with the often to be repeated view that the only reason against cruelty to animals is that it may lead to cruelty to human beings. No argument could reveal the essence of speciesism more clearly.

Aquinas's influence has lasted. As late as the middle of the nineteenth century, Pope Pius IX refused to allow a Society for the Prevention of Cruelty to Animals to be established in Rome, on the grounds that to do so would imply that human beings have duties toward animals.[15] And we can bring this account right up to date without finding significant modifications in the official position of the Roman Catholic Church. The following passage, from a contemporary American Roman Catholic text, makes an instructive comparison with the above passage quoted from Aquinas:

In the order of nature, the imperfect is for the sake of the perfect, the irrational is to serve the rational. Man, as a rational animal, is permitted to use things below him in this order of nature for his proper needs. He needs to eat plants and animals to maintain his life and strength. To eat plants and animals, they must be killed. So killing is not, of itself, an immoral or unjust act.[16]

The thing to notice about this text is that the author sticks so closely to Aquinas that he even repeats the assertion that it is necessary for human beings to eat plants *and* animals. The ignorance of Aquinas in this respect was surprising, but excusable given the state of scientific knowledge in his time: that a modern author, who would only need to look up a standard work on nutrition or take note of the existence of healthy vegetarians, should carry on the same error is incredible.

There have, of course, been many humane Catholics who have done their best to ameliorate the position of their church with regard to animals, and they have had occasional successes. By stressing the degrading tendency of cruelty, some Catholic writers have felt themselves able to condemn the worst of human practices toward other animals. Yet most remain limited by the basic outlook of their religion. The case of St. Francis of Assisi illustrates this.

St. Francis is the outstanding exception to the rule that Catholicism discourages concern for the welfare of non-human beings. "If I could only be presented to the emperor," he is reported as saying, "I would pray him, for the love of God, and of me, to issue an edict prohibiting anyone from catching or imprisoning my sisters the larks, and ordering that all who have oxen or asses should at Christmas feed them particularly well." Many legends tell of his compassion, and the story of how he preached to the birds certainly seems to imply that the gap between them and humans was less than other Christians supposed.

But a misleading impression of the views of St. Francis may be gained if one looks only at his attitude to larks and the other animals. It was not only sentient creatures whom St. Francis addressed as his sisters: the sun, the

moon, wind, fire, all were brothers and sisters to him. His
contemporaries described him as taking "inward and out-
ward delight in almost every creature, and when he handled
or looked at them his spirit seemed to be in heaven rather
than on earth." This delight extended to water, rocks,
flowers and trees. The description is reminiscent of someone who, in more modern terms, is "high"; and the ecstatic
aspect of St. Francis's personality has often been com-
mented upon. This makes the breadth of his love and compassion more readily comprehensible. It enables us to see
how this love for all creatures could coexist with a theological position that was quite orthodox in its speciesism.
St. Francis affirmed that "every creature proclaims: 'God
made me for your sake, O man!'" The sun itself, he
thought, shines for man. These beliefs were part of a cos-
mology that he never questioned; the force of his love for
all creation, however, was not to be bound by such considerations.

While this kind of ecstatic universal love can be a wonderful fountain of compassion and goodness, the lack of
rational reflection can also do much to counteract its beneficial consequences. If we love rocks, trees, plants, larks,
and oxen equally, we may lose sight of the essential differences between them, most importantly, the differences
in degree of sentience. We may then think that since we
have to eat to survive, and since we cannot eat without
killing something we love, it does not matter which we kill.
Possibly it was for this reason that St. Francis's love for
birds and oxen appears not to have led him to cease eating
them; and when he drew up the rules for the conduct of
the friars in the order he founded, he gave no instruction
that they were to abstain from meat, except on certain fast
days.[17]

It may seem that the period of the Renaissance, with
the rise of humanist thought in opposition to medieval
scholasticism, would have shattered the medieval picture
of the universe and brought down with it earlier ideas
about the status of man vis-à-vis the other animals. But
Renaissance humanism was, after all, *humanism;* and the

meaning of this term has nothing to do with humanitar-
ianism, the tendency to act humanely.

The central feature of Renaissance humanism is its insistence on the value and dignity of human beings, and on
man's central place in the universe. "Man is the measure
of all things," a phrase revived in Renaissance times from
the ancient Greeks, is the theme of the period. Instead of
a somewhat depressing concentration on original sin and
the weakness of man in comparison to the infinite power
of God, the Renaissance humanists emphasized man's
uniqueness, his free will, his potential, and his dignity; and
they contrasted all this with the limited nature of the
"lower animals." Like the original Christian insistence on
the sanctity of human life, this was in some ways a very
valuable advance in attitudes to human beings, but it left
nonhumans as far below humans as they had ever been.

So the Renaissance writers wrote self-indulgent essays in
which they said that "nothing in the world can be found
that is more worthy of admiration than man"[18] and
described man as "the center of nature, the middle of the
universe, the chain of the world."[19] If the Renaissance
marks, in some respects, the beginning of modern thought,
so far as attitudes to animals were concerned earlier modes
of thought still maintained their hold.

Around this time, however, we may notice the first
genuine dissenters: Leonardo da Vinci was teased by his
friends for being so concerned about the sufferings of animals that he became a vegetarian;[20] and Giordano Bruno,
influenced by the new Copernican astronomy which allowed for the possibility of other planets, some of which
could be inhabited, ventured to assert that "man is no
more than an ant in the presence of the infinite." Bruno
was burned at the stake for refusing to recant his heresies
in 1600.

Michel de Montaigne's favorite author was Plutarch, and
his attack on the humanist assumptions of his age would
have met with the approval of that gentle Roman:

Presumption is our natural and original disease . . .
Tis by the same vanity of imagination that [man]
equals himself to God, attributes to himself divine

qualities, and withdraws and separates himself from
the crowd of other creatures. . . .[21]

It is surely not a coincidence that the writer who rejects
such self-exaltation should also, in his essay *On Cruelty*,
be the first writer since Roman times to say that cruelty to
animals is wrong in itself, quite apart from its tendency to
lead to cruelty to human beings.

Perhaps, then, from this point in the development of
Western thought the status of nonhumans was bound to
improve? The old concept of the universe, and of man's
central place in it, was slowly giving ground; modern
science was about to set forth on its now-famous rise; and
after all, the status of nonhumans was so low that one
might reasonably think it could only improve.

But the absolute nadir was still to come. The last, most
bizarre, and—for the animals—most painful outcome of
Christian doctrines emerged in the first half of the seventeenth century, in the philosophy of René Descartes.

Descartes was a distinctively modern thinker. He is regarded as the father of modern philosophy, and also of
analytic geometry, in which a good deal of modern mathematics has its origins. But he was also a Christian, and
his beliefs about animals arose from the combination of
these two aspects of his thought.

Under the influence of the new and exciting science of
mechanics, Descartes held that everything that consisted
of matter was governed by mechanistic principles, like
those that governed a clock. An obvious problem with this
view was the nature of man himself. The human body is
composed of matter, and is part of the physical universe.
So it would seem that human beings must also be machines, whose behavior is determined by the laws of science.

Descartes was able to escape the unpalatable and heret-
ical view that man is a machine by bringing in the idea of
the soul. There are, Descartes said, not one but two kinds
of things in the universe, things of the spirit or soul as well
as things of a physical or material nature. Human beings
are conscious, and consciousness cannot have its origin in
matter. Descartes identified consciousness with the im-

mortal soul, which survives the decomposition of the physical body, and asserted that the soul was specially created by God. Of all material beings, Descartes said, only humans have a soul. (Angels and other immaterial beings have consciousness and nothing else.)

Thus in the philosophy of Descartes the Christian doctrine that animals do not have immortal souls has the extraordinary consequence that they do not have consciousness either. They are, he said, mere machines, automata. They experience neither pleasure nor pain, nor anything else. Although they may squeal when cut with a knife, or writhe in their efforts to escape contact with a hot iron, this does not, Descartes said, mean that they feel pain in these situations. They are governed by the same principles as a clock, and if their actions are more complex than those of a clock, it is because the clock is a machine made by man, while animals are infinitely more complex machines, made by God.[22]

This "solution" of the problem of locating consciousness in a materialistic world seems paradoxical to us, as it did to many of Descartes's contemporaries, but at the time it was also thought to have important advantages. It provided a reason for believing in a life after death; something which Descartes thought "of great importance" since "the idea that the souls of animals are of the same nature as our own, and that we have no more to fear or to hope for after this life than have the flies and ants" was an error that was apt to lead to immoral conduct. It also eliminated the ancient and vexing theological puzzle of why a just God would allow animals—who neither inherited Adam's sin, nor are recompensed in an afterlife—to suffer.*

Descartes was also aware of more practical advantages:

. . . my opinion is not so much cruel to animals as indulgent to men—at least to those who are not given

---

* John Passmore describes the question "why do animals suffer?" as "for centuries, the problem of problems. It engendered fantastically elaborate solutions. . . . Malebranche [a contemporary of Descartes] is quite explicit that for purely theological reasons it is necessary to deny that animals can suffer, since all suffering is the result of Adam's sin and the animals do not descend from Adam." See Man's Responsibility for Nature, p. 114n.

to the superstitions of Pythagoras—since it absolves them from the suspicion of crime when they eat or kill animals.[23]

For Descartes the scientist the doctrine had still another fortunate result. It was at this time that the practice of experimenting on live animals became widespread in Europe. Since there were no anesthetics then, these experiments must have caused the animals to behave in a way that would indicate, to most of us, that they were suffering extreme pain. Descartes's theory allowed the experimenter to dismiss any qualms he might feel under these circumstances. Descartes himself dissected living animals in order to advance his knowledge of anatomy, and many of the leading physiologists of the period declared themselves Cartesians and mechanists. The following eye-witness account of some of these experimenters, working at the Jansenist seminary of Port-Royal in the late seventeenth century, makes clear the convenience of Descartes's theory:

They administered beatings to dogs with perfect indifference, and made fun of those who pitied the creatures as if they felt pain. They said the animals were clocks; that the cries they emitted when struck were only the noise of a little spring that had been touched, but that the whole body was without feeling. They nailed poor animals up on boards by their four paws to vivisect them and see the circulation of the blood which was a great subject of conversation.[24]

From this point, the status of animals could only improve.

The Enlightenment and After

The new vogue for experimenting on animals may itself have been partly responsible for a change in attitudes toward animals, for the experiments revealed a remarkable similarity between the physiology of human beings and other animals. Strictly, this was not inconsistent with what

Descartes had said, but it made his views less plausible. Voltaire put it well:

> There are barbarians who seize this dog, who so greatly surpasses man in fidelity and friendship, and nail him down to a table and dissect him alive, to show you the mesaraic veins! You discover in him *all the same organs of feeling as in yourself.* Answer me, mechanist, has Nature arranged all the springs of feeling in this animal *to the end that he might not feel?*[25]

Although there was no radical change, a variety of influences combined to improve attitudes to animals. There was a gradual recognition that other animals do suffer and are entitled to some consideration. It was not thought that they had any rights, and their interests were overridden by human interests; nevertheless the Scottish philosopher David Hume was expressing a common enough sentiment when he said that we are "bound by the laws of humanity to give gentle usage to these creatures."[26]

"Gentle usage" is, indeed, a phrase that nicely sums up the attitude that began to spread in this period: we were entitled to use animals, but we ought to do so gently. The tendency of the age was for greater refinement and civility, more benevolence and less brutality, and animals benefited from this tendency along with humans.

The eighteenth century was also the period in which man rediscovered Nature: Jean-Jacques Rousseau's noble savage, strolling naked through the woods, picking fruits and nuts as he went, was the culmination of the idealization of nature. By seeing himself as part of nature, man regained a sense of kinship with "the beasts." This kinship, however, was in no sense egalitarian. At best, man was seen in the role of benevolent father of the family of animals.

Religious ideas of man's special role did not disappear. They were interwoven with the newer, more benevolent attitude. Alexander Pope, for example, opposed the practice of cutting open fully conscious dogs by arguing that although "the inferior creation" has been "submitted to our power" we are answerable for the "mismanagement" of it.[27]

Finally, and especially in France, the growth of anticlerical feeling was favorable to the status of animals. Voltaire, who delighted in fighting dogmas of all kinds, compared Christian practices unfavorably with those of the Hindu. He went further than the contemporary English advocates of kind treatment when he referred to the "barbarous custom of supporting ourselves upon the flesh and blood of beings like ourselves," although apparently he continued to practice this custom himself.[28] Rousseau, too, seems to have recognized the strength of the arguments for vegetarianism without actually adopting the practice; his treatise on education, Émile, contains a long and mostly irrelevant passage from Plutarch which attacks the use of animals for food as unnatural, unnecessary, bloody murder.[29]

The Enlightenment did not affect all thinkers equally so far as animals are concerned. Immanuel Kant, in his lectures on Ethics, still told his students:

> so far as animals are concerned, we have no direct duties. Animals are not self-conscious, and are there merely as a means to an end. That end is man.[30]

But in the same year that Kant gave these lectures—1780—Jeremy Bentham completed his Introduction to the Principles of Morals and Legislation and in it, in a passage I have already quoted in the first chapter of this book, he gave the definitive answer to Kant: "The question is not, Can they reason? nor Can they talk? but Can they suffer?" In comparing the position of animals with that of black slaves, and looking forward to the day "when the rest of the animal creation may acquire those rights which never could have been withholden from them but by the hand of tyranny," Bentham was perhaps the first to denounce "man's dominion" as tyranny rather than legitimate government.

The intellectual progress made in the eighteenth century was followed, in the nineteenth century, by some practical improvements in the conditions of animals. These took the form of laws against wanton cruelty to animals. The first battles for legal rights for animals were fought in Britain, and the initial reaction of the British Parliament indicates that Bentham's ideas had had little impact on his countrymen.

The first proposal for a law to prevent abuse of animals was a bill to prohibit the "sport" of bull-baiting. It was introduced into the House of Commons in 1800. George Canning, the foreign secretary, described it as "absurd" and asked rhetorically: "What could be more innocent than bull-baiting, boxing, or dancing?" Since no attempt was being made to prohibit boxing or dancing, it appears that this astute statesman had missed the point of the bill he was opposing—he thought it an attempt to outlaw gatherings of "the rabble" that might lead to immoral conduct.[31] The presupposition that made this mistake possible was that conduct which injures only an animal cannot possibly be worth legislating about—a presupposition shared by *The Times,* which devoted an editorial to the principle that "whatever meddles with the private personal disposition of man's time or property is tyranny. . . . Till another person is injured there is no room for power to interpose." The bill was defeated.

In 1821 Richard Martin, M.P., proposed a law to prevent the ill-treatment of horses. The following account conveys the tone of the ensuing debate:

> . . . when Alderman C. Smith suggested that protection should be given to asses, there were such howls of laughter that *The Times* reporter could hear little of what was said. When the Chairman repeated this proposal, the laughter was intensified. Another member said Martin would be legislating for dogs next, which caused a further roar of mirth, and a cry "And cats!" sent the House into convulsions.[32]

This bill failed too, but in the following year Martin succeeded with a bill that made it an offense "wantonly" to mistreat certain domestic animals, "the property of any other person or persons." For the first time, cruelty to animals was a punishable offense. Despite the mirth of the previous year, asses were included; dogs and cats, however, were still beyond the pale. More significantly, Martin had had to frame his bill so that it resembled a measure to protect items of private property, for the benefit of the owner, rather than for the sake of the animals themselves.*

The bill was now law, but it still had to be enforced. Since the victims could not make a complaint, Martin and a number of other notable humanitarians formed a society to gather evidence and bring prosecutions. So began the first animal welfare organization, later to become the Royal Society for the Prevention of Cruelty to Animals.

A few years after the passage of this first, modest statutory prohibition of cruelty to animals, Charles Darwin wrote in his diary: "Man in his arrogance thinks himself a great work, worthy of the interposition of a deity. More humble and, I believe, true, to consider him created from animals."[33] Another twenty years were to pass before, in 1859, Darwin considered that he had accumulated enough evidence in support of his theory to make it public. Even then, in *The Origin of Species*, Darwin carefully avoided any discussion of the extent to which his theory of the evolution of one species from another could be applied to humans, saying only that the work would illuminate "the origin of man and his history." In fact, Darwin already had extensive notes on the theory that man had descended from other animals, but he decided that publishing this material would "only add to the prejudices against my views."[34] Only in 1871, when many scientists had accepted the general theory of evolution, did Darwin publish *The Descent of Man*, thus making explicit what had been concealed in a single sentence of his earlier work.

---

* It has been claimed that the first legislation protecting animals from cruelty was enacted by the Massachusetts Bay Colony in 1641. Section 92 of "The Body of Liberties," printed in that year, reads: "No man shall exercise any Tirranny or Crueltie towards any bruite Creature which are usuallie kept for man's use"; and the following section requires a rest period for animals being driven. This is a remarkably advanced document; one could quibble over whether it was technically a "law," but certainly Nathaniel Ward, compiler of the "Body of Liberties," deserves to be remembered along with Richard Martin as a legislative pioneer. For a fuller account, see Emily Leavitt, *Animals and Their Legal Rights* (Washington: Animal Welfare Institute, 1970).

So began a revolution in human understanding of the relationship between ourselves and the nonhuman animals ... or did it?

One would expect the intellectual upheaval sparked by the publication of the theory of evolution to have made a marked difference in human attitudes to animals. Once the weight of scientific evidence in favor of the theory became apparent, practically every earlier justification of man's supreme place in creation and his dominion over the animals had to be rejected. Intellectually the Darwinian revolution was genuinely revolutionary. Human beings now knew that they were not the special creation of God, made in the divine image and set apart from the animals; on the contrary, human beings came to realize that they were animals themselves. Moreover, in support of his theory of evolution, Darwin pointed out that the differences between human beings and animals are not so great as is generally supposed. Chapter 3 of *The Descent of Man* is devoted to a comparison of the mental powers of man and the "lower animals," and Darwin summarizes the results of this comparison as follows:

We have seen that the senses and intuitions, the various emotions and faculties, such as love, memory, attention and curiosity, imitation, reason, etc., of which man boasts, may be found in an incipient, or even sometimes in a well-developed condition, in the lower animals.[35]

The fourth chapter of the same work goes still further, affirming that man's moral sense can also be traced back to social instincts in animals which lead them to take pleasure in each other's company, feel sympathy for each other, and perform services of mutual assistance. And in a subsequent work, *The Expression of the Emotions in Man and Animals,* Darwin provided additional evidence of extensive parallels between the emotional life of human beings and that of other animals.

The storm of resistance which met the theory of evolution and of the descent of man from animals—a story too well known to need retelling here—is an indication of the

extent to which speciesist ideas had come to dominate
Western thought. The idea that man is the product of a
special act of creation, and that the other animals were
created to serve him, was not to be given up without resistance. The scientific evidence for a common origin of the
human and other species was, however, overwhelming.

With the eventual acceptance of Darwin's theory we
reach a modern mentality, one which has since then
changed in detail rather than in fundamentals. It can no
longer be maintained by anyone but a religious fanatic that
man is the special darling of the whole universe, or that
other animals were created to provide us with food, or that
we have divine authority over them, and divine permission to kill them.

When we add this intellectual revolution to the growth
of humanitarian feeling that had preceded it, we might
think that all would now be well. Yet, as I hope the preceding chapters have made plain, the human "hand of tyranny" is still clamped down over other species, and we
probably inflict more pain on animals now than at any
other time in history. What went wrong?

If we look at what relatively advanced thinkers wrote
about animals from the time when, toward the end of the
eighteenth century, the right of animals to *some* degree of
consideration was beginning to be accepted, we may notice
an interesting fact. With very, very rare exceptions these
writers, even the best of them, stop short of the point at
which their arguments would lead them to face the choice
between breaking the deeply ingrained habit of eating the
flesh of other animals or admitting that they do not live
up to the conclusions of their own moral arguments. There
is an often repeated pattern here. When reading among
sources from the late eighteenth century onward one frequently comes across passages in which the author urges
the wrongness of our treatment of other animals in such
strong terms that one feels sure that here, at last, is someone who has freed himself altogether from speciesist ideas
—and hence, has freed himself too from the most widespread of all speciesist practices, the practice of eating
other animals. With one or two notable exceptions (in the
nineteenth century Lewis Gompertz and Henry Salt),[36]

one is always disappointed. Suddenly a qualification is made, or some new consideration introduced, and the author spares himself the qualms over his diet that his argument seemed sure to create. When the history of the animal liberation movement comes to be written, the era that began with Bentham will be known as the era of excuses.

The excuses used vary, and some of them show a certain ingenuity. It is worthwhile examining specimens of the main types, for they are still encountered today.

First, and this should come as no surprise, there is the Divine Excuse. It may be illustrated by the following passage from William Paley's *Principles of Moral and Political Philosophy* (1785). In setting out "the General Rights of Mankind" Paley asks whether we have a right to the flesh of animals:

> Some excuse seems necessary for the pain and loss which we occasion to brutes, by restraining them of their liberty, mutilating their bodies, and at last, putting an end to their lives (which we suppose to be the whole of their existence) for our pleasure or convenience.
>
> [It is] alleged in vindication of this practice . . . that the several species of brutes being created to prey upon one another affords a kind of analogy to prove that the human species were intended to feed upon them . . . [but] the analogy contended for is extremely lame; since brutes have no power to support life by any other means, and since we have; for the whole human species might subsist entirely upon fruits, pulse, herbs and roots, as many tribes of Hindoos actually do. . . .
>
> It seems to me that it would be difficult to defend this right by any arguments which the light and order of nature afford; and that we are beholden for it to the permission recorded in Scripture, *Genesis* ix, 1, 2, 3.[87]

Paley is only one of many who have appealed to revelation when they found themselves unable to give a rational justification of a diet consisting of other animals. Henry

Salt in his autobiography *Seventy Years Amongst Savages* (an account of his life in England) records a conversation he had when he was a master at Eton College. He had recently become a vegetarian; now for the first time he was to discuss his practice with a colleague, a distinguished science teacher. With some trepidation he awaited the verdict of the scientific mind on his new beliefs; when it came, it was: "But don't you think that animals were *sent* to us for food?"[38]

Another writer, Lord Chesterfield, appealed to Nature, instead of God:

> my scruples remained unreconciled to the committing of so horrid a meal, till upon serious reflection I became convinced of its legality from the general order of nature, which has instituted the universal preying upon the weaker as one of her first principles.[39]

Whether Lord Chesterfield thought this justified cannibalism is not recorded.

Benjamin Franklin used the same argument—the weakness of which Paley exposed—as a justification for returning to a flesh diet after some years as a vegetarian. In his *Autobiography* he recounts how he was watching some friends fishing, and noticed that some of the fish they caught had eaten other fish. He therefore concluded: "If you eat one another, I don't see why we may not eat you." Franklin, however, was at least more honest than some who use this argument, for he admits that he reached this conclusion only after the fish was in the frying-pan and had begun to smell "admirably well"; and he adds that one of the advantages of being a "reasonable creature" is that one can find a reason for whatever one wants to do.[40]

It is also possible for a deep thinker to avoid confronting the troublesome issue of diet by regarding it as altogether too profound for the human mind to comprehend. As Dr. Thomas Arnold of Rugby wrote:

> The whole subject of the brute creation is to me one of such painful mystery that I dare not approach it.[41]

This attitude was shared by the French historian Michelet; being French, he expressed it less prosaically:

> Animal Life, somber mystery! Immense world of thoughts and of dumb sufferings. All nature protests against the barbarity of man, who misapprehends, who humiliates, who tortures his inferior brethren. . . . Life, death! The daily murder which feeding upon animals implies—those hard and bitter problems sternly placed themselves before my mind. Miserable contradiction. Let us hope that there may be another sphere in which the base, the cruel fatalities of this may be spared to us.[42]

Michelet seems to have believed that we cannot live without killing; if so, his anguish at this "miserable contradiction" must have been in inverse proportion to the amount of time he gave to examining it.

Another to accept the comfortable error that we must kill to live was Arthur Schopenhauer. Schopenhauer was influential in introducing Eastern ideas to the West, and in several passages he contrasted the "revoltingly crude" attitudes to animals prevalent in Western philosophy and religion with those of Buddhists and Hindus. His style is sharp and scornful, and there are many acute criticisms of Western attitudes that are still appropriate today. After one particularly biting passage, however, Schopenhauer briefly considers the question of killing for food. He can hardly deny that humans can live without killing—he knows too much about the Hindus for that—but he claims that: "Without animal food the human race could not even exist *in the North.*" No basis is given for this geographical distinction, although Schopenhauer does add that the death of the animal should be made "even easier" by means of chloroform.[43]

Even Bentham, who stated so clearly the need to extend rights to nonhumans, flinched at this point:

> . . . there is very good reason why we should be suffered to eat such of them as we like to eat; we are the better for it, and they are never the worse. They

have none of those long-protracted anticipations of
future misery which we have. The death they suffer
in our hands commonly is, and always may be, a
speedier, and by that means a less painful one, than
that which would await them in the inevitable course
of nature.

One cannot help feeling that in these passages Schopenhauer and Bentham lowered their normal standards of
argument. Quite apart from the question of the morality
of painless killing, neither Schopenhauer nor Bentham considers the suffering necessarily involved in rearing and
slaughtering animals on a commercial basis. Whatever the
purely theoretical possibilities of painless killing may be,
the large-scale killing of animals for food is not and never
has been painless. When Schopenhauer and Bentham wrote,
slaughter was an even more horrific affair than it is today.
The animals were forced to cover long distances on foot,
driven to slaughter by drovers who had no concern but to
complete the journey as quickly as possible; they might then
spend two or three days in the slaughteryards, without
food, perhaps without water; they were then slaughtered
by barbaric methods, without any form of prior stunning.[44]
Despite what Bentham says, they did have some form of
anticipation of what was in store for them, at least from
the time they entered the slaughteryard and smelled the
blood of their fellows. Bentham and Schopenhauer would
not, of course, have approved of this, yet they continued
to support the process by consuming its products, and
justifying the general practice of which it was part. In this
respect Paley seems to have had a more accurate conception of what was involved in eating flesh. He, however,
could safely look the facts in the face, because he had
divine permission to fall back upon; Schopenhauer and
Bentham could not have availed themselves of this excuse,
and so had to turn their gaze away from the ugly reality.

As for Darwin himself, he too retained the moral attitudes to animals of earlier generations, though he had
demolished the intellectual foundations of those attitudes.
He continued to dine on the flesh of those beings who, he
had said, were capable of love, memory, curiosity, reason,

and sympathy for each other; and he refused to sign a petition urging the RSPCA to press for legislative control of experiments on animals.[45] His followers went out of their way to emphasize that although man was a part of nature and descended from animals, this did not mean that his status had been altered. In reply to the accusation that Darwin's ideas undermined the dignity of man, T. H. Huxley, Darwin's greatest champion, said:

> . . . no-one is more strongly convinced than I am of the vastness of the gulf between civilized man and the brutes . . . our reverence for the nobility of mankind will not be lessened by the knowledge that man is, in substance and in structure, one with the brutes. . . .[46]

Huxley is a true representative of modern attitudes; a man who knows perfectly well that the old reasons for deeming there to be a vast gulf between "man" and "brute" no longer stand up, but continues to believe in the existence of such a gulf nevertheless.

It is here that we see most clearly the ideological nature of our justification of the use of animals. It is a distinctive characteristic of an ideology that it resists refutation. If the foundations of an ideological position are knocked out from under it, new foundations will be found, or else the ideological position will just hang there, defying the logical equivalent of the laws of gravity. In the case of attitudes to animals it is the latter that seems to have happened. While the modern view of man's place in the world differs enormously from all the earlier views we studied, in the practical matter of how we act toward other animals there has been little basic change. If animals are no longer quite outside the moral sphere, they are still in a special section near the outer rim. Their interests are allowed to count only when they do not clash with human interests. If there is a clash—even a clash between the life of a nonhuman animal and the gastronomic preference of a human being—the interests of the nonhuman are disregarded. The moral attitudes of the past were too deeply embedded in our thought and our practices to be upset by a mere change in our knowledge of ourselves and of other animals.

NOTES

1. Gen. 1:24-28.
2. Gen. 9:1-3.
3. *Politics*, Everyman's Library, p. 10.
4. *Politics*, Everyman's Library, p. 16.
5. W. E. H. Lecky, *History of European Morals from Augustus to Charlemagne* (London, 1869), 1:280-282.
6. Mark 5:1-13
7. Corinthians 9:9-10.
8. St. Augustine, *The Catholic and Manichaean Ways of Life*, trans. D. A. Gallagher and I. J. Gallagher (Boston: The Catholic University Press, 1966) p. 102. I owe this reference to John Passmore, *Man's Responsibility for Nature* (New York: Charles Scribner's Sons, 1974), p. 11.
9. *History of European Morals*, I:244; for Plutarch see especially the essay "On the Eating of Flesh" in his *Moral Essays*.
10. *Summa Theologica* II, II, Q64, art. 1.
11. *Summa Theologica* II, II, Q159, art. 2.
12. *Summa Theologica* I, II, Q72, art. 4.
13. *Summa Theologica* II, II, Q25, art. 3.
14. *Summa Theologica* II, I, Q102, art. 6; see also *Summa contra Gentiles* III, II, 112 for a similar view.
15. E. S. Turner, *All Heaven in a Rage* (London: Michael Joseph, 1964), p. 163.
16. V. J. Bourke, *Ethics* (New York: Macmillan, 1951), p. 352.
17. *St. Francis of Assisi, His Life and Writings as Recorded by His Contemporaries*, trans. L. Sherley-Price (London, 1959), see especially p. 145.
18. Pico della Mirandola, *Oration on the Dignity of Man*.
19. Marsilio Ficino, *Theologica Platonica* III, 2 and XVI, 3; cf. Giannozzo Manetti, *The Dignity and Excellence of Man*.
20. E. McCurdy, *The Mind of Leonardo da Vinci* (London: Cape, 1932), p. 78.
21. "Apology for Raimond de Sebonde," in his *Essays*.
22. *Discourse on Method*, vol. 5; see also his letter to Henry More, 5 February 1649.
23. Letter to Henry More, 5 February 1649.
24. Nicholas Fontaine, *Memoires pour servir à l'histoire de Port-Royal* (Cologne, 1738), 2:52-53; quoted in L. Rosenfield, *From Beast-Machine to Man-Machine: The Theme of Animal Soul in French Letters from Descartes to La Mettrie* (New York: Oxford University Press, 1940).

25. *Dictionnaire Philosophique,* s.v. *"Bêtes."*

26. *Enquiry Concerning the Principles of Morals,* ch. 3.

27. *The Guardian,* 21 May 1713.

28. *Elements of the Philosophy of Newton,* vol. 5; see also *Essay on the Morals and Spirit of Nations.*

29. *Émile,* Everyman's Library, 2:118-120.

30. *Lectures on Ethics,* trans. L. Infield (New York: Harper Torchbooks, 1963), pp. 239-40.

31. Hansard's Parliamentary History, 18 April 1800.

32. Turner, *All Heaven in a Rage,* p. 127. Other details in this section come from chapters 9 and 10 of this book.

33. Quoted in *All Heaven in a Rage,* p. 162.

34. Charles Darwin, *The Descent of Man* (London, 1871), p. 1.

35. Ibid., p. 193.

36. See Lewis Gompertz, *Moral Inquiries on the Situation of Man and of Brutes* (London, 1824); H. S. Salt, *Animals' Rights* (London, 1892); *The Logic of Vegetarianism* (London, no date); and other works. I am indebted to *Animals' Rights* for some of the quotations in the following pages.

37. Bk. 2, ch. 11; for the same idea, see Francis Wayland, *Elements of Moral Science* (1835, reprinted ed., J. L. Blau, ed. [Cambridge: Harvard University Press, 1963], p. 364), perhaps the most widely used work on moral philosophy in nineteenth-century America.

38. Quoted by S. Godlovitch, "Utilities," in *Animals, Men and Morals* (New York: Taplinger Publishing Co., 1972).

39. Quoted in Salt, *Animals' Rights* (1915 ed.), p. 43.

40. Benjamin Franklin, *Autobiography* (New York: Modern Library, 1950), p. 41.

41. Quoted in Salt, *Animals' Rights,* p. 15.

42. *La Bible de l'humanité,* quoted in H. Williams, *The Ethics of Diet* (abridged ed., Manchester and London, 1907), p. 214.

43. *On the Basis of Morality,* trans. E. F. J. Payne (Library of Liberal Arts, 1965), p. 182; see also *Parerga und Paralipomena,* ch. 15.

44. See Turner, *All Heaven in a Rage,* p. 143.

45. Ibid., p. 205.

46. T. H. Huxley, *Man's Place in Nature* (Ann Arbor: University of Michigan Press, 1959), ch. 2.

6

Speciesism Today . . .

defenses, rationalizations, and
objections to Animal Liberation.

We have seen how, in violation of the fundamental moral
principle of equality of consideration of interests that ought
to govern our relations with all beings, humans inflict suffering on nonhumans for trivial purposes; and we have
seen how generation after generation of Western thinkers
has sought to defend the right of humans to do this. In this
final chapter I shall look at some of the ways in which
speciesist practices are maintained and promoted today,
and at the various arguments and excuses that are still used
in defense of animal slavery. Some of these defenses will,
I expect, be raised against the position taken in this book,
and so this chapter provides an opportunity to answer some
of the objections most often made to the case for Animal
Liberation; but the chapter is also intended as a continuation of the previous one, revealing the continued existence
of the ideology whose history we have traced back to the
Bible and the ancient Greeks. It is important to expose and
criticize this ideology, because although contemporary attitudes to animals are sufficiently benevolent—on a very
selective basis—to allow some improvements in the conditions of animals to be made without challenging basic attitudes to animals, these improvements will always be in

danger of erosion unless we alter the underlying position that sanctions the ruthless exploitation of nonhumans for human ends. Only by making a radical break with more than 2,000 years of Western thought about animals can we build a solid foundation for the abolition of this exploitation.

Our attitudes to animals begin to form when we are very young, and they are dominated by the fact we begin to eat meat at an early age. Interestingly enough, many children at first refuse to eat animal flesh, and only become accustomed to it after strenuous efforts by their parents, who mistakenly believe that it is necessary for good health. Whatever the child's initial reaction, though, the point to notice is that we eat animal flesh long before we are capable of understanding that what we eat is the dead body of an animal. Thus we never make a conscious, informed decision, free from the bias that accompanies any long-established habit, reinforced by all the pressures of social conformity, to eat animal flesh. At the same time children have a natural love of animals, and our society encourages them to be affectionate toward pets and cuddly, stuffed toy animals. From these facts stems the most distinctive characteristic of the attitudes of children in our society to animals —namely, that there is not one unified attitude to animals, but two conflicting attitudes that coexist in the one individual, carefully segregated so that the inherent contradiction between them rarely causes trouble.

Not so long ago children were brought up on fairy tales in which animals, especially wolves, were pictured as cunning enemies of man. A characteristic happy ending would leave the wolf drowning in a pond, weighed down by stones which the ingenious hero had sown into its belly while it was asleep. And in case children missed the implications of these stories, they could all join hands and sing a nursery rhyme like:

> Three blind mice, see how they run!
> They all ran after the farmer's wife
> Who cut off their tails with a carving knife.

Did you ever see such a thing in your life
As three blind mice?

For children brought up on these stories and rhymes
there was no inconsistency between what they were taught
and what they ate. Today, however, such stories and
rhymes have gone out of fashion, and on the surface all is
sweetness and light, so far as children's attitudes to animals
are concerned. Thereby a problem has arisen: what about
the animals we eat?

One response to this problem is simple evasion. The
child's affection for animals is directed toward animals that
are not eaten: dogs, cats, and other pets. These are the
animals that an urban or suburban child is most likely to
see. Cuddly, stuffed toy animals are more likely to be bears
or lions than pigs or cows. When farm animals are mentioned in picture books and stories, however, evasion may
become a deliberate attempt to mislead the child about the
nature of modern farms, and so to screen him from the
reality that we examined in Chapter 3. An example of this
is the popular Hallmark book *Farm Animals,* which pre-
sents the child with pictures of hens, turkeys, cows, and
pigs, all surrounded by their young, with not a cage, shed,
or stall in sight. The text tells us that pigs "enjoy a good
meal, then roll in the mud and let out a squeal!" while
"Cows don't have a thing to do, but switch their tails, eat
grass and moo."[1] British books, like *The Farm* in the best-
selling Ladybird series, convey the same impression of rural
simplicity, showing the hen running in an orchard with her
chicks, and all the other animals living with their offspring
in spacious quarters.[2] With this kind of early reading it is
not surprising that children grow up believing that even if
animals "must" die to provide human beings with food they
live happily until that time comes.

Recognizing the importance of the attitudes we form
when young, the Women's Liberation movement has suggested changes in the stories we read to our children. They
want brave princesses to rescue helpless princes occasionally. To alter the stories about animals that we read to our
children will not be so easy, since cruelty is not an ideal
subject for children's stories. Yet it should be possible to

avoid the most gruesome details, and still give children picture books and stories that encourage respect for animals as independent beings, and not as cute little objects that exist for our amusement and table; and as children grow older, they can be made aware that most animals live under conditions that are not very pleasant. The difficulty will be that nonvegetarian parents are going to be reluctant to let their children learn the full story, for fear that the child's affection for animals may disrupt family meals. Even now, one frequently hears that, on learning that animals are killed to provide meat, a friend's child has refused to eat meat. Unfortunately this instinctive rebellion is likely to meet strong resistance from nonvegetarian parents, and most children are unable to keep up their refusal in the face of opposition from parents who provide their meals and tell them that they will not grow up big and strong without meat. One hopes, as knowledge of nutrition spreads, more parents will realize that on this issue their children may be wiser than they are.*

It is an indication of the extent to which people are now isolated from the animals they eat that a child brought up on storybooks that lead him to think of a farm as a place where animals wander around freely in idyllic conditions might be able to live out his entire life without ever being forced to revise this rosy image. There are no farms in the cities and suburbs where people live and while on a drive through the country one now sees many farm buildings and relatively few animals out in the fields, how many of us can distinguish a storage barn from a broiler shed?

Nor do the mass media educate the public on this topic.

* An example: Lawrence Kohlberg, a Harvard psychologist noted for his work on moral development, relates how his son, at the age of four, made his first moral commitment, and refused to eat meat because, as he said, "it's bad to kill animals." It took Kohlberg six months to talk his son out of his position, which Kohlberg says was based on a failure to make a proper distinction between justified and unjustified killing, and indicates that his son was only at the most primitive stage of moral development. (L. Kohlberg, "From Is to Ought," in T. Mischel, ed., Cognitive Development and Epistemology, New York, Academic Press, 1971, pp. 191–192.) Moral: if you reject a pervasive human prejudice, you can't be morally developed.

On American television there are programs on animals in the wild (or supposedly in the wild—sometimes the animals have been captured and released in a more limited space to make filming easier) almost every night of the week; but film of intensive farms is limited to the briefest of glimpses as part of infrequent "specials" on agriculture or food production. The average viewer must know more about the lives of cheetahs and sharks than he knows about the lives of chickens or veal calves. The result is that most of the "information" about farm animals to be gained from watching television is in the form of paid advertising, which ranges from ridiculous cartoons of pigs that want to be made into sausages and tuna trying to get themselves canned, to straightforward lies about the conditions in which broiler chickens are reared. The newspapers do little better. Their coverage of nonhuman animals is dominated by "human interest" events like the birth of a baby gorilla at the zoo, or by threats to endangered species; but developments in farming techniques that deprive millions of animals of freedom of movement go unreported.*

What goes on in laboratories is no better known than what goes on down on the farm. The public, of course, does not have access to laboratories. Although researchers publish their reports in professional journals, news of experiments only filters out to the public when the experiments are of extraordinary importance. Thus the public never learns that most experiments performed on animals are never published at all, and that most of those published are trivial anyway. Since, as we saw in Chapter 2, no one knows exactly how many experiments are performed on animals in the United States, it is not surprising that the public has not the remotest idea of the extent of animal experimentation. Research facilities are usually designed so that the public sees little of the live animals that go in, or the dead ones that go out. (A standard textbook on the

---

* I had a dramatic confimation of this when, in search of illustrations for this book, I visited the photograph library of the Associated Press in New York. There I found folder after folder of pictures of children holding rabbits, pigs with exceptionally large litters, and zoo animals with their babies; but there was not a single photograph of a modern veal or pig farm.

use of animals in experimentation advises laboratories to install an incinerator, since the sight of dozens of bodies of dead animals left out as ordinary refuse "will certainly not enhance the esteem with which the research center or school is held by the public.")[3]

Ignorance, then, is the speciesist's first line of defense. Yet it is easily breached by anyone with the time and determination to find out the truth. Ignorance has prevailed so long only because people do not *want* to find out the truth. "Don't tell me, you'll spoil my dinner" is the usual reply to an attempt to tell someone just how that dinner was produced. Even people who are aware that the traditional family farm has been taken over by big business interests, and that some questionable experiments go on in laboratories, cling to a vague belief that conditions cannot be too bad, or else the government or the animal welfare societies would have done something about it. Dr. Bernhard Grzimek, director of the Frankfurt Zoo and one of West Germany's most outspoken opponents of intensive farming, has likened the ignorance of Germans today about these farms to the ignorance of an earlier generation of Germans to another form of atrocity, also hidden away from most eyes;[4] and in both cases, no doubt, it is not the inability to find out what is going on as much as a desire not to know about facts that may lie heavy on one's conscience that is responsible for the lack of awareness; as well as, of course, the comforting thought that, after all, it is not members of one's own race (species) that are the victims of whatever it is that goes on in those places.

The thought that we can rely on the animal welfare societies to see that animals are not cruelly treated is a reassuring one. Most countries now have at least one large, well-established animal protection society: in the United States there is the American Society for the Prevention of Cruelty to Animals, the American Humane Association, and the Humane Society of the United States; in Britain the Royal Society for the Prevention of Cruelty to Animals remains unchallenged as the largest group. It is reasonable to ask: why have these associations not brought to the attention of the public the facts that I have presented in Chapters 2 and 3 of this book?

There are several reasons for the silence of the animal welfare establishment on the most important areas of cruelty. One is historical. When first founded, the RSPCA and ASPCA were radical groups, far ahead of the public opinion of their times, and opposed to all forms of cruelty to animals, including cruelty to farm animals which then, as now, was the source of many of the worst abuses. Gradually, however, as these organizations grew in wealth, membership, and respectability, they lost their radical drive and became part of "The Establishment." They built up close contacts with members of the government, and with businessmen and scientists. They tried to use these contacts to improve the conditions of animals, and some minor improvements resulted; but at the same time contacts with those whose basic interests are in the use of animals for food or research purposes blunted the radical criticism of the exploitation of animals which had inspired the founders. Again and again the societies compromised their fundamental principles for the sake of trivial reforms. Better some progress now than nothing at all, they said; but often the reforms proved ineffective in improving the conditions of the animals, and functioned rather to reassure the public that nothing further needed to be done.*

As their wealth increased, another consideration became important. The animal welfare societies had been set up as registered charities. This status brought them substantial tax savings; but it is a condition of being registered as a charity, in both Britain and the United States, that the organization does not engage in political activities. Political action, unfortunately, is sometimes the only thing that can be done to improve the conditions of animals (especially if an organization is too cautious to call for public boycotts of meat) but most of the large groups kept well clear of anything that might endanger their charitable status. This has led them to emphasize safe activities like collecting stray dogs and prosecuting individual acts of wanton

---

* Examples are the 1876 British Cruelty to Animals Act and the 1966–1970 Animal Welfare Act in the United States, both of which were enacted in response to concern about animals being used in experiments but have done little to benefit those animals.

cruelty, instead of broad campaigns against systematic cruelty.

Finally, at some point in the last hundred years the major animal welfare societies lost interest in farm animals. Perhaps this was because the supporters and officials of the societies came from the cities, and knew more and cared more about dogs and cats than about pigs and calves.

It is regrettable to have to criticize organizations that are trying to protect animals from cruelty. But it is a fact that the literature and publicity of the major animal welfare organizations make a significant contribution to the prevailing attitude that dogs and cats and wild animals need protection, but other animals do not. Thus people come to think of "animal welfare" as something for kindly ladies who are dotty about cats, and not as a cause founded on basic principles of justice and morality.

Indeed, not only do most animal welfare societies in the United States fail to educate the public about what happens to animals on farms and in laboratories; they themselves do not know. When, in writing this book, I contacted the American Humane Association and the New York ASPCA for information on these topics, neither of them was able to tell me anything about factory farming, and the information I received on laboratory animals gave the general impression that there was nothing to worry about.*

By failing to attack the major kinds of cruelty to ani-

---

* In fact, the ASPCA even seems concerned to play down the size and nature of the problem of animal experimentation when it reports to its own members. The September/October 1974 issue of *Animal Protection*, the magazine of the New York ASPCA, carried a reassuring item on the report of the US Department of Agriculture on the Animal Welfare Act, omitting, however, the information contained in that report that the testing of cosmetics was responsible for painful experiments on animals, and omitting also to give any indication that the report covers fewer than 5 percent of all animals experimented upon in the United States.

The British sister-organization of the ASPCA, the RSPCA, should to some extent be exempted from the criticisms made in the text of the major humane associations, since in the last two or three years the RSPCA has begun to pay more attention to farm animals and laboratory animals. There is still a long way to go, but the RSPCA once again has some radical reformers among its younger committee members.

mals, these groups have allowed the public to delude itself that all is well; and by actively collaborating with those responsible for cruelty, they have lent an air of respectability to practices that ought to be condemned outright. Some examples: the American Humane Association is so ignorant about food production that when a reporter, shocked at conditions he had witnessed on an egg farm, asked an AHA spokesman for a comment, he was told that "we do have to meet food demand, and mass farming techniques may be the only way to do it."[5] The AHA collaborates with the organizers of rodeos, certifying them as "humane"; although the rodeos thus certified may not indulge in some of the finer cruelties practiced elsewhere, any rodeo is inherently an abuse of animals, as anyone who has watched one can see. The main function of the various state SPCAs today is rounding up stray dogs and cats. Most of these are killed, as humanely as possible; but in some states the SPCA obediently complies with laws that require them to hand over these animals to laboratories for research purposes. In Britain the RSPCA runs an airport hostel, reviving and caring for animals that have suffered from shocking transportation conditions; but often these animals are being transported into Britain to be experimented upon. Should an animal welfare society assist experimenters by keeping their victims alive for them?

Another American group, the Animal Welfare Institute, has such close contact with the International Committee on Laboratory Animals—a committee whose professed aim is the promotion of Laboratory Animal Science all over the world—that the Animal Welfare Institute's Report has carried a call for papers to be read at a symposium organized by the ICLA, on such themes as the training of researchers in laboratory animal science in the developing countries, and the choice of animals for use in research. Moreover the Greek representative of the ICLA also represents Greece on the International Committee of the Animal Welfare Institute![6] And for one last instance look back to page 71 where there is a quotation from an article by a veterinarian to whom animals are not "mere" animals, but also "standardized biological research tools." The reader will no doubt be as surprised as I was to learn that the author of this article, Robert L. Hummer, VMD, MPH, is a veterinary consultant to the American Humane Association, advising the AHA and speaking on its behalf on many occasions.[7] Is it any wonder that the AHA has not taken a strong stand against what goes on in laboratories?

A few smaller organizations have tried to do what the larger ones have failed to do, but they find it hard going.* Among the factors that make it difficult for small groups to arouse public concern about animals perhaps the hardest to overcome is the assumption that "humans come first" and that any problem about animals cannot be comparable, as a serious moral or political issue, to problems about humans. There are a number of things to be said about this assumption. First, it is in itself an indication of speciesism. How can anyone who has not made a thorough study of the topic possibly know that the problem is less serious than problems of human suffering? One can claim to know this only if one assumes that animals really do not matter, and that however much they suffer, their suffering is less important than the suffering of humans. But pain is pain, and the importance of preventing unnecessary pain and suffering does not diminish because the being that suffers is not a member of our species. What would we think of someone who said that "whites come first" and that therefore poverty in Africa does not pose as serious a problem as poverty in Europe?

It is true that there are many problems in the world deserving our time and energy. Famine and poverty, racism, war, Women's Liberation, inflation and unemployment, the environment—all are major issues, and who can say which is the most important? Yet once we put aside speciesist biases we can see that the oppression of nonhumans by humans ranks somewhere along with these issues. The suffering that we inflict on nonhuman beings can be extreme, and the numbers involved are gigantic: hundreds of millions of pigs, cattle, and sheep go through the processes described in Chapter 3 each year, in the

---

* For a list of these organizations, see Appendix 3.

United States alone; billions of chickens do the same; and more than 60 million animals are experimented upon annually. If a thousand human beings were forced to undergo the kind of tests that animals undergo to ensure the safety of cosmetics, there would be a national uproar. The use of millions of animals for this purpose should cause at least as much concern, especially since this suffering is so unnecessary and could easily be stopped if we wanted to stop it. All reasonable people want to prevent war, racial inequality, inflation, and unemployment; the problem is that we have been trying to prevent these things for years, and now we have to admit that we don't really know how to do it. By comparison, the reduction of the suffering of nonhuman animals at the hands of humans will be relatively easy, once human beings set themselves to do it.

In any case, the idea that "humans come first" is more often used as an excuse for not doing anything about either human or nonhuman animals than as a genuine choice between incompatible alternatives. For the truth is that there is no incompatibility here. Granted, everyone has a limited amount of time and energy, and time taken in active work for one cause reduces the time available for another cause; but there is nothing to stop those who devote their time and energy to human problems from joining the boycott of the produce of agribusiness cruelty. It takes no more time to be a vegetarian than to eat animal flesh. In fact, as we saw in Chapter 4, those who claim to care about the well-being of humans should become vegetarians for that reason alone. They would thereby increase the amount of grain available to feed people elsewhere, and since a vegetarian diet is cheaper than one based on meat dishes, they would have more money available to devote to famine relief, population control, or whatever social or political cause they thought most urgent. I would not question the sincerity of vegetarians who take little interest in Animal Liberation because they give priority to other causes; but when nonvegetarians say that "human problems come first" I cannot help wondering what exactly it is that they are doing for humans that compels them to continue to support the wasteful, ruthless exploitation of farm animals.

At this point a historical digression is appropriate. It is often said, as a kind of corollary of the idea that "humans come first," that people in the animal welfare movement care more about animals than they do about humans. No doubt there are some people of whom this is true. Historically, though, the leaders of the animal welfare movement have cared far more about human beings than have other humans who cared nothing for animals. Indeed, the overlap between leaders of movements against the oppression of blacks and women, and leaders of movements against cruelty to animals, is extensive; so extensive as to provide an unexpected form of confirmation of the parallel between racism, sexism, and speciesism. Among the handful of founders of the RSPCA, for example, were William Wilberforce and Fowell Buxton, two of the leaders in the fight against Negro slavery in the British Empire.[8] As for early feminists, Mary Wollstonecraft wrote, in addition to her *Vindication of the Rights of Woman*, a collection of children's stories entitled *Original Stories*, expressly designed to encourage kinder practices toward animals;[9] and a number of the early American feminists, including Lucy Stone, Amelia Bloomer, Susan B. Anthony, and Elizabeth Cady Stanton, were connected with the vegetarian movement. Together with Horace Greeley, the reforming, antislavery editor of *The Tribune*, they would meet to toast "Women's Rights and Vegetarianism."[10]

To the animal welfare movement, too, must go the credit for starting the fight against cruelty to children. In 1874 Henry Bergh, the pioneer of the American animal welfare societies, was asked to do something about a little animal that had been cruelly beaten. The little animal turned out to be a human child; nevertheless Bergh successfully prosecuted the child's custodian for cruelty to an animal, under a New York animal protection statute that he had drafted and bullied the legislature into passing. Further cases were then brought, and the New York Society for the Prevention of Cruelty to Children was set up. When the news reached Britain, the RSPCA set up a British counterpart—the National Society for the Prevention of Cruelty to Children.[11] Lord Shaftesbury was one of the founders of this group; as a leading social reformer,

author of the Factory Acts that put an end to child labor
and fourteen-hour work days, and a notable campaigner
against uncontrolled experimentation and other forms of
cruelty to animals, Shaftesbury's life, like that of many
other humanitarians, clearly refutes the idea that those
who care about nonhumans do not care about humans, or
that working for one cause makes it impossible to work
for the other.

Our conceptions of the nature of nonhuman animals,
and faulty reasoning about the implications that follow
from our conception of nature, form another buttress to
our speciesist attitudes. We have always liked to think ourselves less savage than the other animals. To say that a
person is "humane" is to say that he is kind; to say that
he is "a beast," "brutal," or simply that he behaves "like
an animal" is to suggest that he is cruel and nasty. We rarely stop to consider that the animal that kills with the least
reason to do so is the human animal. We think of lions
and wolves as savage because they kill; but they must kill,
or starve. Humans kill other animals for sport, to satisfy
their curiosity, to beautify their bodies, and to please their
palates. Human beings also kill members of their own
species for greed or power. Moreover humans are not content with mere killing. Throughout history they have shown
a tendency to torment and torture both their fellow-humans
and their fellow-animals before putting them to death. No
other animal shows much interest in doing this.

While we overlook our own savagery, we exaggerate
that of other animals. The notorious wolf, for instance,
villain of so many folk tales, has been shown by the careful
investigations of zoologists in the wild to be a highly social
animal, a faithful and affectionate spouse—not just for a
season, but for life—a devoted parent, and a loyal member
of the pack. Wolves almost never kill anything except to
eat it. If males should fight among themselves, the fight
ends with a gesture of submission in which the loser offers
to his conqueror the underside of his neck—the most vul-
nerable part of his body. With his fangs only an inch away
from the jugular vein of his foe, the victor will be content

with submission, and, unlike a human conqueror, does not kill the vanquished opponent.[12]

In keeping with our picture of the world of animals as a bloody scene of combat, we ignore the extent to which other species exhibit a complex social life, recognizing and relating to other members of their species as individuals. When human beings marry, we attribute their closeness to each other to love, and we feel keenly for a human being who has lost his or her spouse. When other animals pair for life, we say that it is just instinct that makes them do so, and if a hunter or trapper kills an animal or captures it for research, or for a zoo, we do not consider that it might have a spouse who will suffer from its sudden absence. In a similar way we know that to part a human mother from her child is tragic for both; but neither the farmer nor the breeder of pets and research animals gives any thought to the feelings of the nonhuman mothers and children whom he routinely separates as part of his business.[13]

Curiously, while people often dismiss complex aspects of animal behavior as "mere instinct," and therefore not worthy of comparison with the apparently similar behavior of human beings, these same people will also ignore or overlook the importance of simple instinctive patterns of behavior when it is convenient for them to do so. Thus it is often said of laying hens, veal calves, and dogs kept in cages for experimental purposes that this does not cause them to suffer since they have never known other conditions. We saw in Chapter 3 that this is a fallacy. Animals feel a need to exercise, stretch their limbs or wings, groom themselves, and turn around, whether or not they have ever lived in conditions that permit this. Herd or flock animals are disturbed when they are isolated from others of their species, though they may never have known other conditions, and too large a herd or flock can have the same effect through the inability of the individual animal to recognize other individuals. These stresses reveal themselves in "vices" like cannibalism.

Widespread ignorance of the nature of nonhuman animals allows those who treat animals in this manner to brush off criticism by saying that, after all, "they're not human." Indeed, they are not; but neither are they machines for converting fodder into flesh, or tools for research. Considering how far the knowledge of the general public lags behind the most recent findings of zoologists and ethologists who have spent months and sometimes years observing animals with notebook and camera, the dangers of sentimental anthropomorphism are less serious than the opposite danger of the convenient and self-serving idea that animals are lumps of clay which we can mold in whatever manner we please.

The nature of nonhuman animals serves as a basis for other attempts to justify our treatment of them. It is often said, as an objection to vegetarianism, that since other animals kill for food, we may do so too. This analogy was already old when William Paley, in 1785, refuted it by reference to the fact that while humans can live without killing, other animals have no choice but to kill if they are to survive.[14] Perhaps this is an inadequate refutation; but it is important to realize that even if there are other animals that could live on a vegetarian diet, but do sometimes kill for food, this would provide no support for the claim that it is *morally* defensible for us to do the same. It is odd how humans, who normally consider themselves so far above other animals, will, if it seems to support their dietary preferences, use an argument that implies that we ought to look to other animals for moral inspiration and guidance! The point is, of course, that nonhuman animals are not capable of considering the alternatives, or of reflecting morally on the rights and wrongs of killing for food; they just do it. We may regret that this is the way the world is, but it makes no sense to hold nonhuman animals morally responsible or culpable for what they do. Every reader of this book, on the other hand, is capable of making a moral choice on this matter. We cannot evade our responsibility for our choice by imitating the actions of beings that are incapable of making this kind of choice.

(Now, someone is sure to say, I have admitted that there is a significant difference between humans and other animals, and thus I have revealed the flaw in my case for the equality of all animals. Anyone to whom this criticism has occurred should read Chapter 1 more carefully. He will then find that he has misunderstood the nature of the case for equality I made there. I have never made the absurd claim that there are no significant differences between normal adult humans and other animals. My point is not that animals are capable of acting morally, but that the moral principle of equal consideration of interests applies to them as it applies to humans. That it is often right to include within the sphere of equal consideration beings that are not themselves capable of making moral choices is implied by our treatment of young children and other humans who, for one reason or another, do not have the mental capacity to understand the nature of moral choice. As Bentham might have said, the point is not whether they can *choose*, but whether they can *suffer*.)

It must be admitted that the existence of carnivorous animals does pose one problem for the ethics of Animal Liberation, and that is whether we should do anything about it. Assuming that humans could eliminate carnivorous species from the earth, and that the total amount of suffering among animals in the world were thereby reduced, should we do it?

The short and simple answer is that once we give up our claim to "dominion" over the other species we have no right to interfere with them at all. We should leave them alone as much as we possibly can. Having given up the role of tyrant, we should not try to play Big Brother either.

Though it contains part of the truth, this answer is too short and simple. Like it or not, humans do know more than other animals about what may happen in the future, and this knowledge may put us in a situation in which it would be callous not to interfere. For instance, if a landslide blocks the exit to a valley, so that the valley begins to flood and animals are trapped by rising waters, human beings can and should put their knowledge to work in enabling the trapped animals to escape.

So it is conceivable that human interference will improve the conditions of animals, and so be justifiable. But when we consider a scheme like the elimination of carnivorous species, we are considering an entirely different matter. Judging by our past record, any attempt to change

ecological systems on a large scale is going to do far more
harm than good. For that reason, if for no other, it is true
to say that, except in a few very limited cases, we cannot
and should not try to police all of nature. We do enough
if we eliminate our own unnecessary killing and cruelty
toward other animals.*

There is yet another purported justification of our treatment of animals that relies on the fact that in their natural
state some animals kill other animals. People often say
that, bad as modern farm conditions are, they are no
worse than conditions in the wild, where animals are exposed to cold, hunger, and predators; and the implication
is that therefore we should not object to modern farm
conditions.

Interestingly, defenders of Negro slavery often made a
similar point. One of them wrote:

> On the whole, since it is evident beyond all contro-
> versy that the removal of the Africans, from the state
> of brutality, wretchedness and misery, in which they
> are at home so deeply involved, to this land of light,
> humanity and Christian knowledge, is to them so great
> a blessing; however faulty any individuals may have
> been in point of unnecessary cruelty, practised in this
> business; that, whether the general state of subordina-
> tion here, which is a necessary consequence of their
> removal, be agreeable to the law of nature, can by no
> means longer remain a question.[15]

Now it is difficult to compare two sets of conditions as
diverse as those of wild animals and those on a factory
farm (or of "wild" Negroes and those on a plantation);
but if the comparison has to be made surely the life of
freedom is to be preferred. Factory farm animals cannot

---

* Some people also ask: what should we do about our cats and
dogs? Though these animals have a better excuse for eating meat
than we do, some vegetarians are reluctant to buy meat at all, and
have tried to raise cats and dogs on a vegetarian diet. This is,
apparently, possible so long as you give the animal plenty of protein,
for example in the form of "textured" soybeans. Leaflets on vegetarian diets for cats and dogs are available from the British
Vegetarian Society, Altrincham, Cheshire, England.

walk, run, stretch freely, or be part of a family or herd. True, many wild animals die from adverse conditions or are killed by predators; but then animals kept in farms do not live for more than a fraction of their normal lifespan either. The steady supply of food on a farm is not an unmitigated blessing, since it deprives the animal of his most basic natural activity, the search for food. The result is a life of utter boredom, with nothing at all to do but lie in a stall and eat.

In any case, the comparison betwen factory farm conditions and natural conditions is really irrelevant to the justifiability of factory farms, since these are not the alternatives that we face. Abolishing factory farms would not mean returning the animals inside them to the wild. Animals in factory farms today were bred by humans to be raised in these farms and sold for food. If the boycott of factory farm produce advocated in this book is effective, it will reduce the amount of factory farm products that are bought. This does not mean that overnight we will go from the present situation to one in which no one buys these products. (I am optimistic about Animal Liberation, but not totally deluded.) The reduction will be gradual. It will make animal raising less profitable. Farmers will turn to other types of farming, and the giant corporations will invest their capital elsewhere. The result will be that fewer animals will be bred. The number of animals in factory farms will decline because those killed will not be replaced, and not because animals are being sent "back" to the wild. Eventually, perhaps (and now I am allowing my optimism free rein), the only herds of cattle and pigs to be found will be on large reservations, rather like our wildlife refuges. The choice, therefore, is not between life on a factory farm and life in the wild, but whether animals destined to live on factory farms and then be killed for food should be born at all.

At this point a further, somewhat bizarre objection may be raised. Noting that if we were all vegetarians there would be far fewer pigs, cattle, chickens, and sheep, a few meat-eaters have claimed that they are actually doing the animals they eat a favor, since but for their desire to eat meat, those animals would never have come into existence at all!

This defense of meat-eating—which could also be employed on behalf of experimentation—has a ludicrous air about it, but some of those who put it forward appear to be quite serious.[16] It could be refuted merely by pointing out that life for an animal in a modern factory farm is so devoid of any pleasure that this kind of existence is in no sense a benefit for the animal. Assuming that conditions were improved, however, so that the lives of the animals did have a slight positive balance of pleasure over pain, the objection would still be invalid. Its flaw lies in the implication that we confer a favor on a being by bringing it into existence, and that we thereby obtain a right to treat the being with less than equal consideration. A little thought will reveal the error in this reasoning. On whom do we confer the favor of existence? On the nonexistent animal, unborn and unconceived? But this is absurd. There are no such entities as nonexistent beings, waiting around in limbo for someone to bring them into existence. Once a being exists, we have an obligation to avoid making that being suffer unnecessarily, but we have no obligations to nonexistent beings. The very term "nonexistent being" is self-contradictory. Therefore we can neither benefit nor harm a nonexistent being. (The only qualification required is that we can benefit or harm beings who will exist in the future, which is why it is wrong to damage the earth's environment, even when the effects of the damage will not be apparent for fifty years.) Someone may say: it is on the pig, when born, that the benefit of existence has been conferred. But once the pig is born, it is too late to confer this particular favor, so this does not help us. Moreover if to bring a being into existence is to benefit it, then presumably to decide not to bring a being into existence is to harm it. But there is no "it" to be harmed by this decision. In this area it is easy to talk nonsense without realizing it.

Nonsense apart, those who use this ingenious defense of their desire to eat pork or beef rarely follow out its implications. If it were good to bring beings into existence then presumably, other things being equal, we ought to

bring as many humans as possible into existence too; and
if to this we add the view that human lives are more important than the lives of animals—a view the flesh-eater
seems sure to accept—then the argument may be turned
on its head, to the discomfort of its original proponent.
Since more humans may be fed if we do not feed our
grain to livestock, the upshot of the argument is, after all,
that we ought to become vegetarians!

Finally, so far as this particular argument is concerned,
if the fact that we have brought an animal into existence
entitled us to use it for our own ends, the same principle
should apply to humans. Jonathan Swift once made an
ironic proposal that we fatten the babies of poor Irish
women for the table, since, he assures us, "a young healthy
child, well nursed, is at a year old, a most delicious, nourishing and wholesome food; whether stewed, roasted,
baked or boiled."[17] Swift's idea was not that the babies
would not otherwise have been born, but that since their
mothers were too poor to care for them, they would lead
miserable lives as beggars on the street, and that a single
year with ample food and comfort was preferable to that
life; but we can alter the proposal so that the women are
paid to breed extra children for the gourmet's table. Then,
if these children had a pleasant year before being humanely slaughtered, it would seem that the gourmet who wished
to dine on roast human child would have as good a defense
of his practice as those who claim that they are entitled to
eat pork because the pig would not otherwise have existed.
George Bernard Shaw once described the meat-eater's diet
as "cannibalism with its heroic dish omitted," and it should
be obvious that there is a point to the remark.[18] If, for
some reason, we do not consider Swift's proposal morally
acceptable, we should also reject the parallel defense of
killing nonhuman animals that have been bred to be raised
for food.

Speciesism is so pervasive and widespread an attitude
that those who attack one or two of its manifestations—
like the slaughter of wild animals by hunters, or cruel experimentation, or bull-fighting—often participate in other
speciesist practices themselves. This allows those attacked

to accuse their opponents of inconsistency. "You say we are cruel because we shoot deer," the hunters say, "but you eat meat. What is the difference, except that you pay someone else to do the killing for you?" "You object to killing animals to clothe ourselves in their skins," say the furriers, "but you are wearing a suede jacket and leather shoes." The experimenter plausibly asks why, if people accept the killing of animals to please their palates, they should object to the killing of animals to advance knowledge; and if the objection is just to suffering, he can point out that animals killed for food do not live without suffering either. Even the bull-fight enthusiast can argue that the death of the bull in the ring gives pleasure to thousands of spectators, while the death of the steer in a slaughterhouse gives pleasure only to the few people who eat some part of it; and while in the end the bull may suffer more acute pain than the steer, for most of his life it is the bull who is better treated.

The charge of inconsistency really gives no logical support to the defenders of cruel practices. As Brigid Brophy has put it, it remains true that it is cruel to break people's legs, even if the statement is made by someone in the habit of breaking people's arms.[19] Yet someone whose conduct is inconsistent with his professed beliefs will find it difficult to persuade others that his beliefs are right; and he will find it even more difficult to persuade others to act on those beliefs. Of course, it is always possible to find some reason for distinguishing between, say, wearing furs and wearing leather—many fur-bearing animals die only after hours or even days spent with a leg caught in a steel-toothed trap, while the animals from whose skins leather is made are spared this agony.[20] There is a tendency, however, for these fine distinctions to blunt the force of the original criticism; and there are some cases where I do not think distinctions can validly be drawn at all. Why, for instance, is the hunter who shoots wild ducks for his supper subject to more criticism than the person who buys a chicken at the supermarket? Over-all, it is probably the intensively reared bird who has suffered more.

The first chapter of this book sets out a clear ethical principle by which we can determine which of our prac-

tices affecting nonhuman animals are justifiable and which
are not. By applying this principle to our own lives we can
make our actions fully consistent. Thus we can deny to
those who ignore the interests of animals the opportunity
to charge us with inconsistency.

For reasons spelled out often enough in this book, following the principle of equal consideration of interests requires us to be vegetarians. This is the most important
step, and the one to which I have given most attention;
but we should also, to be consistent, stop using other animal products for which animals have been killed or made
to suffer. We should not wear furs. We should not buy
leather products either, since the sale of hides for leather
plays a significant role in the profitability of the meat
industry.

For the pioneer vegetarians of the nineteenth century,
giving up leather meant a real sacrifice, since shoes and
boots made of other materials were scarce. Lewis Gompertz, the second secretary of the RSPCA and a strict
vegetarian who even refused to ride in horse-drawn ve-
hicles, suggested that animals should be reared in pastures
and allowed to grow old and die a natural death, after
which their skins would be used for leather.[21] The idea is
a tribute to Gompertz's humanity rather than his economics, but today the economics are on the other foot. Shoes
and boots made of plastic and other synthetic materials
are now available in many cheaper stores, at prices considerably lower than those for leather shoes; and canvas
sneakers are now almost the standard footwear for American youth. Belts, bags, and other goods once made of
leather are now easily found in other materials.

Other problems that once daunted the most advanced
opponents of the exploitation of animals have also disappeared. Candles, once made only of tallow, are no longer
indispensable, and can, for those who still want them, be
obtained in nonanimal materials. Soaps made from vegetable oils rather than animal fats are obtainable from
health food stores. We could do without wool, if we wanted
to, though since the sheep is not killed for its fleece, and
is allowed to roam freely, perhaps this is not a major
issue.[22] Cosmetics and perfumes, often made from wild

animals like the musk deer and the Ethiopian civet cat, are hardly an essential item anyway, but those who wish to wear them can obtain animal-free cosmetics from an organization called Beauty Without Cruelty.[23]

Although I mention these alternatives to animal products to show that it is not difficult to refuse to participate in the major areas of exploitation of animals, I do not believe that consistency is the same as, or implies, a rigid insistence on standards of absolute purity in all that one consumes or wears. The point of altering one's buying habits is not to keep oneself untouched by evil, but to reduce the economic support for the exploitation of animals, and to persuade others to do the same. So it is not a sin to continue to wear leather shoes you bought before you began to think about Animal Liberation. When your leather shoes wear out, buy nonleather ones; but you will not reduce the profitability of killing animals by throwing out your present ones. With diet, too, it is more important to remember the major aims than to worry about such details as whether the cake you are offered at a party was made with a factory farm egg.

We are still a long way from the point at which it is possible to put pressure on restaurants and food manufacturers to eliminate animal products altogether. That point will come when a significant section of the population is boycotting meat and other factory farm products. Until then consistency demands only that we do not contribute *significantly* to the demand for animal products. Thus we can demonstrate that we have no need of animal products. We are more likely to persuade others to share our attitude if we temper our ideals with common sense than if we strive for the kind of purity that is more appropriate to a religious dietary law than to an ethical and political movement.

Usually it is not too difficult to be consistent in one's attitudes to animals. We do not have to sacrifice anything essential, because in our normal life there is no serious clash of interests between human and nonhuman animals. It must be admitted, though, that it is possible to think of more unusual cases in which there is a genuine clash of interests. For instance, we need to grow crops of vegetables and grain to feed ourselves; but these crops may be threatened by rabbits, mice, or other "pests." Here we have a clear conflict of interest between humans and nonhumans. What would be done about it, if we were to act in accordance with the principle of equal consideration of interests?

First let us note what is done about this situation now. The farmer will seek to kill off the "pests" by the cheapest method available. This is likely to be poison. The animals will eat poisoned baits, and die a slow, painful death. The poison will remain in the environment, spreading into the water or soil. No consideration at all is given to the interests of the "pest"—the very word "pest" seems to exclude any concern for the animal itself.[24] But the classification "pest" is our own, and a rabbit that is a pest is as capable of suffering, and as deserving of consideration, as the cutest white rabbit in a pet store. The problem is how to defend our own essential food supplies while respecting the interests of these animals to the greatest extent possible. It should not be beyond our technological abilities to find a solution to this problem which, if not totally satisfactory to all concerned, at least causes far less suffering than the present "solution." The use of baits which cause sterility, instead of a lingering death, would be an obvious improvement.

When we have to defend our food supplies against rabbits, or our houses and our health against mice and rats, it is as natural for us to lash out violently at the animals that invade our property as it is for the animals themselves to seek food where they can find it. At the present stage of our attitudes to animals, it would be absurd to expect people to change their conduct in this respect. Perhaps in time, however, when more major abuses have been remedied, and attitudes to animals have changed, people will come to see that even animals which are in some sense "threatening" our welfare do not deserve the cruel deaths we inflict upon them; and so we may eventually develop more humane methods of limiting the numbers of those species whose interests are genuinely incompatible with our own.

A similar reply may be given to those hunters and controllers of what are misleadingly called "wildlife refuges" who claim that to prevent overpopulation by deer, seals, or whatever the animal in question may be, hunters must periodically be allowed to "harvest" the excess population —this allegedly being in the interests of the animals themselves. The use of the term "harvest"—often found in the publications of the hunters' organizations—gives the lie to the claim that this slaughter is motivated by concern for the animals. The term indicates that the hunter thinks of deer or seals as if they were corn or coal, objects of interest only in so far as they serve human interests. This attitude, which is shared to a large extent by the US Fish and Wildlife Service, overlooks the vital fact that deer and other hunted animals are capable of feeling pleasure and pain. They are therefore not means to our ends, but beings with interests of their own. If it is true that in special circumstances their population grows to such an extent that they damage their own environment and the prospects of their own survival, or that of other animals who share their habitat, then it may be right for humans to take some supervisory action; but obviously if we consider the interests of the animals, this action will not be to let hunters go in, killing and wounding the animals, but rather to reduce the fertility of the animals. If we made an effort to develop more humane methods of population control for wild animals in reserves, it would not be difficult to come up with something better than what is done now. The trouble is that the authorities responsible for wildlife have a "harvest" mentality, and are not interested in finding techniques of population control which would reduce the number of animals to be "harvested" by hunters.

I have said that the difference between animals like deer —or pigs and chickens for that matter—which we ought not to think of in "harvesting" terms, and crops like corn which we may harvest, is that the animals are capable of feeling pleasure and pain, while the plants are not. At this point another common objection may be raised: "How do we know that plants do not suffer?"

This objection may arise from a genuine concern for plants; but more often the objector does not seriously contemplate extending consideration to plants if it should be shown that they suffer; instead he hopes to show that if we were to act on the principle I have advocated we would have to stop eating plants as well as animals, and so would starve to death. The conclusion he draws is that if it is impossible to live without violating the principle of equal consideration, we need not bother about it at all, but may go on as we have always been doing, eating plants and animals.

The objection is weak in both fact and logic. There is no reliable evidence that plants are capable of feeling pleasure or pain. Although a recent popular book, *The Secret Life of Plants*, claimed that plants have all sorts of remarkable abilities, including the ability to read people's minds, the most striking experiments cited in the book were not carried out at serious research institutions, and more recent attempts by researchers in major universities to repeat the experiments have failed to obtain any positive results. These failures are explained by those who made the original startling claims as a result of the fact that only those "in tune" with the psychic properties of the plants can get the plants to perform, but as Arthur Galston, a biologist at Yale University, has said of the experiments made by Cleve Backster and his lie detector machine:

> What do you want to believe—results that are obtained when carefully described experiments are repeated by competent investigators anywhere in the world, or results that can be obtained only by a select few in "special contact" with their test material?[25]

In the first chapter of this book I gave three distinct grounds for believing that nonhuman animals can feel pain: behavior, the nature of their nervous systems, and the evolutionary usefulness of pain. None of these gives us any reason to believe that plants feel pain. In the absence of scientifically credible experimental findings, there is no observable behavior that suggests pain; nothing resembling a central nervous system has been found in plants; and it is difficult to imagine why species that are incapable of moving away from a source of pain or using the perception of pain to avoid death in any other way should have evolved the capacity to feel pain. Therefore the belief that plants feel pain appears to be quite unjustified.

So much for the factual basis of this objection. Now let us consider its logic. Assume that, improbable as it seems, researchers do turn up evidence suggesting that plants feel pain. It would still not follow that we may as well eat what we have always eaten. If we must inflict pain or starve, we would then have to choose the lesser evil. Presumably it would still be true that plants suffer less than animals, and therefore it would still be better to eat plants than to eat animals. Indeed this conclusion would follow even if plants were as sensitive as animals, since the inefficiency of meat production means that those who eat meat are responsible for the indirect destruction of at least ten times as many plants as are vegetarians! At this point, I admit, the argument becomes farcical, and I have pursued it this far only to show that those who raise this objection but fail to follow out its implications are really just looking for an excuse to go on eating meat.

Up to this point we have been examining, in this chapter, attitudes that are shared by many people in Western societies, and the strategies and arguments that are commonly used to defend these attitudes. We have seen that from a logical point of view these strategies and arguments are very weak. They are rationalizations and excuses rather than arguments. It might be thought, however, that their weakness is due to some lack of expertise that ordinary people have in discussing ethical questions. It may be interesting, therefore, to consider what contemporary philosophers, who have made a special study of ethics and moral reasoning, have to say about our relations with nonhuman animals.

Philosophy ought to question the basic assumptions of the age. Thinking through, critically and carefully, what most of us take for granted is, I believe, the chief task of philosophy, and the task that makes philosophy a worthwhile activity. Regrettably, philosophy does not always live up to its historic role. Aristotle's defense of slavery will always stand as a reminder that philosophers are human beings and are subject to all the preconceptions of the society to which they belong. Sometimes they succeed in breaking free of the prevailing ideology: more often they become its most sophisticated defenders. So it is in this case. Philosophy, as practiced in our universities today, does not challenge anyone's preconceptions about our relations with other species. By their writings, most philosophers who tackle problems that touch upon the issue reveal that they make the same unquestioned assumptions as most other human beings, and what they say tends to confirm the reader in his comfortable speciesist habits.

To see this, let us look at what contemporary philosophers have said about the topic I discussed in the first chapter of this book, the problem of equality, and the related problem of what beings have rights.

It is significant that discussions of equality and rights in moral and political philosophy are almost always formulated as problems of human equality and human rights. The effect of this is that the issue of the equality of animals never confronts the philosopher or his students as an issue in itself—and this is already an indication of the failure of philosophy to challenge accepted beliefs. Still, philosophers have found it difficult to discuss the issue of human equality without raising questions about the status of nonhumans. The reason for this—which may already be apparent from what I said in the first chapter—has to do with the way in which the principle of equality must be interpreted and defended, if it is to be defended at all.

Very few philosophers today are prepared to support rigidly elitist and hierarchic political arrangements. Overt racists or believers in the rights of a natural aristocracy are hardly ever encountered in the pages of philosophy journals. The dominant tone of contemporary philosophy favors the idea that all human beings are equal. The problem is how to interpret this slogan in a manner that does not make it plainly false. In most ways, humans are not equal; and if we seek some characteristic that all of them possess then this characteristic must be a kind of lowest common denominator, pitched so low that no human lacks this characteristic. The catch is that any such characteristic that is possessed by *all* human beings will not be possessed *only* by human beings. For example all humans, but not only humans, are capable of feeling pain; and while only humans are capable of solving complex mathematical problems, not all humans can do this. So it turns out that in the only sense in which we can truly say, as an assertion of fact, that all humans are equal, at least some members of other species are also "equal"—equal, that is, to some humans.

If, on the other hand, we decide that, as I argued in Chapter 1, these characteristics are really irrelevant to the problem of equality, and equality must be based on the moral principle of equal consideration of interests rather than on the possession of some characteristic, it is even more difficult to find some basis for excluding animals from the sphere of equality.

This result is not what the egalitarian philosopher originally intended to assert. Instead of accepting the outcome to which their own reasonings naturally point, however, most philosophers try to reconcile their beliefs in human equality and animal inequality by arguments that can only be described as devious.

As a first example, consider the following quotation from an article by William Frankena, a well-known professor of philosophy who teaches at the University of Michigan.

> . . . all men are to be treated as equals, not because they are equal, in any respect but simply because they are human. They are human because they have emotions and desires and are able to think and hence are capable of enjoying a good life in a sense in which other animals are not.[26]

But what is this capacity to enjoy the good life which all humans have but other animals do not? Surely every sentient being is capable of leading a life that is happier or less miserable than some other possible life, and therefore has a claim to be taken into account. In this respect the distinction between humans and other animals is not a sharp division but rather a continuum along which we move gradually and with overlaps between the species, from simple capacities for enjoyment and satisfaction to more complex ones.

Another philosopher who has been prominent in recent philosophical discussions of equality, this time arguing in terms of rights, is Richard Wasserstrom, professor of philosophy and law at the University of California, Los Angeles. In his article "Rights, Human Rights and Racial Discrimination," Wasserstrom defines "human rights" as those rights that humans have and nonhumans do not have. He then argues that there are human rights to well-being and to freedom. In defending the idea of a human right to well-being, Wasserstrom says that to deny someone relief from acute physical pain makes it impossible for that person to live a full or satisfying life. He then goes on: "In a real sense, the enjoyment of these goods differentiates human from nonhuman entities."[27] But this statement is incredible, for when we look back to find what the expression "these goods" is supposed to refer to, we find that the *only* example we have been given is relief from acute physical pain—and this, surely, is something that nonhumans may appreciate as well as humans. So if human beings have a right to relief from acute physical pain, it is not a specifically human right, in Wasserstrom's sense. Animals would have it too.

Faced with a situation in which they see a need for some basis for the moral gulf that is commonly thought to separate humans and animals, but can find no concrete difference that will do this without undermining the equality of humans, philosophers tend to waffle. They resort to high-sounding phrases like "the intrinsic dignity of the human individual."[28] They talk of "the intrinsic worth of all men" as if men had some worth that other beings do not have[29] or they say that human beings, and only human beings, are "ends in themselves" while "everything other than a person can only have value for a person."[30]

As we saw in the preceding chapter, the idea of a distinctive human dignity and worth has a long history. Contemporary philosophers have cast off its original metaphysical and religious shackles, and freely invoke the idea of human dignity without feeling any need to justify the idea at all. Why should we not attribute "intrinsic dignity" or "intrinsic worth" to ourselves? Why should we not say that we are the only things in the universe that have intrinsic value? Our fellow human beings are unlikely to reject the accolades we so generously bestow upon them, and those to whom we deny the honor are unable to object. Indeed, when we think only of humans it can be very liberal, very progressive, to talk of the dignity of all human beings. In so doing we implicitly condemn slavery, racism, and other violations of human rights. We admit that we ourselves are in some fundamental sense on a par with the poorest, most ignorant members of our own species. It is only when we think of human beings as no more than a small subgroup of all the beings that inhabit our planet that we may realize that in elevating our own species we are at the same time lowering the relative status of all other species.

The truth is that the appeal to the intrinsic dignity of human beings appears to solve the egalitarian philosopher's problems only as long as it goes unchallenged. Once we ask *why* it should be that all humans—including infants, mental defectives, criminal psychopaths, Hitler, Stalin, and the rest—have some kind of dignity or worth that no elephant, pig, or chimpanzee can ever achieve, we see that this question is as difficult to answer as our original request for some relevant fact that justifies the inequality of humans and other animals. In fact, these two questions are really one: talk of intrinsic dignity or moral worth does not help, because any satisfactory defense of the claim that all and only humans have intrinsic dignity would need to refer to some relevant capacities or characteristics that only human beings have, in virtue of which they have this unique dignity or worth. To introduce ideas of dignity and worth as a substitute for other reasons for distinguishing humans and animals is not good enough. Fine phrases are the last resource of those who have run out of arguments.

In case anyone still thinks it may be possible to find some relevant characteristic that distinguishes all humans from all members of other species, let us consider again the fact that there are some humans who quite clearly are below the level of awareness, self-consciousness, intelligence, and sentience of many nonhumans. I am thinking of humans with severe and irreparable brain damage, and also of infant humans; to avoid the complication of the potential of infants, however, I shall concentrate on permanently retarded humans.

Philosophers who set out to find a characteristic that will distinguish humans from other animals rarely take the course of abandoning these groups of humans by lumping them in with other animals. It is easy to see why they do not; to take this line without rethinking our attitudes to other animals would mean we have the right to perform painful experiments on retarded humans for trivial reasons; similarly it would follow that we had the right to rear and kill them for food.

For philosophers discussing the problem of equality, the easiest way out of the difficulty posed by the existence of mentally defective humans beings is to ignore it. The Harvard philosopher John Rawls, in his long book *A Theory of Justice*, comes up against this problem when trying to explain why we owe justice to humans but not to other animals, but he brushes it aside with the remark: "I cannot examine this problem here, but I assume that the account of equality would not be materially affected."[31] This is an extraordinary way of handling an issue which would appear to imply either that we may treat mental defectives as we now treat animals, or that, contrary to Rawls's own statements, we do owe justice to animals.

What else can the philosopher do? If he honestly confronts the problem posed by the existence of humans with no morally relevant characteristics not also possessed by nonhumans, it seems impossible to cling to the equality of human beings, without suggesting a radical revision in the status of nonhumans. In a desperate attempt to save the usually accepted views, it has even been argued that we should treat beings according to what is "normal for the species" rather than according to their actual characteristics.[32] To see how outrageous this is, imagine that at some future date evidence were to be found that, even in the absence of any cultural conditioning, it was normal for more females than males in a society to stay at home looking after the children instead of going out to work.

This finding would, of course, be perfectly compatible with the obvious fact that there are some women who are less well suited to looking after children, and better suited to going out to work, than some men. Would any philosopher then claim that these exceptional women should be treated in accordance with what is "normal for the sex"—and therefore, say, not be admitted to medical school—rather than in accordance with their actual characteristics? I do not think so. I find it hard to see anything in this argument except a defense of preferring the interests of members of our own species because they are members of our own species.

Like the other philosophical arguments we have examined, this one stands as a warning of the ease with which not only ordinary people, but also those most skilled in moral reasoning, can fall victim to a prevailing ideology.

The core of this book is the claim that to discriminate against beings solely on account of their species is a form of prejudice, immoral and indefensible in the same way that discrimination on the basis of race is immoral and indefensible. I have not been content to put forward this claim as a bare assertion, or as a statement of my own personal view, which others may or may not choose to accept. I have *argued* for it, appealing to reason rather than to emotion or sentiment. I have chosen this path, not because I am unaware of the importance of kind feelings and sentiments of respect toward other creatures, but because reason is more universal and more compelling in its appeal. Greatly as I admire those who have eliminated speciesism from their lives purely because their sympathetic concern for others reaches out to all sentient creatures, I do not think that an appeal to sympathy and good-heartedness alone will convince most people of the wrongness of speciesism. Even where other human beings are concerned, people are surprisingly good at limiting their sympathies to those of their own nation or race. Almost everyone, however, is at least nominally prepared to listen to reason. Admittedly, there are some who flirt with an excessive subjectivism in morality, saying that any morality is as good as any other; but when these same people are pressed to say if they think the morality of Hitler, or of the slave traders, is as good as the morality of Albert Schweitzer or Martin Luther King, they find that, after all, they believe some moralities are better than others.

So throughout this book I have relied on rational argument. Unless you can refute the central argument of this book, you must now recognize that speciesism is wrong, and this means that, if you take morality seriously, you must try to eliminate speciesist practices from your own life, and oppose them elsewhere. Otherwise no basis remains from which you can, without hypocrisy, criticize racism or sexism.

I have generally avoided arguing that we ought to be kind to animals because cruelty to animals leads to cruelty to humans. Perhaps it is true that kindness to humans and to other animals often go together; but whether or not this is true, to say, as Aquinas and Kant did, that this is the real reason why we ought to be kind to animals is a thoroughly speciesist position. We ought to consider the interests of animals because they have interests and it is unjustifiable to exclude them from the sphere of moral concern; to make this consideration depend on beneficial consequences for humans is to accept the implication that the interests of animals do not warrant consideration for their own sakes.

Similarly, I have avoided an extensive discussion of whether a vegetarian diet is healthier than a diet that includes animal flesh. There is a good deal of evidence to suggest that it is, but I have contented myself with showin that a vegetarian can expect to be at least as healthy as one who eats meat. Once one goes beyond this it is difficult to avoid giving the impression that if further studies should show that a diet containing flesh is acceptable from the point of view of health, then the case for becoming a vegetarian collapses. From the standpoint of Animal Liberation, however, so long as we can live without inflicting suffering on animals, that is what we ought to do.

I believe that the case for Animal Liberation is logically cogent, and cannot be refuted; but the task of overthrowing speciesism in practice is a formidable one. We have seen that speciesism has historical roots that go deep into

the consciousness of Western society. We have seen that
the elimination of speciesist practices would threaten the
vested interests of the giant agribusiness corporations, and
the professional associations of research workers and vet-
terinarians. Should it appear necessary, these corporations
and organizations would be prepared to spend millions of
dollars in defense of their interests, and the public would
be bombarded with advertisements denying allegations of
cruelty. Moreover the public has—or thinks it has—an interest in the continuance of the speciesist practice of raising and killing animals for food and this makes people
ready to accept reassurances that, in this area at least,
there is little cruelty. As we have seen, people are also
ready to accept fallacious forms of reasoning, of the type
we have examined in this chapter, which they would never
entertain for a moment were it not for the fact that these
fallacies appear to justify their preferred diet.

Against these ancient prejudices, powerful vested interests, and ingrained habits, does the Animal Liberation
movement have any chance at all? Other than reason and
morality, does it have anything in its favor? Difficult as it
is to take any consolation from the threat of world-wide
famine, the food crisis has made us more conscious of the
inefficiency of animal production as a method of feeding
people. It is possible that out of this terrible crisis a more
rational and humane diet will emerge.

The environmental movement, itself the result of another crisis, has led people to think about our relations
with other animals in a way that seemed impossible only
a decade ago. To date environmentalists have been more
concerned with wildlife and endangered species than with
animals in general, but it is not too big a jump from the
thought that it is wrong to treat whales as giant vessels
filled with oil and blubber to the thought that it is wrong
to treat pigs as machines for converting grains to flesh.

These factors are a ground for hope in the future of the
Animal Liberation movement. No doubt in the early days of
the movement for the abolition of slavery, prospects looked
just as bleak. Nevertheless, Animal Liberation will require
greater altruism on the part of human beings than any
other liberation movement. The animals themselves are in-

capable of demanding their own liberation, or of protesting against their condition with votes, demonstrations, or bombs. Human beings have the power to continue to oppress other species forever, or until we make this planet unsuitable for living beings. Will our tyranny continue, proving that we really are the selfish tyrants that the most cynical of poets and philosophers have always said we are? Or will we rise to the challenge and prove our capacity for genuine altruism by ending our ruthless exploitation of the species in our power, not because we are forced to do so by rebels or terrorists, but because we recognize that our position is morally indefensible?

The way in which we answer this question depends on the way in which each one of us, individually, answers it.

NOTES

1. Dean Walley and Frieda Staake, *Farm Animals* (Kansas City: Hallmark Children's Editions, no date).

2. M. E. Gagg and C. F. Tunnicliffe, *The Farm* (Loughborough, England: Ladybird Books, 1958).

3. W. I. Gay, ed., *Methods of Animal Experimentation* (New York: Academic Press, 1965), p. 191; quoted in Richard Ryder, *Victims of Science* (London: Davis-Poynter, 1974).

4. Bernard Grzimek, "Gequaelte Tiere: Unglueck fuer die Landwirtschaft," in *Das Tier* (Bern, Switzerland), special supplement.

5. *Daily News*, 1 September 1971.

6. Animal Welfare Institute, *Information Report*, vol. 23, no. 3 (July-September 1974). For a statement of the aim of the ICLA, see *ICLA Constitution and Aims* (ICLA Secretariat, Oslo, 1972); see also the introduction to M. L. Conalty, ed., *Husbandry of Laboratory Animals*, Proceedings of the Third ICLA International Symposium (New York: Academic Press, 1967).

7. See the *National Humane Review*, published by the American Humane Association, November 1974, pp. 3, 4.

8. E. S. Turner, *All Heaven in a Rage* (London: Michael Joseph, 1964), p. 129.

9. Ibid., p. 83.

10. Gerald Carson, *Cornflake Crusade* (New York: Rinehart and Co., 1957), pp. 19, 53-62.

11. Turner, *All Heaven in a Rage*, pp. 234-235; Gerald Carson, *Men, Beasts and Gods* (New York: Charles Scribner's Sons, 1972), p. 103.

12. See Farley Mowat, *Never Cry Wolf* (Boston: Atlantic Monthly Press, 1963), and Konrad Lorenz, *King Solomon's Ring* (London: Methuen, 1964), pp. 186-189. I owe the first reference to Mary Midgley, "The Concept of Beastliness: Philosophy, Ethics and Animal Behavior," *Philosophy*, vol. 48 (1973), p. 114.

13. See, in addition to the references in footnote 12, works by Niko Tinbergen, Jane van Lawick-Goodall, George Schaller, and Irenäus Eibl-Eibesfeldt.

14. See page 216, above.

15. "On the Legality of Enslaving the Africans," by a Harvard Student; quoted in Louis Ruchames, *Racial Thought in America* (Amherst, Mass.: University of Massachusetts Press, 1969), pp. 154-156.

16. H. S. Salt, in *The Humanities of Diet* (Manchester: The Vegetarian Society, 1914), p. 35, cites Leslie Stephen's *Social Rights*

and Duties and D. G. Ritchie's *Natural Rights* as places in which this argument is to be found. My own objections to the argument are similar to those of Salt.

17. Jonathan Swift, *A Modest Proposal for Preventing the Children of Poor People from Becoming a Burden to Their Parents and Country* (first published in 1729).

18. Hesketh Pearson, *G. B. S.: A Full-Length Portrait* (New York, 1942), p. 48.

19. Brigid Brophy, "In Pursuit of a Fantasy," in S. and R. Godlovitch and J. Harris, eds., *Animals, Men and Morals* (New York: Taplinger Publishing Co., 1972), p. 132.

20. See Cleveland Amory, *Man Kind?* (New York: Harper & Row, 1974), p. 237.

21. Lewis Gompertz, *Moral Inquiries on the Situation of Man and of Brutes* (London, 1824).

22. Although the annual shearing process does appear to be a terrifying one for the sheep, and sheep farmers are responsible for poisoning a lot of wildlife, especially coyotes. See J. Olsen, *Slaughter the Animals, Poison the Earth* (New York: Simon & Schuster, 1971).

23. For the address, see Appendix 3.

24. For examples of how brutal and painful the killing of "pests" can be, see *Slaughter the Animals, Poison the Earth*, pp. 153-164.

25. *Natural History*, 83 (3) p. 18 (March 1974).

26. In R. Brandt, ed., *Social Justice* (New York: Prentice-Hall, 1962), p. 19.

27. In A. I. Melden, ed., *Human Rights* (Belmont, Cal.: Wadsworth, 1970), p. 106.

28. Frankena, in *Social Justice*, p. 23.

29. H. A. Bedau, "Egalitarianism and the Idea of Equality," in *Nomos IX: Equality*, ed. J. R. Pennock and J. W. Chapman (New York, 1967).

30. G. Vlastos, "Justice and Equality," in *Social Justice*, p. 48.

31. J. Rawls, *A Theory of Justice* (Cambridge: Harvard University Press, Belknap Press, 1972), p. 510. For another example, see Bernard Williams, "The Idea of Equality," in *Philosophy, Politics and Society* (second series), ed. P. Laslett and W. Runciman (Oxford: Blackwell, 1962), p. 118.

32. For an example, see Stanley Benn's "Egalitarianism and Equal Consideration of Interests," *Nomos IX: Equality*, pp. 62ff.

APPENDIX 1.

Cooking for Liberated People

The following pages are intended to help you start to make the ideas expressed in this book part of your everyday practice. They are not a substitute for a good vegetarian cookbook (some of which are listed at the end of this section), but they may ease the transition to vegetarianism.

Because most people have only a limited amount of time for cooking, most of the recipes below are fairly simple to prepare. They are also economical, appetizing, and nutritious. Those who enjoy more elaborate cooking may start with these recipes and graduate to one of the vegetarian cookbooks I shall recommend.

Equipment

You don't really need any special equipment to cook vegetarian meals, but an electric blender or liquidizer will save you a lot of effort on soups and other dishes. A pressure cooker saves time and fuel, and eliminates the need to plan ahead when cooking beans, chickpeas, and other foods that would otherwise have to be soaked overnight before cooking; but it is not essential. A minor item that I find indispensable is a garlic press, but not everyone likes garlic as much as I do.

Shopping

You do need to get to know some new foods, and some new places to shop: this is half the fun of becoming a vegetarian. You should try to locate a health food shop—avoiding those which are overpriced—and ask the proprietor if the eggs they sell come from hens that have access to outside runs. (Check up if possible.) A health food shop will probably also stock the following items, uses for which will be suggested below: soybeans, lentils, chickpeas (garbanzos), mung beans, brown rice, millet, buckwheat, whole wheat berries, tahini, yeast extract, soy flour, and meat substitutes. Bear in mind that if you can get the same items at a supermarket or other grocery store they will probably be cheaper.

Next, find a Chinese or Indian specialty food store—if possible both. You will find them useful for many of the ingredients in the recipes that follow. If your city has a Chinese or Indian/Pakistani community, you are in luck, as the shops used by the community will probably be inexpensive, as well as fascinating to browse in and find new things to try.

Finally, many basic items of a vegetarian diet can be obtained through the Seventh Day Adventist Church, whose members are vegetarians. Look them up in the phone book and call to ask if they have a food store open to the general public. Usually they do, and for those with limited access to other sources they can be very helpful. They carry an especially wide range of meat substitutes.

Light Meals: Salads and Soups

You already know at least two kinds of food which are often vegetarian, and can serve as the basis for a nourishing light meal. In summer, salad and bread make an excellent lunch; and a really thick soup with bread serves the same purpose when the weather is colder.

The salad, of course, need not be lettuce and tomatoes. Use the following fresh raw vegetables: bean sprouts, peas, mushrooms, green pepper, avocado, cucumber, cabbage (red and white), celery, radishes. All of these go well with an oil and vinegar, or oil and lemon juice, dressing. Raw grated carrot is good with lemon juice and raisins. Add walnuts and dried fruits to salads. Sesame seeds, lightly roasted in a pan until they begin to turn brown, add flavor, protein, and calcium to salads. Experiment with salads using the following high-protein ingredients, which should be cooked and cooled first: red kidney beans, large white lima beans, soybeans, brown lentils, whole-wheat berries, chickpeas (garbanzos).

You probably know several recipes for bean and split pea soups, both of which are economical forms of protein. My favorite winter soup is *Austrian Lentil Soup*, made like this:

Soak ½ lb. brown lentils overnight (unnecessary if you use a pressure cooker, but you will then need more water). Slice an onion and a carrot, and fry in oil or margarine. Add the lentils, drained, together with 1 tbsp. flour and 1 large potato, peeled and chopped. Continue frying for a few minutes, then add 2½ pints water, flavor with salt, pepper, thyme, and 2 bay leaves. If you like the traditional flavor of a soup made from ham stock, add some imitation bacon bits (sold at many supermarkets). Simmer until the lentils are soft—about 1 hour. Mash the lentils, or put in blender, adjust the seasoning, add a tbsp. of lemon juice, and serve.

Incidentally this recipe, with about half the amount of water, and omitting the mashing, makes a thick lentil stew that can be served with rice or potatoes for a simple, peasant-style meal.

Some soup recipes in nonvegetarian cookbooks call for a meat stock. Health food stores sell vegetable stock cubes that can be used instead. Alternatively, use a teaspoon of Marmite or yeast extract for a beeflike stock, and imitation bacon bits for a ham or bacon stock.

Soups made from lentils, peas, or beans have plenty of protein, especially when eaten together with whole-wheat bread. Other soups, like tomato or potato soup, can be made more nourishing by adding 1–2 tbsp. of soy flour, which is one of the most concentrated and economical forms of protein you can buy. Unlike wheat or corn flour, it contains almost no starch, and so will not thicken a soup.

Iced soups are good for a hot day. With a blender they can be prepared in minutes. To make the famous Spanish cold soup, *Gazpacho*, for instance, roughly chop raw tomatoes (canned will do), cucumber, a spring onion, a green pepper, and a few black olives. Put everything in a blender, except for a few pieces to be floated in the soup afterward. Add 2 tbsp. olive oil, a lot of crushed garlic, 1 tbsp. vinegar, salt, pepper, a pinch of cayenne, marjoram, mint, and parsley. Blend it all together with iced water, but not too much, as it should be thick. Serve with ice cubes floating in it.

After this, try a cold carrot soup, made by putting cooked carrots in the blender with salt, pepper, garlic, and lemon juice. Then try other vegetables for yourself.

Bread . . .

A soup is not a meal without bread to go with it, and the same is true of most salads, but not just any bread will do. Whole-wheat breads are more nourishing than white bread, and they taste better and have a more satisfying texture too. Although good whole-wheat breads are usually not difficult to obtain, you may like to try baking your own. Many cookbooks give directions; and you can increase the protein content of any recipe by using 10 percent soy flour instead of wheat flour.

. . . and something to put on it

Unless you have decided to give up milk products, you still have cheese to put on your bread. Peanut butter is another economical form of protein everyone knows, although those who have not tried the crunchier kinds available at health food stores may not know how good peanut butter can taste. You can probably think of many other vegetarian foods that go well on bread, but there are some high-protein spreads you may not know about. One is *tahini*, or sesame paste, available at health food stores and Middle Eastern food stores. Taken straight, tahini is too thick and oily for most tastes, but it has the curious property of changing texture entirely when mixed with an equal quantity of water. You can then flavor the spread with herbs, or garlic, or curry powder, or tomato sauce, or whatever you like. Once mixed with water, however, tahini must be refrigerated.

Tahini may be mixed with *miso*, a dark brown soybean paste that is available in Chinese groceries and some health food stores. Miso can be used as a spread on its own, and as a base for soups.

Tahini leads naturally to *hummus*, the classic Arab dip, a recipe for which you will find under Middle Eastern Food, below.

Health food stores stock a variety of other nutritious spreads. One I particularly like is called *Tartex*, a kind of vegetarian pâté. If your health food store can't get it for you, try the Seventh Day Adventists.

Cooking Vegetables

Those who regard vegetables as an accompaniment to meat seldom do them justice when cooking them. I read somewhere that the secret of cooking vegetables properly is never, never boil them. Although I sometimes violate that rule, it is true that boiling destroys the flavor and nutrients of many vegetables. Instead, try sautéing them. Slice the vegetables—onions, carrots, potatoes, beetroot, broccoli, cabbage, etc.—and brown for a few minutes in a little oil or margarine. Add salt and herbs if you like. Then cover the pan and turn the heat down low. Stir occasionally. Depending on the vegetables, they will be cooked in 20–30 minutes.

Nicely cooked vegetables are sufficient for a simple meal. Try corn on the cob; or baked potatoes, served really hot with butter or margarine, and a selection of accompaniments like mushrooms or grated cheese. Steam or boil a small cauliflower until just tender, then cover with grated cheese and bake in the oven for a few minutes until the cheese has melted. Try slicing zucchini squash, or courgettes, together with tomatoes and mushrooms; add herbs and spices according to taste, and fry together for a few minutes.

All these are quick, light meals. Those that follow tend to be more filling. They are sample dishes from various cuisines, intended to illustrate the range of cooking that vegetarians can draw from.

Chinese Recipes

The Chinese cook vegetables properly, and their stir-fry method can be used on many vegetables. The vegetables should be sliced, then fried in a little oil to which a crushed garlic clove, some onion, and a little ginger has been added. Stir while frying, on a high heat, for 2–3 minutes, then add 2 tsp. soy sauce and continue a little longer. For a thicker gravy, add a little water and corn flour. Serve with rice—unpolished rice is best. Good vegetables to use are bean sprouts, celery, mushrooms, cabbage, and cauliflower. For the best flavor, cook, and keep them hot in individual bowls while you cook the next vegetable.

If you like Chinese food, you may like to grow your own bean sprouts. Buy dried mung beans at a health food store or Chinese grocery. A small quantity produces a lot of sprouts, so start by soaking ½ cup overnight. In the morning, wash and drain them. Take a medium-sized flower pot or any other receptacle with a hole in the bottom for drainage. Cover the hole with a scrap of linen or cheesecloth. Put the beans in the bottom, and pour water over them. Then cover the top to exclude all light, and stand in a warm place. Water them two or three times daily, making sure the water drains away completely each time. They will be ready in 2–5 days. Once grown, they can be stored for a few days in the refrigerator, or frozen.

Bean sprouts grown at home are an amazingly economical vegetable, since 1 lb. of mung beans provides you with an enormous amount of sprouts. Since mung beans are a variety of soybean, the sprouts are high in protein and low in calories. Apart from using them with other vegetables, as described above, you may try them raw, or if you prefer very lightly stir-fried, in a salad. They can also be fried up with left-over rice, or cooked with curry powder or in a tomato sauce. Finally, they can be made into *Egg Foo Yong*. For this, beat up some eggs—free-range, of course—add the sprouts, soy sauce, some chopped mushrooms, chopped scallions or onion, and a little ginger. Heat some oil in a frying pan and drop large spoonfuls of the mixture into it. Fry until brown on both sides and serve immediately.

Another Chinese soybean product you ought to get to know is bean curd, sometimes called bean cake, or *tofu*. It too is comparable to steak in the amount of protein it provides per calorie. If your city has a Chinatown, you should be able to buy it ready made. If not, try making your own from dry soybeans or from soy flour. Recipes are given in Dorothea Jones, *The Soybean Cookbook* (see below). Tofu is bland in taste, but absorbs flavors when cooked in any kind of sauce. Because it resembles a kind of curd cheese, those who do not use dairy products can flavor it with herbs and spices to make a spread that resembles cheese.

Indian Recipes

Because millions of Hindus and Sikhs are vegetarians, Indian cuisine provides an unrivaled range of vegetarian dishes. The basic Indian meal is lentil curry, or *dal*, served over a mound of rice. This dish can be made from various kinds of lentils, or from split peas. I find the small red lentils best. Dal is easy to make. Chop an onion and 2 cloves of garlic and fry them in a little oil. Add 1 cup lentils, 3 cups water, and curry powder to taste. Some cloves and a stick of cinnamon may also be added. Bring to the boil, then cover and simmer until the lentils are very soft (about 20 minutes). Then add a can of tomatoes, and if you have it, 2 oz. creamed coconut (available from health food stores and Indian groceries). Mix very well, mashing the lentils a little. The final product should flow freely; add water if it is too stodgy. Serve over brown rice, with Indian pickles and chutney. Sliced raw cucumber, sprinkled with coriander powder and yoghurt, or sliced banana sprinkled with grated coconut, make cooling accompaniments. If you manage to find an Indian grocery, you can also get some pappadams to serve with the dal. They are very flat wafers that you dip into a pan of hot oil. They then swell rapidly and are lifted out, drained, and served.

After you have made this simple Indian meal, you may like to try more elaborate ones, consisting of vegetable curries, chakees, bhajis, and biryanis, accompanied by savories like samosas and fulouries. You will find recipes for all these in Sally and Lucien Berg, *Vegetarian Gourmet*. *The Vegetarian Epicure*, by Anna Thomas, also has a chapter of Indian dishes. Still more are to be found in *The Hare Krishna Cookbook*. (See the end of this section for information about these books.)

Middle Eastern Recipes

I have already mentioned *hummus*, which with bread can make a good light meal. To make it, soak and then cook 4–6 oz. of chickpeas until they are very soft. Drain, saving some of the cooking water. Then mash the chickpeas well—your blender may do the job if you add some of the cooking water. Then add salt, a generous amount of lemon juice, a few crushed garlic cloves, and ½ cup tahini paste. Blend it all until smooth, adding more of the cooking water if necessary. Spread on a shallow dish and garnish with olive oil, paprika, and parsley. It is then ready to dip your bread into. Flat Arabian bread is the best, if you can get it.

Chickpeas, known in Spanish as garbanzos, and available at any Spanish-American grocery, are yet another species of the protein-rich family known as pulses—a family that includes peas, beans, and lentils. They are also the main ingredient in a dish that goes by the name of *Chickpea and Bread Puree*, but tastes much better than it sounds. To make this, soak and cook ¾ lb. chickpeas, until tender. Drain, keeping the cooking water. Flavor the chickpeas with crushed garlic and salt, and mash them with a potato masher, or by putting them through a grinder. Add some olive oil. Now toast 5 or 6 slices of whole-wheat bread, break the toast into pieces, and put the pieces into the bottom of a shallow serving dish. Sprinkle the chickpea water over them until they are soaked. Cover with the

pureed chickpeas, sprinkle with more oil, and garnish with
paprika. May be served hot or cold. A good variation is to
pour yoghurt flavored with herbs over the top, before
sprinkling with paprika.

Stuffed vegetables are another very popular Middle
Eastern dish. Almost anything can be stuffed: zucchini
squash, eggplant, tomato, green pepper, cabbage leaves,
onions, a small pumpkin, or a potato. One very popular
Turkish dish is called *Imam Bayildi*, which means "the
Imam (priest) fainted"—presumably with delight. This
may be made with eggplant, or zucchini (otherwise known
as courgettes). To stuff eggplant, cut in half lengthwise,
scooping out the centers. Sprinkle with salt and leave upside down to drain for 30 minutes, then rinse with cold
water. Zucchini may be hollowed out from one end with
an apple corer or knife, leaving the peel on.

The filling is made from ¾ lb. onions, lightly cooked in
olive oil, some crushed garlic cloves, a can of tomatoes
(drained), finely chopped parsley, and some salt. Stuff the
vegetables with this mixture and lay them side by side in
a large pan. Pour some olive oil over them, and about ¼
pint water, mixed with a little sugar, salt, and lemon juice.
Cover and simmer until tender (about 1 hour). Traditionally, this is served cold, but we have found it excellent
hot too, with rice.

The Middle Eastern equivalent of America's hamburger
is the vegetarian felafel sandwich. *Felafel* are little fried
balls, made from ground chickpeas or beans, and flavored
with spices. Although it is possible to make your own mixture, it is easier to buy a prepared mix, which can be found
at any Middle Eastern grocery and (since it is a great
favorite in Israel) at some Jewish delicatessens. Then all
you have to do is add water to the mixture, shape into
balls, and deep fry. They are usually eaten tucked into the
hollow center of Arabian bread, with salad and tahini
dressing packed in around them. Served on a plate with
hummus, bread, and salad, they make a complete meal.

If you would rather make your own than buy a mix,
there are recipes in *Vegetarian Gourmet* and in Claudia
Roden's *A Book of Middle Eastern Food*.

Italian Recipes

It is easy to make pasta dishes without meat. To get extra protein from your spaghetti, buy the high-protein varieties that are made with added wheat germ; if your supermarket doesn't have them, your health food store may; or else it may have spaghetti made from soy flour. You can then have a balanced meal using simply a sauce made from tomatoes, garlic, and oregano, or a pesto (basil) sauce that can be prepared from fresh basil, or bought ready made in a tin from Italian food stores.

If you use cheese, there are many other Italian dishes available: ravioli stuffed with spinach and cheese, eggplant parmigiana, or the following simple meatless *lasagna:*

In a greased casserole dish, make several layers of: cooked lasagna noodles, grated cheese, mushroom, oregano, and tomato sauce. Cover the top with sliced cheese, preferably mozzarella, and bake at 350° for 30–35 minutes. (Textured vegetable protein, described below, is also good in this dish, though not at all necessary.)

How about making your own *pizza?* Combine 1 cup flour, 1 tsp. baking powder, ½ tsp. salt, and blend with ¼ cup olive oil. Sprinkle 6 tbsp. water over the mixture and work in well. Cover and let rise in a warm place for 10 minutes. Shape the dough on a tray to form a pizza about 10 inches across, and build up the edge into a ridge. Spread this with: 1 onion, finely chopped and mixed with 1 tin of tomatoes, oregano, crushed garlic, mushrooms, olives, green pepper, grated mozzarella cheese, or any combination of these ingredients. Bake at 450° for 20 minutes.

Jewish Recipes

Because ancient religious laws prohibit the mixing of meat and dairy products in one meal, Jewish cooking has many dishes for vegetarians.

The traditional sabbath dish for Eastern European Jews is *Cholent,* of which there are many varieties. Modern versions often contain meat, but this is an innovation due to affluence, and was not part of the original dish. To make cholent, take 2 cups dried white lima beans, and soak overnight. Brown 3 sliced onions with 6 tbsp. of corn oil in a large casserole dish. Add the soaked, drained beans, 3 or 4 potatoes, peeled and cut into large pieces, sprinkle with salt, 2 tbsp. flour, and 2 tsp. paprika. Add boiling water to a level one inch above the mixture, and cover tightly. Religious Jews allow this dish to bake for 24 hours at 250°, thus observing the law which forbids them to light the oven on the sabbath. You may prefer to bake at 350° for about 4 hours.

Potato Latkes are another well-known Jewish specialty. They are simple to make. Take 2 cups of raw, grated potatoes and drain them well. Mix with 1 egg, 1 minced onion, salt, and 1 tbsp. flour. Heat some oil in a frying pan, and drop the mixture in by the spoonful. Fry until brown on both sides, and serve with apple sauce.

A more recent addition to Jewish cuisine is *eggplant steak*. Take a medium-sized eggplant, peel it and cut lengthwise into slices 1 inch thick. Soak these in cold salted water for 1 hour (this removes a slight tartness that some people find objectionable). Place the slices side by side in a greased baking pan. Sprinkle with salt and pepper and brush with the yolks of 2 beaten eggs; then sprinkle with grated cheese. Bake at 350° for 30 minutes.

If you want to try kreplach and kugels and knishes and piroshki and blintzes, buy yourself a copy of Jennie Grossinger's *The Art of Jewish Cooking*.

Macrobiotic Recipes

You may not accept all the principles of the macrobiotic theory—principles that have been seriously criticized by nutrition experts—but still find the typical macrobiotic meal of whole grains and vegetables a pleasant change. Most health food stores sell a variety of whole grains, like brown rice, wheat berries, millet, and buckwheat. Millet especially is a grain that deserves to be better known in the West. It has a delicious, nutty flavor. To cook millet (or buckwheat), brown the grains for a few minutes in a little oil, then cover with water and allow to simmer until tender.

The best way to cook rice and whole-wheat berries is to take 1¼ cups of water for every cup of the grain, bring to the boil, then cover and turn the heat down *very* low. After about 30 minutes for rice, and 45 for wheat, the water should have been absorbed and the grains should be tender. If the grains are tender and still too wet, raise the heat and remove the lid; if the grains are dry but hard, add more water. Different varieties of rice and wheat take different amounts of water and time to cook.

Serve these grains with sautéed vegetables, flavored with herbs or soy sauce. You can make a more elaborate risotto by adding cooked chickpeas, soybeans, or nuts.

Meat Substitutes

Very few vegetarian cookbooks tell you about the use of meat substitutes. Most long-established vegetarians rarely or never use them. Some find the idea of eating something that tastes like beef or bacon repugnant, even though they know the product is entirely vegetarian. Others object to the substitutes as "plastic food," although they are generally made out of soybeans with flavorings like caramel, which are also natural in origin; certainly they are as "natural" as animal flesh that comes from animals raised on hormones and antibiotics.

While both these objections are quite understandable, there is much to be said for meat substitutes, especially for people with no experience of vegetarian cooking. Once you have been a vegetarian for a year or two you will find there are so many delicious dishes to make from the natural products of the earth that there is no need to use products that pretend to be something else. But for the meat-eater thinking about becoming a vegetarian, it is reassuring to know that by using a vegetarian substitute for ground (minced) beef, one can instantly transform dozens of recipes—spaghetti with meat sauce, hamburgers, shepherd's pie, etc.—into vegetarian recipes that you can eat with a clear conscience.

Moreover, the substitutes are generally much cheaper than meat, contain as much protein (and no saturated fats), are more convenient, since they keep without refrigeration in their dehydrated state, and when mixed with a sauce or other flavorings are indistinguishable in taste and texture from "the real thing." So, simply in order to make a quick, nutritious meal when there is not much in the house, a packet of ground beef substitute is a handy thing to have in the kitchen.

As a general rule, meat substitutes sold dry, in a dehydrated form, are cheaper and better tasting than those sold in cans. These products are technically known as "textured vegetable protein," or TVP. The variety shaped and flavored to resemble ground beef is now being sold in supermarkets as "hamburger extender." In health food stores and Seventh Day Adventist stores in America it is sold under the brand name "Granburger"; in England, health food stores carry various brands, including "Protoveg," "Itona," and "Vitpro." Directions for use are on the packet, but you can improve the texture of the reconstituted TVP by frying it in a little oil for a few minutes before using. In addition to the ground or mince type, a chunky variety is available in England, suitable for casseroles and stews; but I have not been able to obtain this in the United States.

There are a greater variety of meat substitutes available in cans, but they tend to be expensive. Those who are saddened by the thought of giving up hot dogs, however, will be pleased to know that Loma Linda meatless frankfurters are as tasty as those made from animal flesh.

New meatlike products of soybean origin are slowly coming onto the market. Imitation bacon bits are now widely available, and both steaks and bacon strips have been tested, apparently with good results.

Some food scientists see these "meat analogues" as the best hope of winning Americans away from the present wasteful and unhealthy demand for meat. Nevertheless the manufacturers of these products appear to be pursuing an ultracautious marketing policy—perhaps, it has been suggested, because some of these manufacturers are members of agribusiness corporations also involved in meat production. (See Folke Dovring, "Soybeans," *Scientific American*, February 1974, p. 18.)

Milk substitutes are also available in some health food stores and from Seventh Day Adventists; they too are made from soybeans. At present they are expensive, especially when compared to nonfat milk powder, but as the volume increases it should be possible for them to be produced at a lower cost than cow's milk. Vegetable cheeses have also been produced. No doubt when people are ready to end animal exploitation completely, milk and cheese substitutes will be produced on a large scale.

Miscellaneous Hints
Protein:

Many Americans worry too much about protein and end up consuming more than their bodies can use. Adults do not need to take in large amounts of protein at every meal. Nonetheless, the recipes I have given nearly all provide protein comparable to that of a meal containing meat. Any meal using pulses—lentils, beans, chickpeas—or products derived from soybeans, like bean curd or textured vegetable protein, supplies adequate protein. If you combine different types of protein at the same meal, your body can use more of the protein than it would otherwise do. This is known as protein complementarity, and is due to the fact that protein consists of different amino acids. Some foods are high in certain amino acids and lower in others, while other foods have the opposite properties. Basically, grains and grain products—rice, wheat, millet, whole-wheat bread, and even, although to a lesser extent, white bread, should be eaten together with foods made from pulses or nuts. The protein compositions of these two groups of food complement each other. Fortunately, one normally eats beans with rice and peanut butter with bread anyway, so balancing one's proteins does not require too much thought.

If you have young children, protein is more important for them than it is for you. You also need more protein if you are pregnant or breast feeding a baby. In these cases, those who do not consume eggs or dairy products must make sure that they eat a nutritiously adequate substitute. One way to make sure your children get enough protein and calcium is to see that their snacks are not store-bought cookies, which provide calories but very little else, but homemade cookies to which you have added wheat germ, soy flour, or nonfat milk powder.

For more details about nutrition and proteins, see the books by Lappé, Ewald, and Null, listed below.

Saving Time:

Some vegetarian dishes may take longer to prepare than meat meals, but you do not have to spend a lot of time in the kitchen if you don't want to. Most casseroles, soups, curries, and similar dishes keep well in the refrigerator. So cook large quantities, put half away, and eat it again two or three days later; alternatively, freeze the leftovers, and have them again next month.

Dining Out:

I may by now have convinced you that you can cook well at home on a vegetarian diet, but you may still feel that you are going to miss the pleasures of eating in restaurants. We have not found this to be the case. We still go out to dinner quite often, and our search for places with suitable dishes has led us to visit some wonderful restaurants we would never have tried otherwise. It is true, however, that you have to choose your restaurant more carefully than you did before.

In major cities, there is almost always at least one vegetarian restaurant. Ask at the tourist bureau if you are traveling. Apart from strictly vegetarian establishments, though, vegetarians usually have no difficulty eating at Indian, Chinese, and Italian restaurants, at Jewish dairy restaurants, or at pizza houses. Then there are soup-and-salad cafeterias. If you fancy French cooking, try somewhere that specializes in crepes, or else call up first and ask if they will make something special for you. In general, don't be afraid to ask a restaurant to prepare a vegetarian meal if there is none on the menu, but try to give them advance notice. Sometimes they will do it and sometimes they won't —but the more people who ask for vegetarian meals, the more likely the restaurants are to put them on the menu.

Some Cookbooks

The following list makes no attempt to be comprehensive, but all of the books on it are worthwhile, and all are reasonably priced.

Sally and Lucien Berg, *Vegetarian Gourmet* (New York: McGraw-Hill, 1971). The best cookbook I know, containing recipes from fourteen different nations, including splendid chapters on Indian, Arabic, and Chinese cooking. This is a book for those who really enjoy food. Some of the recipes are a little elaborate, but can be simplified without great loss.

Anna Thomas, *The Vegetarian Epicure* (New York: Alfred A. Knopf, 1972; also published in paperback by Vintage Books). Many delicious gourmet recipes. Especially good on breads and soups. Not so good for "vegans," as there is too much emphasis on cheese and egg recipes.

Sonya Richmond, *International Vegetarian Cookery* (New York: Arco, 1965; also published in paperback by Arc Books). Recipes from a wide range of countries, though generally modified for Western tastes and cooking methods.

Patty Fisher, *500 Recipes for Vegetarian Cookery* (London: Hamlyn, 1969). A very inexpensive basic book, including nutritional information and a surprising range of recipes.

Frances Moore Lappé, *Diet for a Small Planet* (New York: Friends of the Earth/Ballantine, 1971). Tells you everything you need to know about protein, and has some recipes as well.

Ellen Buchman Ewald, *Recipes for a Small Planet* (New York: Ballantine, 1973). A sequel to the preceding; more about protein, and a lot more recipes.

Frances Moore Lappé and Ellen Buchman Ewald, *Great Meatless Meals* (New York: Ballantine, 1974). Thirty complete menus, with recipes, for excellent and nutritious vegetarian meals.

Edith Brown and Sam Brown, *Cooking Creatively with Natural Foods* (New York: Ballantine, 1973). Recipes from Brownies Health Food Restaurant, in New York City.

Mildred Lager and Dorothea van Gundy Jones, *The Soybean Cookbook* (New York: Arco, 1968; also published in paperback by Arc Books). Three hundred and fifty recipes for using soybeans, including directions for growing bean sprouts and making bean curd.

Eva Batt, *What's Cooking?* (Vegan Society, England; to obtain a copy, write to the society at the address given on page 284). Over 250 completely vegan recipes, with other valuable information for vegans.

Freya Dinshah, *The Vegan Cookbook* (American Vegan Society; address on page 282). Just what the name implies.

Dr. and Mrs. Frank Hurd, *Ten Talents* (published by the authors, Chisholm, Minnesota; available through the Seventh Day Adventist Church). A natural food cookbook and health manual. It is more expensive than the other books on this list, but worthwhile for vegans, as most recipes are vegan.

The Hare Krishna Cookbook (Radnor, Pennsylvania: Chilton Book Co., 1974). An Indian vegetarian cookbook. Many good recipes, but with some religious quirks which forbid such ingredients as garlic and onions!

Jennie Grossinger, *The Art of Jewish Cooking* (New York: Bantam, 1972). Not vegetarian, but you will find enough vegetarian recipes to keep you gaining weight happily, if you like Jewish food.

Claudia Roden, *A Book of Middle Eastern Food* (New York: Alfred A. Knopf, 1972; also published in paperback by Vintage Books). Also not vegetarian, but has recipes for hummus, felafel, and stuffed vegetables of all kinds. Especially worthwhile for those who use a ground beef substitute, since many of the meat dishes use ground or minced meat, and work well with textured vegetable protein instead.

APPENDIX 2.

Further Reading

This is not a complete list of sources—reference to which will be found in the footnotes—but a select list of especially valuable books in the field. Many of the earlier volumes are now out of print; they are included for those who have access to a major reference library.

Lewis Gompertz, *Moral Inquiries on the Situation of Man and of Brutes* (London, 1824). One of the first carefully argued proposals for a radically different attitude to animals, with a discussion of the effect this would have on our lives. The author, who was a driving force in the early animal welfare movement, later published another work, *Fragments in Defence of Animals* (1852), but the former is the more thorough treatment.

Henry S. Salt, *Animals' Rights* (London, 1892, and later revised editions until 1915). The first chapter contains a strong argument for granting rights to animals, if we grant them to humans. Later chapters discuss cruelties to domestic and wild animals. There are many valuable references to earlier works on the subject. Salt was an active reformer, campaigning against the death penalty, and for improved prison conditions, as well as for animals. He published several other works about animals, including *The Logic of Vegetarianism* and *The Humanities of Diet*.

Howard Williams, *The Ethics of Diet* (London, 1896). A compilation of extracts from writers advocating vegetarianism, from the Ancient Greeks to the nineteenth century. An invaluable reference for anyone interested in the history of vegetarianism.

E. S. Turner, *All Heaven in a Rage* (London: Michael Joseph, 1964). A history of the fight against cruelty to animals in Britain that manages to be both informative and entertaining.

Ruth Harrison, *Animal Machines* (London: Stuart, 1964). The first book to reveal the effects of factory farm techniques on animal welfare. Still the best source of information on many aspects of modern farming.

Report of the Technical Committee to Enquire into the Welfare of Animals kept under Intensive Livestock Husbandry Systems (The Brambell Report), Command Paper 2836, London, Her Majesty's Stationery Office, 1965. The full report of the most authoritative impartial study of animal welfare under modern farming conditions.

Stanley and Roslind Godlovitch and John Harris, eds., *Animals, Men and Morals: An Enquiry into the Mal-Treatment of Non-Humans* (London: Gollancz, and New York: Taplinger, 1972). A collection of thirteen contributions detailing the facts of our treatment of animals, placing these facts within a critical moral framework, and suggesting sociological perspectives from which to understand our attitudes to animals. The most radical book about animals to be published since *Animals' Rights*.

Cleveland Amory, *Man Kind? Our Incredible War on Wildlife* (New York: Harper & Row, 1974). This book is worth reading for its account of what humans have done to wild animals.

Richard Ryder, *Victims of Science* (London: Davis-Poynter, 1975). The most complete and up-to-date account of the use of animals in experimentation, by a psychologist who was once himself an experimenter.

Tom Regan and Peter Singer, eds., *Animal Rights and Human Obligations* (Englewood Cliffs, New Jersey: Prentice Hall, 1976). A collection of writings, from the Old Testament to the present, for and against the view that animals have rights, or that we have obligations to animals.

APPENDIX 3.

Organizations

The following list is confined to organizations in the United States and Britain that are working for radical changes in our attitudes to, and treatment of, nonhuman animals. It does not include organizations that accept the prevailing attitudes and try only to correct isolated instances of cruelty. At the same time the list is selective, corresponding to some extent to those organizations with which I have had contact, and the omission of an organization from this list should not be taken as an indication that it is unsatisfactory in any way.

United States

Friends of Animals, Inc., 11 West 60th Street, New York, N.Y. 10023. Although its recent activities have been mainly against hunting and the problem of overpopulation of dogs and cats in urban areas, Friends of Animals has also opposed various forms of cruelty to farm animals. Friends of Animals works with the Committee for Humane Legislation, 910 Sixteenth Street, NW, Washington, DC 20006, a nonprofit body that is free to lobby for legislative change.

Society for Animal Rights, 900 First Avenue, New York, N.Y. 10022. An activist group, organizing demonstrations and protests against specific cruelties, while taking a strong position in favor of animal rights in its educational material.

United Action for Animals, 205 East 42nd Street, New York, N.Y. 10017. Concentrates exclusively on exposing and protesting cruelty to animals used in research, against which it has waged an unrelenting and uncompromising campaign.

American Anti-Vivisection Society, 1903 Chestnut Street, Philadelphia, Pa. 19103. Not as thorough as United Action, but has done valuable work in exposing painful experiments.

The Fund for Animals, Inc., 140 West 57th Street, New York, N.Y. 10019. Although less radical than other organizations in this list, The Fund for Animals is included because it has done valuable work in opposing cruelty to wild animals.

American Vegetarians, Box 5424, Akron, Ohio 44313. An activist vegetarian group, emphasizing the cruelty to animals involved in meat production. It acts as a communications center for smaller groups throughout the country.

American Vegan Society, Box H, Malaga, N.J. 08328. Promotes the vegan diet, for both ethical and health reasons.

Animal Liberation, Inc., 319 West 74th Street, New York, N.Y. 10023. Advocates an end to the raising and killing of animals for food, on grounds of cruelty and health. (No connection with this book, the title of which was arrived at independently.)

Vegetarian Activist Collective, 616 6th Street, Brooklyn, N.Y. 11215. An active political grouping of people who promote vegetarianism for the sake of animals, to ease the food problem, and for health. It manages to function without organized leadership. Send $1 for literature kit.

Beauty Without Cruelty, 175 West 12th Street, New York, N.Y. 10012. The American branch of the British organization of the same name (see below) promoting substitutes for furs and cosmetics that use animal products and are tested on animals.

Argus Archives, 228 East 49th Street, New York, N.Y. 10017. A research center, with information on all aspects of cruelty to animals, emphasizing those within New York State.

Vegetarian World, Box 46664, Los Angeles, California. Publishes a vegetarian newspaper.

United Kingdom

Royal Society for the Prevention of Cruelty to Animals, 105 Jermyn Street, London, SW1. Though not at present a radical organization, the society has some members who are attempting to redirect attention from dogs and cats toward the basic cruelties to farm animals and to animals used in experimentation. An influx of new, more committed members could bring this venerable institution back to the strong position taken by its founders 150 years ago.

Farm and Food Society, 4 Willifield Way, London NW11 7XT. Does outstanding work in opposing factory farming, and proposing alternatives.

Compassion in World Farming, Copse House, Greatham, Liss, Hampshire. Fights factory farming and promotes more rational ways of feeding the world. It has produced an excellent film of farming conditions in Britain.

National Anti-Vivisection Society, 51 Harley Street, London W1N 1DD. Works to phase out painful experiments on animals.

The Scottish Society for the Prevention of Vivisection, 10 Queensferry Street, Edinburgh EH2 4PG. Also aims at the abolition of vivisection.

Fund for the Replacement of Animals in Medical Experiments (FRAME), 312A Worple Road, Wimbledon, London SW20 8QU. Issues information on and promotes research into alternatives to methods of experimentation involving animals.

The Vegetarian Society, Parkdale, Dunham Road, Altrincham, Cheshire, and 53 Marloes Road, Kensington, London W8. Embraces all vegetarians, for whatever reason. Useful information on nutritional aspects of vegetarianism and also on the treatment of animals.

The Vegan Society, 47 Highlands Road, Leatherhead, Surrey. Advocates doing without all animal foods, for the sake of the animals and to produce more food for humans.

Beauty Without Cruelty, 1 Calverley Park, Tunbridge Wells, Kent TN1 2SG, England. Promotes and supplies fake furs and cosmetics that have no animal ingredients and have not been tested on animals.

Index

285

People for the Ethical Treatment of Animals (PETA) is a non-profit charity organization headquartered in Washington, D.C. PETA was incorporated to educate policy-makers and the public to the issues involving the intense, prolonged, and unjustifiable abuse of animals; and to promote an understanding of the inherent rights of sentient animals to be treated with respect and decency.

Founded in 1980, PETA has been the fastest growing animal protection organization in the United States. Readers of "AGENDA", the animal protection community's national, independent news magazine, voted PETA the Number 1 organization in the country that has done the most to further the protection of animals.

A 1983 study conducted by the Office of government and Community Affairs at Harvard University stated:

> *"PETA, based in Washington, D.C., is headed by Alex Pacheco, who became a national folk hero to the animal rights movement when he 'exposed' the mistreatment of animals by Dr. Edward Taub in 1981 in his Silver Spring, Maryland lab. Ingrid Newkirk, a well known animal rights advocate, also is a leader in PETA, which works with the Animal Rights Network, MFA, and other groups in an attempt to connect the array of animal rights crusaders.... PETA may pose the greatest grass-roots challenge to the scientific and medical research communities. Its members are young, articulate and dedicated."*

Since its inception, PETA has been responsible for such breakthroughs as the closing down of the largest horse slaughter operation in the United States; the first and only arrest and criminal conviction of an animal experimenter in the U.S. on charges of cruelty to animals; the first confiscation of abused laboratory animals under a court ordered search and seizure warrant; and an order by U.S. Secretary of Defense Caspar Weinberger that stopped all military wound laboratories engaged in shooting live animals in bullet wound experiments, pending a national review of military experimentation on animals.

PETA's animal protection case work brings members of the scientific community together with members of the judicial and legislative communities to halt abusive operations and practices. Such cases, aided by thorough investigative work, Congressional involvement, and international media coverage frequently result in widespread primary as well as secondary changes that improve the quality of life for many thousands of animals.

As a non-profit charity, PETA is registered with the Internal Revenue Service as a tax-exempt 501(c)3 organization, IRS #52-1218336. It is soley supported by tax-deductible contributions. All PETA officers and staff either receive no monetary compensation or are paid minimum wage. PETA headquarters are open to the public every day of the year.